ABU

THE CODE OF THE
EXTRAORDINARY MIND

THE
CODE
— OF THE —
EXTRAORDINARY
MIND

**TEN UNCONVENTIONAL LAWS TO REDEFINE
YOUR LIFE & SUCCEED ON YOUR OWN TERMS**

VISHEN LAKHIANI
FOUNDER OF MINDVALLEY

RODALE.

RODALE *wellness*

Live happy. Be healthy. Get inspired.

Sign up today to get exclusive accesss to our authors, exclusive bonuses, and the most authoritative, useful, and cutting-edge information on health, wellness, fitness, and living your life to the fullest.

**Visit us online at RodaleWellness.com
Join us at RodaleWellness.com/Join**

Book design by Christine Gaugler

Library of Congress Cataloging-in-Publication Data is on file with the publisher.

ISBN-13: 978–1–62336–708–4 hardcover
ISBN-13: 978–1–62336–758–9 paperback

Distributed to the trade by Macmillan

  4 6 8 10 9 7 5   hardcover
2 4 6 8 10 9 7 5 3   paperback

RODALE.

We inspire and enable people to improve their lives and the world around them.
rodalebooks.com

To my family: Kristina, Hayden, and Eve.
You're the most important thing in my life.

And to our parents, Mohan and Roopi, Virgo and Ljubov, for allowing us
to forge our own beliefs and question the Brules, even as kids.

CONTENTS

PART III: RECODING YOURSELF: TRANSFORMING YOUR INNER WORLD

PART IV: BECOMING EXTRAORDINARY: CHANGING THE WORLD

BEFORE YOU BEGIN: KNOW THAT THIS IS NOT YOUR TYPICAL BOOK

In fact, I would be hesitant to call this a personal growth book. It's more of a personal disruption book. This book forces you to rethink aspects of your life that may have been running on autopilot for years.

Which means that within months of reading this book, you may find yourself no longer accepting certain aspects of your current reality. Your relationships, your career, your goals, your spiritual beliefs may all be forced to change as you come to understand that many of your beliefs and past decisions were never taken on by choice—but were installed by default.

This book is designed to disrupt the way you see the world and to give you the tools to shift the world through cognitive changes in your mind. In short, it creates an awakening. Once you see the patterns this book unveils, you cannot "unsee" them.

Depending on your worldview, you will either *love* this book or *hate* this book. That's by design. It's because we grow through discomfort or insight. But never through apathy.

In addition to the ideas it contains, this book is also unique in several ways:

NEW WORDS: This book contributes more than 20 new words to the English language. I had to create new words to describe (sometimes humorously) the new models for living that you'll be introduced to. Words are powerful, as they influence how we see the world. Once you understand these words, your perspective of certain things will change.

THE ONLINE EXPERIENCE: This book comes with its own custom-designed app with hours of additional content, practices, training, and more. Do you especially like a particular idea from one of the thinkers I mention in the book—for example, Peter Diamandis? You can use the app to dive in deeper and listen to my full interview with him. Do you really enjoy a particular technique I share? The app will let you play a video of me guiding you through the technique. You'll find gorgeous images, photos, ideas, and more, all on the Online Experience available for web, Android, and iOS. You can therefore read this book in a few hours, or you can choose to spend days exploring and deep-diving into the full content. Access it from www.mindvalley.com/extraordinary.

THE SOCIAL LEARNING PLATFORM: Since this book is about questioning life, as I wrote it, I began questioning the traditional ways books are made. One of my biggest annoyances with the idea of a "book" in today's world is that you cannot easily interact with fellow readers or with the author. For this book, I decided to fix this flaw. I had my team develop a social learning platform to allow authors and readers to interact and learn from each other. This is the first of its kind in the world. You can interact with other readers, share ideas, and even communicate with me directly from your mobile device or computer when you sign up for the online experience. This makes this book perhaps one of the most technologically hooked-up volumes in history. You can access the Social Learning Platform via the Online Experience on www.mindvalley.com/extraordinary.

LEARNING METHODOLOGY: This book is designed to help you learn through a learning model upgrade I call Consciousness Engineering. Once you understand this, every idea in the book starts to connect. Furthermore, you'll learn HOW TO learn. After reading this book, every other book you read on personal growth will make more sense and you'll absorb their ideas better.

WRITING STYLE: My best and most meaningful conversations tend to happen with friends over a few drinks in a social setting. We're vulnerable, we're honest, we're open, we're transparent. When I have these conversations on life and business (often over a glass of wine), I love sketching on napkins to illustrate ideas. I bring this same style into this book. You'll find the napkin illustrations, the personal stories, the raw vulnerability. I wrote things down I never thought I'd share publicly, but I share here because I feel others can learn from my errors.

COLLABORATION: This book involves more than 200 hours of interviews with many of the leading players on the world stage today. Arianna Huffington and Dean Kamen edited chapters. Richard Branson, Peter Diamandis, Michael Beckwith, and Ken Wilber gave me hours of one-on-one discussions and interviews. I even got to pose a question (via my wife) to the Dalai Lama. I integrate all of these ideas into the Code because I consider these men and women to be role models we can all learn from.

THIS IS FOUR BOOKS IN ONE: I consider my time (and yours) precious, and I dislike reading personal growth books that drag on and on for 70,000 words trying to teach a relatively simple concept. I have no wish to stretch out an idea—that just means wasted time for busy readers who understand concepts fast. So this book is really packed with knowledge. To offer you the best value possible, in each of the book's four parts, I've tried to provide a richly detailed yet cohesive set of ideas. Each part stands well alone, yet together, they form a philosophy for living. My aim was to deliver maximum wisdom, in a fun way, in minimal time.

CONNECT WITH ME: I love being in touch with my readers.

Facebook.com/vishen

Instagram.com/vishen

Twitter.com/vishen
(Use hashtag #codeXmind)

MY WEB SITES: To learn more about me and my work:

MindvalleyAcademy.com

VishenLakhiani.com

Mindvalley.com

INTRODUCTION

I think it's possible for ordinary people to choose to be extraordinary.

—ELON MUSK

I was going on stage to speak. But it was no ordinary stage. At this particular event in Calgary, Alberta, they had slotted me last—in a spot reserved for the *least* popular speakers. Before me, a whole procession of awe-inspiring names had taken the stage. His Holiness the Dalai Lama—who dished out wisdom like Yoda in orange robes. Then Nobel Prize winner F. W. de Klerk, former President of South Africa. Then Sir Richard Branson, founder of the Virgin Group. Followed by Tony Hsieh, CEO of Zappos.

And finally on day three, it was my turn. I was a gap filler—not a brand name that drew people to a conference like this but a random speaker slotted in to fill a space when budgets to book the big-name speakers were spent.

I stepped on stage to the biggest audience I had ever spoken to: waiting expectantly. I was nervous but had secretly downed a shot of vodka at the lobby bar to calm my nerves. My ripped jeans and untucked shirt bespoke nothing other than the fact that I was a man with poor fashion sense. I was thirty-three years old.

When I got on stage, I spoke about an idea very dear to me—about the way human beings view life, goals, happiness, and meaning. By the end, I saw that I had the audience in joy and in tears. Even more surprising, at the end of the conference, the audience had voted me best speaker. (I tied with Zappos' Tony Hsieh.) This was a big deal, given the major names I was sharing that stage with and the fact that I had little experience as a speaker. But I had gotten more votes than the Dalai Lama (the fact that I take mild pride in this while he probably doesn't care is the reason his title is His Holiness and mine is just Mr.).

I spoke that day about what it means to have an extraordinary life. It does not happen by chance, or through hard work, or through a unique set of skills. There is actually a methodology that anyone can employ—a code you can learn—that will catapult your life into the realm of the extraordinary.

These ideas have worked not just for a few individuals but also for hundreds of thousands of people. This code is being used in schools around the world, in corporations to train their staff, and by individuals in countries all over the world to find meaning and happiness in their lives. It is a code that I have learned through trial and error and by paying very close attention to some of the most extraordinary people in the world.

My speech went on to get almost half a million views on YouTube despite being almost an hour long, and I received suggestions to write a book. But I didn't feel I was ready. Who was I to be an author?

Then three years later, something else happened. I was sitting with Richard Branson on Necker Island after a party, and when most of the other guests had left and it was just the two of us, I shared with him some of my ideas and theories on what made him and others extraordinary. Branson turned to me and said, "You should write a book." Branson wasn't just an entrepreneur I admired. Because of his book *Losing My Virginity*, he was also my favorite author. This was the push I needed to get cracking on *The Code of the Extraordinary Mind*. It would still take another three years before the first chapter would be written. But the book is now complete, and I'm honored to place it in your hands.

I share these thoughts with you only to impress upon you how powerful the ideas in this book can be. This is not your typical personal growth book. In fact, it's not a regular nonfiction book of any sort. It's designed and written in a way to take really complex ideas (the keys to success, meaning, and happiness, for instance) and break them down into frameworks and models that anyone can understand. And I mean anyone (as I was writing this, I received a video showing a teacher in India teaching some of the ideas in this book to several hundred Indian schoolchildren).

And these ideas work. If you knew my full background (more about that in the chapters to come), you would know that I should never have had the success I have today. The odds should have been squarely stacked against me. Yet, I've been blessed to live a life that's "extraordinary"—in short, a life that by reasonable odds I should never have experienced, including:

- Turning a hobby—personal growth—into a company, Mindvalley, with 500,000 students, 2 million subscribers, and a passionate fan base that loves what we stand for.

- Starting Mindvalley with no bank loans or venture capital and, despite impossible odds, building it into one of the most innovative companies in our space.

- Creating an award-winning workplace that employs people from more than 40 countries and that was voted one of the coolest offices on the planet in 2012 in an *Inc.* magazine readers' poll.

- Marrying an incredible woman and having two wonderful kids we're in the process of raising.

- Starting my own festival, A-Fest, that takes place in exotic locations around the world and attracts thousands of incredible people to apply for sought-after tickets.

- Experiencing spiritual awakenings that changed my understanding of physical reality.

- Raising and donating millions of dollars for charities.

- Getting an incredible offer to write this book (thank you, Rodale Inc.!).

Yet I can tell you with certainty that I was not born extraordinary. My life should have been fairly ordinary. I grew up in Malaysia before moving to the United States. I always considered myself a geek and dealt with self-esteem issues most of my life.

I almost flunked out of the University of Michigan, and just two years after graduation in 1999, I had the proud honor of being fired twice, losing my businesses twice, and being dead broke on multiple occasions.

I failed at over a dozen start-up ideas before one idea—Mindvalley—clicked. Then, at age twenty-eight, I had to leave the country I dreamed of living in, and I moved back to my parents' house. I spent the next six years struggling to get my little business going while living with my wife in a bedroom in my parents' home and driving a tiny Nissan March.

Just one year before my speech in Calgary, I was nowhere close to accomplishing my goals. I was in greater debt than I would have been if I had never started my business.

And then at the age of thirty-two, I experienced a shift so powerful that in a few short years, my life went through a total and radical transformation.

All of this happened because despite my ordinary beginnings, I do have one unique skill that has served me time and again. It's a skill I used to develop the framework for this book—a framework I've designed to help you step out of whatever ordinary circumstances you'd like to move beyond.

If I had to summarize this skill, it's this—I'm a sponge when it comes to learning from others and connecting the dots. I am fortunate to have the ability to soak up knowledge and wisdom easily from all sorts of people—from billionaires to monks—and then "codify" these ideas, connect those bits of knowledge, and construct unique new models for understanding the world. This is my gift.

In the world of computers, you might call this being a hacker. To hack, in that world, is to cut something apart, break it to the core, and then reassemble it to make it better than before.

That's what I do. I was trained as a computer engineer, but I was born with a mind that loved learning how to hack life. I see patterns that others sometimes miss and connect dots in very unusual ways.

In this book, I'm going to share with you some of these dots—10, in particular. I've collected them through my life experiences and from listening to brilliant thinkers, leaders, creators, and artists who pursue greatness in their everyday lives.

As I learned from these extraordinary people, my life grew exponentially. I became who I am because when I was broke and struggling, I made it a point to consistently seek out and listen to people who were just a step ahead of me. I'd take in their wisdom, assimilate the lessons, and grow. Then I'd level up, make new connections, and learn from people a step ahead from that level. And on and on.

Eventually, I got to pose questions to people like Elon Musk, Richard Branson, Peter Diamandis, Arianna Huffington, and Ken Wilber. Their wisdom is shared in this book along with the distilled wisdom from more than 200 hours of interviews with more than 50 extraordinary minds who live life by their own rules while making an amazing impact on the planet.

I also founded Mindvalley, which grew to become one of the world's leading companies in human transformation. With more than 2 million subscribers, we've been at the forefront of much of the new ideas happening globally on personal growth. The access to wisdom and minds I get from Mindvalley's network gives me another unique edge in writing this book.

My talent is to take all of these ideas and knowledge and unify them into a single path, a path you can follow to break the bounds of the ordinary and to take you to all those beautiful places you may have dreamed of going as a kid.

Here's an overview of what we'll be exploring.

TEN LAWS FOR AN EXTRAORDINARY LIFE

There's an invisible code as to how the world operates—how human beings interact with each other, how we worship, relate with our parents, perform at work, fall in love, make money, and stay healthy and happy. I started my career as a computer programmer spending hours in front of a screen trying to understand the code of machines. Today, I'm more obsessed with the code of how the human world operates—and, believe me, this code is just as hackable.

Just as a programmer can program a computer to do specific tasks by understanding its code, you can program your life and the world around you to improve, enhance the way you live and the experiences you have in this lifetime.

But first, you have to *see* this code. And that's where this book comes in.

This book is divided into four parts and ten chapters. Each part looks at a different level of the code and represents an expansion of your state of awareness. Each chapter provides and describes a law that takes you further into this expansion.

PART I. Living in the Culturescape: How You Were Shaped by the World Around You

PART II. The Awakening: The Power to Choose Your Version of the World

PART III. Recoding Yourself: Transforming Your Inner World

PART IV. Becoming Extraordinary: Changing the World

These four parts represent a gradual expansion of your levels of awareness of who you are and just what you're capable of. The illustration below shows these levels as an expanding circle of awareness.

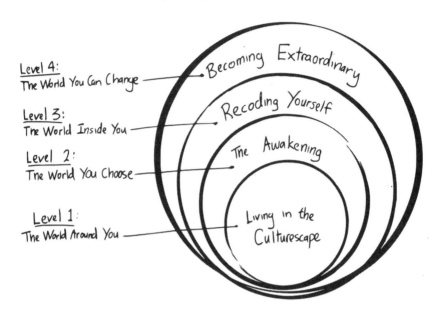

Level 4:
The World You Can Change — Becoming Extraordinary

Level 3:
The World Inside You — Recoding Yourself

Level 2:
The World You Choose — The Awakening

Level 1:
The World Around You — Living in the Culturescape

Within these four worlds I'll be sharing 10 laws, each of which builds on the one before. This is the Code of the Extraordinary Mind.

Part I. Living in the Culturescape: How You Were Shaped by the World Around You

This section looks at the world we live in with all its messy and conflicting ideas, beliefs, and patterns that we've invented in an attempt to keep humanity safe and under control. The problem is that many of these patterns and rules long moved past their expiration date. In this section, you learn to question the rules of the world around you—from your religion to your relationships to your career and education. Here we introduce you to Laws 1 and 2.

1. TRANSCEND THE CULTURESCAPE. We'll explore the tangled web of the culturescape—humanity's collective rules, beliefs, and practices about life. These are the rules that tell you how to exist, how to plan your life,

how to define success and happiness. Following them is a sure path to being ordinary and safe. But I'm going to urge you to instead jump on the thrilling, sometimes uncertain, yet exciting ride of an *unrestricted* life. It all starts with asking a few disruptive questions.

2. QUESTION THE BRULES. Here you'll discover how to identify *bulls**t rules* or *Brules* that should have expired generations ago but that still infect our lives. Getting rid of our Brules is like shedding old dirty clothing and putting on something fresh. It's liberating. Extraordinary people tend to have an allergy to Brules. You will, too, as we explore how Brules can keep us tied up in older ways of living and limit our creativity and growth.

Part II. The Awakening: The Power to Choose Your Version of the World

As you learn to question the Brules of the culturescape, you also learn that you can *choose* your own rules. Here we look at the interface between you and the world around you. What ideas and values do you choose to believe? What do you choose to reject? You'll learn to consciously mold the beliefs, habits, and practices that shape your life while you discard old beliefs and systems that you no longer need. The method for doing this is a process I call "consciousness engineering."

3. PRACTICE CONSCIOUSNESS ENGINEERING. Here's where you'll learn how to think like a hacker and discover the crucial framework for understanding HOW your beliefs and practices shape you. You'll learn to see beliefs as "models of reality" and habits and practices as "systems for living." You'll cut to the core of who you are and learn to rebuild and remake yourself anew through this powerful mental model for growth and awakening.

4. REWRITE YOUR MODELS OF REALITY. These are the beliefs ingrained in you since you were a child. Many are disempowering and keep you stuck in troublesome, painful, or mediocre ways of viewing the world. Here you'll learn how to swap out disempowering models and replace them with newer, more empowering ones. The world reflects your beliefs—so imagine what happens when you take on the beliefs of extraordinary minds.

5. UPGRADE YOUR SYSTEMS FOR LIVING. Your systems for living are your daily practices for getting on with life, from eating to working to parenting to making love. New systems for living are being discovered all the time.

Most just never make it into our formal education system. So most of us learn, love, work, meditate, and parent using models that are suboptimal or even damaging. You'll learn how to observe the systems that run the world (and your life) and how to optimize them to be more powerful than ever before. You'll also learn how to curate and install updated systems for living to make you a far more optimized human being.

And then we get to the second half the book.

Thus far the book has been about your functioning in the outer world and how to first break the rules, and then create new ones that lead to greater growth and happiness for yourself. As you get better at this, the next step is to explore your inner world. How can you transform the world *within* you? We'll be bringing a beautiful order and balance to this world.

Part III. Recoding Yourself: Transforming Your Inner World

In Part III we explore how to hack consciousness itself, including alternate ideas of what it is to be human, to be happy, and to pursue goals that will ultimately lead to a fulfilling life. We also explore the idea that consciousness can shape the world you experience—an idea I call "bending reality."

6. BEND REALITY. This is a model of reality that suggests that there is an optimal state of living where everything seems to just *click* and luck seems to be something you can control. I've met many remarkable people who seem to exist in this state. Some were monks. Some were billionaires. I'll dissect this state of being and share with you how you, too, can get there.

7. LIVE IN BLISSIPLINE. Happiness is hackable, and Blissipline is a beautiful discipline for leveling up your happiness every day and feeling limitless. We'll explore why happiness can be so elusive, and you'll discover some of the best practices I've discovered for hacking happiness and other positive emotions.

8. CREATE A VISION FOR YOUR FUTURE. Most of us are trained by the Brules of the world to pursue the wrong goals. I think much of modern goal setting is absolute rubbish. I'll show you how to set goals that truly, deeply lead to happiness, create meaning, and allow you to live a life that's exciting and purposeful.

Part IV. Becoming Extraordinary: Changing the World

In this section you learn how to go from creating your own rules for the world and mastery of your inner self to going forth and actually *changing* the world. This is the point when you can truly say you've become extraordinary. You've not just mastered your inner and outer worlds—you're using this power to push humanity forward and make a positive dent in the universe. In order to do this, you need two things: to be unfuckwithable and to find your quest.

9. BE UNFUCKWITHABLE. Here you learn how to be so rock solid in your own self that judgments from others or fear of loss no longer affect you. You're unshakeable in your journey through the world. Changing the world is tough. This chapter shows you how to be strong enough to weather the storm.

10. EMBRACE YOUR QUEST. And then we come to Chapter 10. Here you learn to go beyond just living in the world to actually *changing it* by discovering your *quest*. When you find it (and I'll teach you a method for doing so), you take that final step toward living an extraordinary life.

After you finish the 10 chapters that unveil and teach you the code, I did not want to keep you hanging as you voyage out into the world. So I've included two bonus chapters on how to take all the ideas and tools and practices in this book and unify them into a daily practice.

Bonus Section: Tools for Your Journey

PRACTICE TRANSCENDENCE. In this section I'll teach you a 20-minute daily practice called the Six-Phase. It's a workout for the mind that helps lock in the elements of the code and accelerate your awakening. It's one of the greatest personal growth and productivity tools I've discovered.

FOLLOWING THE CODE OF THE EXTRAORDINARY MIND. In this section I summarize in one place all the key tools and practices you can bring into your life to live the code.

The bonus sections are supported by the Online Experience. You can download the app to get specific trainings, deeper interviews, and further models to apply. You can also join the online learning community to stay in touch with me and learn and share with other readers. All of this comes free with this book and is available at www.mindvalley.com/extraordinary.

MY PROMISE TO YOU

The ideas and techniques you'll learn in this book are based on the best models and systems I've found for performance, growth, and success from years of working with experts in personal development and human transformation.

I will give you the tools to bend the universe to attain the success, pleasure, and purpose that may have eluded you despite your best efforts. I know these methods work because I've used them myself, and I've helped millions around the world adopt them through various online programs, apps, and talks. This book will be the first time I bring it all together in one place.

You'll discover mental models for radically shifting your understanding of the world and your role within it. Chapter by chapter, you'll learn specific systems to create the biggest leaps in your life—of body, mind, heart, and soul.

Now, let's get started.

PART I

LIVING ^{IN THE} CULTURESCAPE

HOW YOU WERE SHAPED BY THE WORLD AROUND YOU

We're all swimming in a massive sea of human beliefs, ideas, and practices. Some are beautiful and bring joy; others are unnecessary, limiting, and sometimes even crippling. A fish is the last to see that it's swimming in a substance called water. Likewise we're often last to see how this mass of human thoughts—what I call the culturescape—completely saturates and influences our lives.

The culturescape sets up rules on how to love, how to eat, how to marry, how to get a job. It establishes benchmarks to measure your self-worth. Are you good enough if you don't have a college degree? Do you need to settle down and have kids? Embrace a religion? Choose a particular profession?

In this section we dive into the culturescape, where you'll discover things about its absurdity that you might have missed before.

In Chapter 1 you'll learn how the culturescape has been governing your life with a series of "shoulds." You *should* be doing this. You *should* be living like that. You'll see why life is best lived outside the *shoulds* and how there can be beauty in the wilder ride of an unrestricted life.

In Chapter 2 you'll learn how to detect the outdated rules that hold so

1

many people back, stop them from infecting you (and your children), and forge ahead by deciding your own rules. We'll take a look at some of the most stifling rules about work, spirituality, culture, and life and ask some important questions to see if they should still apply in our lives.

It's going to be a fun journey—a little controversial in some aspects because we'll be challenging some ideas that have been around for more than 2,000 years. But by the time we're through, you'll be able to walk toward a new version of the world—a version that *you* get to choose based on *your* truth and *your* vision.

CHAPTER I

TRANSCEND ^{THE} CULTURESCAPE

Where We Learn to Question the Rules of the World We Live In

> When you grow up, you tend to get told that the world is the way it is and your life is just to live your life inside the world. Try not to bash into the walls too much. Try to have a nice family life, have fun, save money. That's a very limited life. Life can be much broader once you discover one simple fact. That is—everything around you that you call life was made up by people no smarter than you. And you can change it. You can influence it. . . . Once you learn that, you'll never be the same again.
>
> **—STEVE JOBS**

The gleaming waters of Lake Washington were stunning from where I stood on the grassy lawn of a grand home. Conversation hummed around me. Glasses clinked as wine was poured. The sweet, spicy aroma of barbecue filled the air.

Just behind me stood Bill Gates, the owner of that home. One of the wealthiest men in the world and the legendary founder of tech giant Microsoft, he was chatting with his other young guests.

I was twenty-two and a few weeks into my job as a Microsoft intern, celebrating at the annual barbecue at Bill Gates's home to welcome Microsoft's newbies. Back then, Microsoft was the company to get into, equivalent to working for Apple or Google today. And I was *in!*

There was so much excitement in the air—we were like young Hogwarts students meeting Dumbledore for the first time.

I'd labored toward this goal for years, first working my butt off to get good grades in high school so I could gain admission to one of the best engineering colleges in the world—the University of Michigan, where I studied electrical engineering and computer science. In Malaysia, where I'd lived until the age of nineteen, as in other parts of Asia, it was the norm for families and educators to promote the idea of growing up to become an engineer, lawyer, or doctor. As a kid, I remember being told that if you were smart, that's what you did. It was just kind of how that world operated.

Yet the sad truth was that I dreaded my computer engineering classes in college. What I really wanted to be was a photographer or a stage actor. Photography and performing arts were the only classes where I got As. But those were not acceptable careers at all, according to the rules. So, I gave them up for programming. After all, I had to be *practical* and *realistic*. Get good grades. Get a good job. Work the nine-to-five. Save my money for a healthy retirement. Do it right and I would be a "success."

And I was beginning to succeed. It felt amazing to be honored with this opportunity to be in Bill's home and to be working at this company, then in its heyday. My professors were elated for me. My parents were thrilled. It made the hours of study and my parents' sacrifices worthwhile. I'd done everything that had been asked of me. Now it was time to reap the rewards. I had arrived. And I was standing in the home of Bill frickin' Gates with my career laid out before me.

But deep inside, I knew I had a problem.

On that fateful day in the summer of 1998, I had simultaneously accomplished two things: first, the completion of a long, many-year journey, and second, the painful realization that I had been walking in the wrong direction the entire damn time.

See, I genuinely disliked my job. I'd sit in my private office at Microsoft headquarters, staring at my triple-screen monitor, and count the minutes until I could escape. I disliked the work so much that, even though Bill Gates was standing just a few feet away from me surrounded by my colleagues, I felt too ashamed to shake his hand. I felt I shouldn't be there.

So a few weeks later, I quit.

Okay, I got fired.

I was too chicken to take charge and quit. To study at a top computer engineering college, get the coveted interview, and then snag the even-more-coveted job at the company my fellow students were dying to get into—to get that far and then quit was going to disappoint a lot of people.

So I did the next best thing a spineless twenty-two-year-old could do. I deliberately got myself fired. I simply goofed off and got caught playing video games at my desk way too many times during office hours until my manager was forced to fire me. So, as they say, *that* happened.

I went back to college and limped to the finish line. I had no idea what I was going do after graduation and felt almost stupid for blowing my huge opportunity with Microsoft.

As it turns out, getting out of there was the smart thing to do. I wasn't just quitting a job (and a career path)—I had also decided to quit following the socially approved rules for how life is supposed to work.

LET'S ADMIT IT'S NOT WORKING

When I went my own way rather than choosing the path of the practical and realistic job, it wasn't because I thought there was anything wrong with being a computer engineer. But I did—and still do—think there's something wrong with the idea that we should work at something we have no passion for, just because it's the norm or the rule in the world we're born into.

Yet many of us do just that. According to a Gallup study surveying more than 150,000 Americans, 70 percent of respondents said they were "disengaged" from their jobs. Given the amount of time we spend at work, a job we have no passion for puts us at risk of living a life we have no passion for. But it's not just our ideas about careers that are faulty. Consider these additional stats:

- 40 to 50 percent of US marriages end in divorce.

- A Harris poll showed that only 33 percent of Americans polled claimed to be "very happy."

- According to CNBC, "a new report by the Pew Charitable Trusts, which examined debt through the generations . . . found that eight in ten Americans are in debt in some fashion, most often because of a mortgage."

- According to the Centers for Disease Control and Prevention, more than one-third of adults in the United States are now obese.

Thus, our careers, our love lives, our happiness, our financial standing, and our health are all in conditions that are pretty inadequate. How did we get here, and how do we escape?

There are many reasons why these things happen. But I submit to you that one big reason is the tyranny of rules—rules that suggest we "should" do life in a particular way because everyone else seems to be doing it, too:

I *should* take this job.

I *should* date/marry this type of person.

I *should* go to this college.

I *should* major in this subject.

I *should* live in this city.

This is how I *should* look.

This is how I *should* feel.

Don't get me wrong. People sometimes have to take jobs they dislike in order to make ends meet. They have to live in places they wouldn't choose because it's all they can afford at the time or because they have family responsibilities.

But there's a big difference between bending to life's necessities and blindly accepting that you must live your life according to preconceived rules. One of the keys to being extraordinary is knowing what rules to follow and what rules to break. Outside the rules of physics and the rules of law, all other rules are open to questioning.

To understand this, we first have to understand why these rules exist in the first place.

THE DAWN OF THE RULES

Who made up the rules of the modern world anyway? To try to answer that question, let's take a quick leap into the beginnings of human history.

In his fascinating book *Sapiens,* historian Yuval Noah Harari, PhD, puts forward the idea that at a certain point in history, there could have been as many as six different types of humans living on the planet at once. There was *Homo sapiens,* which is what we all are. But there were also *Homo neanderthalensis, Homo soloensis,* and *Homo erectus,* among others.

But over time, all of the nonsapiens, such as the Neanderthals, died out, leaving *Homo sapiens* as our prehistoric grandmother or grandfather.

What helped sapiens survive?

The reason for our ultimate dominance, according to Dr. Harari, was our use of language—and specifically, its complexity in comparison to others'. Primatologists who have studied monkeys have found that monkeys can alert others in their group to danger, along the lines of, say, "Look out—tiger!"

But our sapiens forebears had very different brains. In contrast, sapiens could say, in effect, "Hey, this morning I saw a tiger by the river, so let's chill here until the tiger leaves to hunt, and then we can go there to eat, okay?"

Our sapiens ancestors had the ability to communicate complex information important to survival through the effective use of language. Language allowed us to organize groups of people—to share news of dangers or opportunities. To create and teach practices and habits: to communicate not just where the berries were on the riverbank but also how to pick, cook, and preserve them, what to do if someone ate too many, and even who should have the first and biggest helping. Language allowed us to preserve knowledge by passing it from person to person, parent to child, generation to generation.

It's difficult to overstate the power successive generations gained from literally not having to reinvent the wheel. Language gave rise to beautiful complexity on every level.

But the biggest advantage of language is that it allowed us to create a whole new world within our heads. We could use it to create things that didn't exist in the physical world but simply as "understandings" in our heads: to form alliances, establish tribes, and develop guidelines for cooperation within and between larger and larger groups. It allowed us to form cultures, mythologies, and religions. On the flip side, though, it also allowed us to go to war over those cultures, mythologies, and religions.

These changes and more, driven by advances in our thinking and enhanced by our ability to use language to share what we knew, were truly revolutionary—indeed, taken together, Dr. Harari calls this the cognitive revolution.

CAN YOU SEE SOMETHING IF YOU DON'T HAVE A WORD FOR IT?

If you don't believe how pervasively language shaped us and our world, here's some intriguing research pointing to its power.

Did the color blue exist in ancient cultures? According to a Radiolab podcast entitled "Why Isn't the Sky Blue?" in ancient times there was no word for blue in numerous languages. Homer, in *The Odyssey,* didn't mention the color blue for the sky or for the Aegean Sea, which he called wine-dark. Nor did the word blue appear in other ancient writings otherwise rich with description and visual detail.

So the question arises: If there's no word for a thing, can you see it?

Researcher Jules Davidoff studied this question among a particular tribe called the Himba, in Namibia. The Himba have many different words for green but no word for blue.

As part of the research, the tribe members were shown a circular pattern of squares. All of the squares were green except for one that was obviously blue like in the image below:

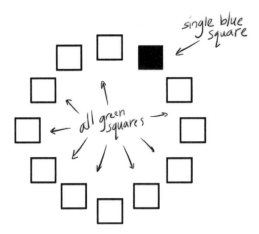

Oddly, when tribe members were shown the image and were asked to point to the outlier, they either couldn't select the blue square as the different one, were slower to do so, or chose the wrong square.

But when shown a similar circular pattern of green squares with one square a subtly different (and to many of us difficult to discern) shade of green, they quickly found it.

What would be easy for us was not easy for them. What would be difficult for us was easy for them. The Himba had no word for blue and thus could not easily identify a blue square from a collection of green squares—a task simple enough for most of us. Yet they could discern shades of green we would never notice.

So it seems that what language delineates, we can more easily discern. Our language shapes what we "see."

THE DUAL WORLDS WE LIVE IN

How miraculous was this ability language gave us to step back and observe our lives—to scope out that riverbank, assess risk and opportunity, and then seek not only advantage for ourselves but also go back to our tribe and share our thoughts with others. Together we became more aware, better able to plan for and prevail over challenges, and capable of inventing solutions to problems and then being able to teach those solutions to others. Language became the building blocks to culture.

These guidelines for living, developed and passed on through language, eventually evolved into the rules that govern our cultures. Our cultures helped us make sense of our world, process events quickly, create religions and nation-states, train our children so they'd be more likely to thrive, and open up mental and physical bandwidth to do more with our big brains than just try to survive until tomorrow.

Of course, there's a darker side to culture: when we get so focused on our rules that we turn them into decrees about how life "should" be and label people or processes as good or bad if they don't follow the rules. This is how you should live. This is how you should dress. This is how women, children, the sick, the elderly, or the "different" should be treated. My tribe is superior to your tribe. My ways are right, which means that yours are wrong. My beliefs are right, and yours are wrong. My God is the only God. We create these complex worlds and then literally defend them with our lives. The language and rules that define our culture can cost lives as much as cultivate them.

WELCOME TO THE CULTURESCAPE

With this vast structure of beliefs and practices that we developed for navigating the world, we actually created a new world layered on top of the one we lived every day on the proverbial riverbank. We've been living in two worlds ever since.

There's the physical world of absolute truth. This world contains things we're all likely to agree on: This is the riverbank; rocks are hard; water is wet; fire is hot; tigers have big teeth and it hurts when they bite you. No arguments there.

But there's also the world of relative truth. It's the mental world of ideas, constructs, concepts, models, myths, patterns, and rules that we've developed and passed from generation to generation—sometimes for thousands of years. This is where concepts such as marriage, money, religion, and laws reside. This is relative truth because these ideas are true only for a particular culture or tribe. Socialism, democracy, your religion, ideas about education, love, marriage, career, and every other "should" are nothing more than relative truths. They are simply not true for ALL human beings.

I call this world of relative truth the culturescape.

From the moment we're born, we're swimming in the culturescape. Our beliefs about the world and our systems for functioning in the world are all embedded in us through the flow and progression of culture from the minds of the people around us into our baby brains. But there's just one problem. Many of these beliefs and systems are dysfunctional, and while the intention is that these ideas should guide us, in reality they keep us locked into lives far more limited than what we're truly capable of. A fish is the last to discover water because it's been swimming in it all its life. Similarly, few people discover how pervasive and powerful the secondary world of our culturescape really is. We are not as independent and freethinking as we'd like to think we are.

The world of absolute truth is fact-based. The world of the culturescape is opinion-based and agreement-based. Yet even though it exists solely in our heads, it is very, very real.

How can a world that exists in our heads be real? Consider these examples of mental constructs we have created that do not exist in the physical world—but that are very real to us:

- We can't draw a *calorie* or point to one, but we believe that eating too many will give us love handles.

- We can't touch or see *meditation,* but more than 1,400 scientific studies show that it influences body and mind in positive ways, from improving longevity to enhancing creativity.

- You and I may not agree on how to define *God,* but God exists in different and unique ways to many people and much of human society is based on it. Even if one takes the view that God is imaginary, it remains a powerful syntax in the brain that influences how billions live their lives.

- *Corporations* don't actually exist in the physical world—you fill out forms and get a piece of paper declaring the formation of the entity. But that piece of paper establishes a series of laws and constructs that allow a group of people to come together and build something they couldn't have built on their own.

- We can't see or touch *laws*—they're just agreements among groups clustered in communities called *cities, states,* and *countries.* But they allow enormous groups of people to live in relative harmony.

- There's a widespread construct called *marriage* in which two people are expected to commit to each other for the rest of their lives, and yet every culture has different ideas of what that commitment should mean—physically, emotionally, and financially.

- In many cultures, there's a construct called *retirement* in which people are expected to alter their activities dramatically after a certain age.

- There are no actual borders drawn on the Earth, and the subjectivity of borders becomes painfully obvious when we summarily redraw them, as often happens at treaty time. Yet billions of people belong to border-defined places called *nations.*

In this way our thoughts literally do construct our world. We create and receive these constructs. We transmit them from generation to generation. They can be incredibly empowering or completely restrictive. For the convenience of being able to operate mindlessly in a complex world, we accept many of these culturescape constructs as true. The problem is—much of them are long past their expiration dates.

STEPPING OUT OF THE CULTURESCAPE

If so much of what we call life is mostly created by our thoughts and beliefs, then much of what we take to be real—all the constructs, rules, and "shoulds" of the culturescape—is nothing more than an accidental tweak of history. For the most part there's no rational basis to prove that what we're doing is the right way or the only way to do things. Much of what you think is true is all in your head.

How'd it get there? As Steve Jobs said, it was "made up by people no smarter than you." Once you understand that the rules aren't absolute, you can learn to think outside the box and live beyond limits imposed by the culturescape.

Realizing that the world you're living in exists inside your head puts you in the driver's seat. You can use your own mind to deconstruct the beliefs, systems, and rules you've been living with. The rules are very real in the sense that they actually govern how people and societies act, but very real does not mean very *right*.

The culturescape is so strong, so self-reinforcing that it convinces us that life must unfold in a particular way. This is fine if you'd like to live a regular, safe life. There's nothing wrong with that. The problem happens when "safety" gives rise to boredom and eventually stagnation.

We start our lives strong; as children we learn, grow, and change at an exhilarating pace. Yet for most people, once they graduate from college and start their careers, that growth slows down and eventually leads to a creeping, boring stagnation. If you were to draw this as a graph, it would look something like this:

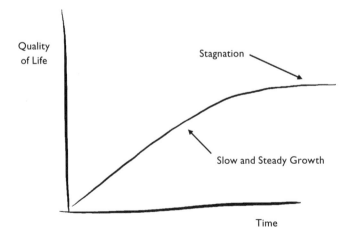

But what if we changed the definition of life from the drawing above to the drawing below:

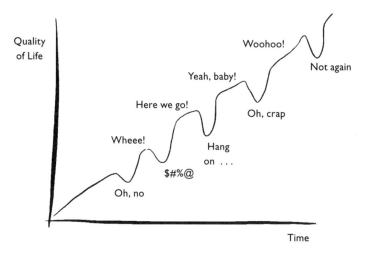

Notice the shift from slow, steady growth to irregular, up-and-down growth. Different, right? What if life was not meant to be safe? Instead, what if it was meant to be a beautiful joyride, with ups and downs as we take off the training wheels of the culturescape and try out things outside what is practical or realistic?

What if we accepted that things *will* go wrong—but that this is simply part of life's beautiful unfolding and that even the biggest failures can have within them the seeds of growth and possibility?

Our culturescape evolved to keep us safe—but in this day and age, we no longer need to fear tigers by the riverbank. Safety is overrated; taking risks is much less likely to kill us than ever before, and that means that playing it safe is more likely just holding us back from the thrills of a life filled with meaning and discovery.

Give me the thrill and excitement of the unsafe, rule-breaking, dogma-questioning life anytime over the boring unfolding of a safe life.

The common thread between every extraordinary individual we'll talk about in this book is that they all questioned their culturescape. They questioned the meaning of careers, degrees, religions, ways of living, and other "be safe" rules. In many cases, their willingness to break away from the culturescape has resulted in innovations and new beginnings that will shift the future of humanity. One such person is Elon Musk.

In 2013 I got to visit the SpaceX headquarters in Hawthorne, California, where I met the legendary Elon Musk. Elon is a living icon—a man who is changing the course of human history with innovations to electric cars via Tesla Motors, solar energy via Solar City, transportation via his Hyperloop idea, and space travel via SpaceX. He is arguably the greatest entrepreneur on the planet today.

I had a simple question to ask Elon. Being in the presence of a living legend made me a little nervous, so my question came out awkwardly: "Elon, you've done some pretty epic things, stuff most people would never even dream about. Yet what makes Elon Musk? I mean, if we could put you in a blender and blend you to distill your essence, what would that essence be?"

Elon laughed at the oddness of my question and the idea of being "blended," but then shared the following story:

"When I was just starting out, I walked into Netscape to get a job. I just sat in the lobby holding my résumé, waiting quietly for someone to talk to me. No one did. I waited and waited."

Elon mentioned that he had no idea what protocol to follow. He just waited, hoping someone would come and invite him for an interview.

"But no one spoke to me," he said.

"So I said: 'Fuck it! I'll just start my own company.'"

The world was forever changed that day.

Elon went on to start a little classified ad company in 1995 that was called Zip2 with $28,000. He sold it in 1999 and pocketed $22 million. He then used the windfall to start a company to challenge the rules of commercial online banking—which evolved into PayPal. But he didn't stop there.

In 2002 he started SpaceX to build a better rocket. And in 2008 he assumed the leadership of Tesla Motors to help make electric cars mainstream.

From banking to space exploration to electric cars, Elon challenged rules that few others dared question and in the process is leaving the planet with a legacy that is jaw-droppingly huge.

Elon shared a lot more, too. And we'll explore those other nuggets of wisdom in later chapters.

But first, let me introduce Law 1.

Law 1: Transcend the culturescape.

Extraordinary minds are good at seeing the culturescape and are able to selectively choose the rules and conditions to follow versus those to question or ignore. Therefore, they tend to take the path less traveled and innovate on the idea of what it means to truly *live*.

WHY SAFETY IS OVERRATED

The culturescape is designed to keep us safe. But as I've mentioned, safety is often overrated. Elon Musk answered my question, he spoke at length about his journey and what drove him—but he ended with one memorable line: "I have a high tolerance for pain."

Elon bounced back from amazing dips as he built his companies. He spoke about how, in 2008, SpaceX's first three rockets had blown up. A fourth failure would have made the company go bust. At the same time, Tesla Motors had failed a financing round and was running out of cash. Elon had to use up most of his windfall from the PayPal sale to finance these companies, and he had to borrow money to pay rent. Yet he came through.

While breaking away from the rules of the culturescape may indeed feel scary, I've often noticed a repeated pattern. The dips contain amazing learnings and wisdom that lead to sharper rises in the quality of life afterward. But you will need to brave the momentary pain of these dips. I assure you it will be worthwhile, and in this book you'll learn how to have the power to weather those downturns.

Every crappy experience I've had—from having my heart broken, to almost having to leave my own company due to a conflict with a business partner, to depression and staring down gaping dark holes of the mind—led to some small-but-significant insight or awakening that boosted the quality of my life and made me stronger. I now welcome these dips with an inner delight: *Wow, this sucks! I can't wait to see what I'm going to learn here!*

One of these dips, of course, was my Microsoft mishap, followed by my mediocre graduation. With no other job prospects after losing my Microsoft opportunity, I moved to New York City and went to work at a nonprofit at a salary level officially below the poverty line. My family and friends thought I was crazy.

Earning a salary officially below the poverty line meant that I could not afford my own apartment. At Microsoft I had a killer apartment with my own bedroom. In New York City I shared a studio in Chelsea with a coworker named James—a dirty little apartment with furniture that the previous tenants had salvaged from the street. Our sofa and mattresses were covered with black marks that could have been soot, mold, or worse. I dared not imagine what. But I do vividly remember one night in May 2000.

I had convinced the hot redhead from Estonia whom I had met on a work-related trip to Europe to come to New York to visit me. The only problem was that she was going to be staying with me in my awful Chelsea apartment—something I was deeply embarrassed about. Kristina arrived at my apartment and was so thrilled to be in New York that she immediately hopped onto James's bed and started jumping up and down in the excitement of finally visiting New York.

"Um, that's my roommate's bed," I said. "Mine is over there."

"You have a roommate? So you don't live here by yourself? But how do we . . . you know . . . have some privacy?" she asked, shocked and a little bewildered.

I pointed to the inspired solution I had rigged up so we could have privacy: a pink shower curtain that, with a few pulls, created a mock "wall" separating my little nook in the studio from the rest of the shared space with James. (Yes, I was too broke to afford real curtains.) It was plastic and ugly—but it offered just enough privacy to, um, make our nights memorable.

I seriously don't know what Kristina saw in me, but three years later we got married. Today we have two beautiful kids and a home with really nice curtains.

I would never have met my wife if I had not quit Microsoft, lost all my other job options, and ended up broke in New York—a series of unfortunate dips lined up one by one by one that resulted in one sharp, booming spike: meeting the woman I would marry and having the children I have today.

See, there is beauty in the dips. We try to avoid them by sticking to the passed-down rules of the culturescape, only to wake up one day wondering how we missed out on so much. Don't let that be you. Life has a way of taking care of you no matter how dark it can sometimes feel—I promise. There's more to it, of course. You need to learn how to change the rules (Chapter 2), how to heal your mind (Chapter 3), how to remove dangerous beliefs (Chapter 4), how to learn new things incredibly fast (Chapter 5), how to be lucky (Chapter 6), how to find happiness (Chapter 7), how to know what to seek (Chapter 8). And then there's weathering the inevitable storm (Chapter 9), finding your calling (Chapter 10), and lots, lots more. But when we set forth on this path, anyone can become truly extraordinary.

I love this quote by American football player and actor Terry Crews: "I constantly get out of my comfort zone. Once you push yourself into something new, a whole new world of opportunities opens up. But you might get hurt. But amazingly when you heal—you are somewhere you've never been."

You can be 12 or 80—it's never too late to question the rules and step out of your comfort zone.

WHAT'S NEXT

In the coming chapters, I'll help you examine the beliefs and systems of your life and decide which ones are moving you forward and which are holding you back. I'll provide keys for unlocking your potential to become extraordinary. This means shaking off the shackles from cultural baggage of the past, expanding your vision of your future, and experiencing a dramatic shift in how you view life, function in the world, pursue goals, and interact with others.

Together, let's seek a level of advanced awareness in which we can see our patterns and go beyond them and understand that, while we may belong to a particular culture or nation or religion, we're only part of that culture or nation or religion because we happen to be born in a particular family at a particular time and place, and that the same is true of every other human being on the Earth. Our individual experiences of the culturescape made us who we are. But what happens when we learn to transcend the culturescape? When we learn that no one is better off than another? That none of us is more superior? And that each of us can be extraordinary?

A SERIOUS WORD OF WARNING

Before we continue, I must issue a word of warning. Questioning many rules of the culturescape will not be easy. Here's a partial list of all the things that could go "wrong" if you continue reading this book:

- You might anger loved ones as you decide to question their expectations of you.
- You might decide to leave your current relationship.
- You might decide to raise your kids with different beliefs.
- You might choose to question your religion or create your own customized religious system.
- You might rethink your career.
- You might become obsessed with being happy.
- You might decide to forgive someone who hurt you in the past.
- You might rip apart your current goal sheet and start anew.
- You might start a daily spiritual practice.
- You might fall out of love with someone and fall in love with yourself.
- You might decide to leave your career and start a business.
- You might decide to leave your business and start a career.
- You might find a mission that excites you a lot and scares you a little.

It all starts with questioning the accepted rules of the culturescape. My friend Peter Diamandis, founder and chairman of the X Prize Foundation, famously said:

> *If you can't win, change the rules. If you can't change the rules, ignore them.*

I love this advice. But before you can challenge the rules of the culturescape, you have to identify the limiting rules that might be holding you back. It starts with discovering the ones you're locked into and operating under right now (whether you know it or not).

Maybe you won't be surprised to know that the process starts with language—with a new word, to be precise—for what language delineates, we can more easily discern.

The new word is Brule.

CHAPTER 2

QUESTION
THE BRULES

Where We Learn That Much of How the World
Runs Is Based on Bulls**t Rules Passed Down
from Generation to Generation

You will find that many of the truths we cling to depend
greatly on our own point of view.

Who's more foolish, the fool? Or the fool who follows him?

—SAYINGS OF OBI-WAN KENOBI, *STAR WARS*

THE LIES WE CHOOSE TO BELIEVE

In Chapter 1, we looked at how human beings simultaneously exist in two
worlds. There's the physical world of absolute truth and the culturescape of
relative truth. In the culturescape all the ideas we hold dear—our identity,
our religion, our nationality, our beliefs about the world—are nothing more
than mental constructs we've *chosen* to believe. And like all mental constructs, many are merely opinions we believe because they were drilled into
us as children and accepted by the culture we grew up in.

Human beings are far less rational than we think. Many ideas we hold
dear and cling to as "truth" fall apart under close inspection. Our mental
constructs of the world can change, pivot, expand, and shrink as human
cultures, ideologies, and opinions collide, dance, and clash with each other.
Just as disease is spread by contagion from host to victim, so ideas are
spread in the same way. We often take on ideas not through rational choice

but through "social contagion"—the act of an idea spreading from mind to mind without due questioning.

Thus our so-called "truths" are rarely optimal ways of life. As consumer psychologist Paul Marsden, PhD, wrote in a paper called "Memetics and Social Contagion: Two Sides of the Same Coin?":

> Whilst we may like to believe that we consciously and rationally decide on how to respond to situations, social contagion evidence suggests that some of the time this is simply not the case. Rather than generating and "having" beliefs, emotions, and behaviours, social contagion research suggests that, in some very real sense, those beliefs, emotions, and behaviours "have" us. . . . When we are unsure of how to react to a stimulus or a situation, these theories suggest that we actively look to others for guidance and consciously imitate them.

It's a stunning statement. Dr. Marsden is saying that when we make decisions, we're more likely to defer to the hive mind than to make a decision based entirely on our own thoughts and best interests. *We don't have beliefs so much as beliefs "have" us.*

Dr. Marsden continues:

> The evidence shows that we inherit and transmit behaviours, emotions, beliefs, and religions not through rational choice but contagion.

This is perhaps one of the most important lines in Dr. Marsden's paper. We *think* we're making a rational decision. But often, the decision has little to do with rationality and more to do with ideas our family, culture, and peers have approved.

There's nothing wrong with taking on ideas from the society we live in. But as our world is undergoing exponential change at a staggering pace, following the masses and doing what's always been done isn't a path that leads to being extraordinary. Ideas, memes, and culture are meant to evolve and change, and we are best served when we question them.

We know intellectually that this sort of change happens, yet billions of us cling to self-defeating rules from the past that should not exist in today's world because technology, society, and human consciousness have simply evolved beyond them.

In Chapter 1, you learned about the Himba tribe and their difficulty with seeing the color blue because they have no word for it. Words play an important role in cognition. So I coined a name for these outdated rules so we can see them better: The word I use is "Brules."

Brule: A Definition

A Brule is a bulls**t rule that we adopt to simplify our understanding of the world.

We use Brules to categorize things, processes, and even people. Brules are handed down by our tribe—often our family, culture, and educational system. For example, do you remember choosing your religion? Or how you got your ideas about love, money, or the way life works? Most of us don't. Many of our most formative rules about how to live come through others. And these rules are tightly bound to ideas of what is good and bad, right and wrong.

Each of us lives by thousands of rules. When we aren't sure what to do, we follow the example of those who came before us. Kids follow their parents, who followed their parents, who followed theirs, and so on back in time.

This means that often we are not Christian or Jewish or politically right or left because we decided we wanted to be, but simply because we happened to be born in a particular family at a particular time and, through memetics and social conditioning, adopted a particular set of beliefs. We may decide to take a certain job (as happened to me when I became a computer engineer), go to law school, get an MBA, or join the family business, not because we made a rational decision that this was the path we wanted to follow but because society programmed us that we should.

You can see from an evolutionary standpoint how it would be efficient to mimic the patterns modeled by those who came before. Ideas such as how to harvest, hunt, cook, and communicate get passed down from generation to generation, allowing civilization to steadily grow in complexity and scale. But it means we may be living our lives according to models that haven't been upgraded for years, decades, even centuries. Blindly following may be efficient, but it's not always smart.

When we look at them closely, we often find that Brules were imposed on us for convenience. To question and dissect these Brules is to take a step into the extraordinary.

My life of questioning the Brules started at age nine. That's when a McDonald's opened close to my home. Everywhere I turned, it seemed, there were ads showing mouthwatering pictures of McDonald's cheeseburgers. Man, they looked good. And I so so so craved a Happy Meal. But I had been brought up as a Hindu and therefore had been told that I could absolutely, positively not eat beef. Ever.

McDonald's had created a phenomenon of manufactured demand. I had never tasted beef, but thanks to all those ads and images of people "lovin' it," I concluded that McDonald's burgers were going to be the greatest meal I'd ever tasted in my nine years on planet Earth. The only thing stopping me was that, culturally, I wasn't supposed to eat beef, since it would anger the gods (or something similarly dreadful).

My parents had always encouraged me to question things, so I felt comfortable asking my mom to explain to me why I couldn't eat beef. She replied that it was part of our family's culture and religion. "But other people eat beef. Why can't Hindus eat it, too?" I persisted.

Wise teacher that she was, she said, "Why don't you go find out?" There was no Internet back then, but I pored over my *Encyclopedia Britannica* and developed a theory about ancient India, Hindus, cows, and beef eating that I took back to my mother. Basically, it went like this: "Mom, I think the ancient Hindus loved having cows as pets because they were gentle and had big, beautiful eyes. Cows were also very useful: They could plow the fields and provide milk. So maybe that was why Hindus back then wouldn't eat beef when they could so easily eat goat, pig, or any other less awesome animal. But last I checked, we have a dog and not a cow, and so I think I should be allowed to eat beef burgers."

I don't know what was going on in my mom's head, but she agreed, and that's how I got to taste my first beef burger. Frankly, it was overrated. But still—boom! Just like that, a dogmatic model of reality I'd grown up blindly following was shattered.

I started questioning everything else. By nineteen, I had discarded religion—not because I wasn't spiritual but because I felt that calling myself a Hindu was separating myself from the billions of spiritual people who weren't Hindu. I wanted to embrace the spiritual essence of every religion, not just one. Even as a teen, I could not understand the whole idea of being bound to one singular religion for life.

I was fortunate to have parents who challenged me and allowed me to create my own beliefs. But if a nine-year-old can bust a Brule, the rest of us should be able to question them, too.

Take a moment and think about the religious or cultural norms that were transmitted to you. How many would you say are truly rational? They may be outmoded or proven untrue by today's thinkers or researchers. Many might even cause terrible pain. I'm not advocating that you instantly reject all the rules you've ever followed, but you must question your rules constantly in order to live by the code that is most authentic to your goals and needs. "My family/culture/people have always done it this way" is not an acceptable argument.

COMMON BRULES WORTH CHALLENGING

As you get on the path to the extraordinary, you must remember that within the culturescape there are no sacred cows that cannot be questioned. Our politics, our education and work models, our traditions and culture, and even our religions all contain Brules that are best discarded.

Below are some common Brules we live by, often without even realizing it, and some different ways I've come to think about them. They're among the biggest Brules I challenged. Escaping them shifted my life forward in dramatic ways. These are the four areas in which I decided to eliminate a Brule from my worldview:

1. The college Brule
2. The loyalty to our culture Brule
3. The religion Brule
4. The hard work Brule

As you read this, ask yourself if you might be held back by any of these Brules.

1. We should get a college degree to guarantee our success.

In addition to saddling many young people with massive debt for decades, studies have shown that a college education really doesn't guarantee success. And does a college degree guarantee high performance on the job? Not necessarily. Times are changing fast. While Internet giant Google looks at good grades in specific technical skills for positions requiring them, a 2014 *New York Times* article detailing an interview with Laszlo Bock, Google's senior vice president of people operations, notes that college degrees aren't as important as they once were. Bock states that "When you look at people who don't go to school and make their way in the world, those are exceptional human beings. And we should do everything we can to find those people." He noted in a 2013 *New York Times* article that the "proportion of people without any college education at Google has increased over time"—on certain teams comprising as much as 14 percent.

Other companies are taking note. According to a 2015 article in iSchoolGuide, Ernst and Young, "the largest recruiter in the United Kingdom and one of the world's largest financial consultancies, recently announced that they will no longer consider grades as the main criteria for recruitment." The article quoted Maggie Stilwell, Ernst and Young's Managing Partner for Talent: "Academic qualifications will still be taken into account and indeed remain an important consideration when assessing candidates as a whole, but will no longer act as a barrier to getting a foot in the door."

I've personally interviewed and hired more than 1,000 people for my companies over the years, and I've simply stopped looking at college grades or even at the college an applicant graduated from. I've simply found them to have no correlation with an employee's success.

College degrees as a path to a successful career may thus be nothing more than a mass societal Brule that's fading away quickly. This is not to say that going to college is unnecessary—my life at college was one of the best memories and growth experiences I've ever had. But little of that had to do with my actual degree or what I was studying.

2. We should marry within our religion or ethnicity.

I come from a very small minority ethnicity from western India. My culture is called Sindhi. The Sindhis left India after 1947 and are living as a diaspora; that is, scattered all over the world. Like many cultures that live as a diaspora, there's a firm desire to protect and preserve the culture and the tradition. As part of that, in my culture, it is considered absolutely taboo to marry anyone outside our ethnicity—not even another Indian. So you can imagine how shocked my family was when I told them I wanted to marry my then-girlfriend, Kristina (now my wife), who is Estonian. I remember well-meaning relatives asking me, "Do you really want to do this? . . . Your children are going to be so confused! . . . Why would you disappoint your family like this?"

At first I feared following my heart because I felt I would cause great disappointment for those I loved. But I realized that with a huge life decision such as this, I shouldn't do something to make someone else happy that would make me so unhappy. I wanted to be with Kristina. So I married her. I rejected the Brule, so common in my generation, that we should marry only people of our ethnicity, religion, and race as it was the safest way to happiness and the "right" thing to do for the family or creed. Kristina and I have been together for sixteen years, married for thirteen. Our two kids, far from being "confused," are learning multiple languages and happily becoming citizens of the world (my son, Hayden, had traveled to eighteen countries by the time he was eighteen months old). My children participate in Russian Orthodox, Lutheran, and Hindu traditions with their grandparents. But they aren't limited to any *one* religion. They get to experience all the beauty of human religions without being locked into any one path. Which brings us to the next big Brule.

3. We should adhere to a single religion.

Okay, here's a touchy question. Do we really need religion? Can spirituality exist without religious dogma? These are only a few of the questions being asked about religion today. Right alongside a rise in fundamentalism, we're seeing a rise in questioning of the fundamentals. Do you remember the day you chose your religion? Few people do because few people get to choose their religion. Generally, it's a series or cluster of beliefs implanted in our minds at a young age, based on our parents' religious beliefs. And for many, the desire to belong to a family or tribe overrides our rational decision-making process and gets us to adopt beliefs that may be highly damaging.

While religion can have immense beauty, it can also have immense dogma that causes guilt, shame, and fear-based worldviews. Today the majority of people on planet Earth who are religious choose a single religion to subscribe to. But this percentage is shrinking as more and more people, especially millennials, are adopting the model "Spiritual But Not Religious."

I believe that religion was necessary for human evolution, helping us develop guidelines for good moral conduct and cooperation within the tribe hundreds and thousands of years ago. But today, as humanity is more connected than ever and many of us have access to the various wisdom and spiritual traditions of the world, the idea of adhering to a singular religion might be obsolete. Furthermore, I believe that the blind acceptance of religious dogma is holding us back in our spiritual evolution as a species.

The core of a religion may be beautiful spiritual ideas. But wrapped around them are usually centuries of outdated Brules that few bother to question.

Can a person be a good Muslim without fasting during Ramadan? A good Christian without believing in sin? A good Hindu who eats beef? Is religion an aging model that needs to be updated?

A better alternative, in my opinion, is not to subscribe to one religion but to pick and choose beliefs from the entire pantheon of global religions and spiritual practices.

I was born in a Hindu family, but over the years, I've created my own set of beliefs derived from the best of every religion and spiritual book I've been exposed to. We don't pick one food to eat every day. Why must we pick one religion? Why can't we believe in Jesus' model of love and kindness, donate 10 percent of our income to charity like a good Muslim, and also think that reincarnation is awesome?

There is much beauty in the teachings of Christ, the Sufism of Islam, the Kabbalah from Judaism, the wisdom of the *Bhagavad Gita*, or the Buddhist teachings of the Dalai Lama. Yet humanity has widely decided that religion should be absolutist: In short, pick one and stick to it for the rest of your life. And worse—pass it on to your children through early indoctrination, so they feel they have to stick to one true path for the rest of *their* lives. Then repeat for generations.

Choose a religion if it gives you meaning and satisfaction, but know that you don't have to accept all aspects of your religion to fit in. You can believe in Jesus and not believe in hell. You can be Jewish and enjoy a ham sandwich. Don't get trapped in preset, strict definitions of one singular path, thinking you must accept all of a particular tribe's beliefs. Your spirituality should be discovered, not inherited.

4. We must work hard to be successful.

This may start as a worthy idea and morph into a tyrannical Brule. Parents want to encourage their kids to stick with challenges, work toward goals, and not give up. But that can get twisted into a Brule: If you aren't working hard all the time, you're lazy and won't be successful.

This Brule also leads to a corollary Brule that work must feel like a slog. It can't be exciting or meaningful and certainly not fun. Yet a Gallup study shows that people who work in jobs that provide them with a sense of meaning and joy retire much later than those who work in jobs that provide no sense of meaning. When you aren't suffering for your paycheck, you're likely to be more engaged and committed to what you're doing. And how long can you afford to not like what you do given that most of us spend the majority of our waking hours at work? As educator and minister Lawrence Pearsall Jacks wrote:

> A master in the art of living draws no sharp distinction between his work and his play; his labor and his leisure; his mind and his body; his education and his recreation. He hardly knows which is which. He simply pursues his vision of excellence through whatever he is doing, and leaves others to determine whether he is working or playing. To himself, he always appears to be doing both.

In my life I've always made a conscious choice to work in fields where I love what I do so much that it ceases to feel like work. When you love what you do, life seems so much more beautiful—in fact, the very idea of "work" dissolves. Instead, it feels more like a challenge, a mission, or a game you play. I encourage everyone to try to move toward work that feels this way. It does not make any sense to spend the majority of our waking hours at work, to earn a living, so we can continue living a life where we spend the majority of our waking hours at work. It's a human hamster wheel. Therefore, always seek work that you love. Any other way of living misses the point of life itself. It won't happen overnight, but it's doable. As you progress through this book, I'll share some mental models and practices to get you there faster.

FIVE WAYS WE TAKE ON BRULES

How can we spot Brules that limit us and break free? The first step is to know how they got installed within you in the first place. There are five ways I believe we take on Brules. When you understand these *infection mechanisms*, you'll be better able to identify which rules of the culturescape might be reasonable to use for planning your life and which ones may be Brules.

I. Childhood Indoctrination

We absorb most beliefs uncritically as children during our extremely long maturity period. While other animals mature relatively quickly or can run or swim for their lives soon after birth, we human beings are helpless at birth and remain highly dependent for years afterward. During this time we are, as *Sapiens* author Yuval Noah Harari describes, like "molten glass"—highly moldable by the environment and the people around us:

> Most mammals emerge from the womb like glazed earthenware emerging from a kiln—any attempt at remolding will only scratch or break them. Humans emerge from the womb like molten glass from a furnace. They can be spun, stretched, and shaped with a surprising degree of freedom. This is why today we can educate our children to become Christian or Buddhist, capitalist or socialist, warlike or peace loving.

Our malleable brains as children make us amazing learners, receptive to every experience and primed to take any shape our culture decrees. Think, for example, about how a child born in a multicultural home can grow up to speak two or three languages fluently. But it also causes us to take on all forms of childhood conditioning.

Ever notice how often a child asks why? The typical parent's response to the steady barrage of why, why, why is usually something along the lines of:

"Because I said so."

"Because that's the way it is."

"Because God wanted it this way."

"Because Dad says you need to do it."

Statements like these cause children to get trapped in a thicket of Brules they may not even realize are open to question. Those children grow up to become adults trapped by restrictions and rules that they have taken to be "truth."

Thus we absorb the rules transmitted by culture and act in the world based on these beliefs. Much of this conditioning is in place before the age of nine, and we may carry many of these beliefs until we die—until or unless we learn to challenge them.

As a parent myself, I know how difficult it can be to answer with honesty and sincerity every question a child poses. I was in the car with my son in the summer of 2014 when Nicki Minaj's song "Anaconda" came on the radio without my noticing. As the key verse rang out about a particular "anaconda" who doesn't "want none unless" it's "got buns hun," my seven-year-old son, Hayden, asked me, "Dad, why does the anaconda only want buns?"

I turned red, as most parents would. And then in an act I know you're going to forgive me for, I did what I think any other dad in my situation would do. I lied.

"It's a song about a snake that only loves bread," I said.

Hayden bought it. Phew. Later that day, he told me he wanted to write a song about a snake with healthier eating habits.

I've fielded my share of difficult "why" questions from my kids. I certainly asked my parents a lot of them. I bet you did, too. And your parents probably did their best to answer you. But some of their answers, especially phrases such as, "because that's the way it is," might sometimes have set up Brules you're still following.

2. Authority Figures

The men and women of our tribe whom we see as authority figures, usually people we depend on in some way, are powerful installers of rules. Certainly that includes our parents but also relatives, caregivers, teachers, clergy, and friends. Many may be wise people with our best interests in mind who want to impart rules that will serve us well in life—such as the

Golden Rule about treating others as we would want to be treated. But because we give them authority, we're also vulnerable to those who pass down Brules that they either seek to manipulate us with or that they genuinely believe themselves, however wrongly.

Authority has proved to have an astonishing, and potentially dangerous, hold over us.

During our evolution as a sentient species, we needed leaders and authority figures to help us organize and survive. With the advent of literacy and other skills for acquiring, retaining, and sharing information, knowledge is now far more evenly distributed and widely available. It's time we stopped behaving like submissive prehistoric tribe members and started questioning some of the things our leaders say.

Take for example, fear-based politics. It's common in the world today for politicians to gain support by creating fear of another group. The Jews, the Muslims, the Christians, the Mexican immigrants, the refugees, the gays are all blamed in one country or another by a politician seeking votes. We need to stop buying into this type of misuse of authority.

But of course it's not just authority figures on the largest scale who dominate us. Interestingly, some people express feeling a sense of freedom after their parents die, because they finally feel able to follow their own desires, opinions, and goals, free of parental expectations and the pressure to conform to rules their parents approved of.

3. The Need to Belong

We have a tendency to take on Brules because we want to fit in. We're a tribal species, evolved to find security and kinship with each other in groups. It was safer than going it alone. Thus survival depended on being accepted within the tribe. But sometimes in order to be part of a tribe, we take on the tribe's beliefs, irrational as those may be. So in exchange for acceptance, we pay a price in individuality and independence. It's almost a cliché, for example, that teenagers struggle to balance individuality with succumbing to peer pressure.

Tribe here refers to any kind of group with a set of beliefs and traditions— it can be a religion, a political party, a club, team, and so on. As soon as we define ourselves by a particular view, even if it's something that we genuinely agree with, we automatically become more likely to start taking on other beliefs of the party—even if these beliefs challenge facts and science.

We see this need for belonging at its strongest when looking at the irrational beliefs people take on when they join cults. The desire to be accepted causes them to shut down their ability to question, and they accept highly illogical, irrational beliefs.

Tim Urban, who runs the amazing blog waitbutwhy.com, calls this blind tribalism. Tim writes:

> Humans also long for the comfort and safety of certainty, and nowhere is conviction more present than in the groupthink of blind tribalism. While a scientist's data-based opinions are only as strong as the evidence she has and inherently subject to change, tribal dogmatism is an exercise in faith, and with no data to be beholden to, blind tribe members believe what they believe with certainty.

You can take on the beliefs of your tribe, but you don't have to take on *all* of their beliefs, especially if their beliefs are unscientific, unhelpful, or untrue.

4. Social Proof

When we take on rules because someone says, in effect, "everyone's doing it," we're adopting beliefs through social proof. Think of it as approval by proxy: We believe what someone else tells us to save ourselves the effort of assessing the truth of it ourselves. If we're led to think that "everyone" is doing it, believing it, or buying it, then we decide maybe we should, too. A modern-day example is advertising: Everyone eats this, buys this, wears this . . . this is healthy; that is unhealthy . . . this is what you need in order to make people notice you . . . and so on. You've seen the ads. The modern advertising age has gotten incredibly slick at using social proof to create what I call manufactured demand. Nobody really needs that much high-fructose corn syrup packaged as Happiness in a Red Can. Nor do we need the thousands of other products that exist solely to fill a void that their own commercials create. But manufactured demand turns products that are unhealthy into must-haves through the effective use of social proof to create desire. If everyone's doing it—it must be legit.

5. Our Internal Insecurities

Suppose you go on a date with someone you're really attracted to. After the date, the person doesn't call you back. For many of us, our internal insecurities go into overdrive: *I didn't dress well enough . . . maybe I talked too much . . . I shouldn't have told that joke . . .* and on and on. Then, without actually finding out why the person hasn't called, we invent a bunch of Brules about love, dating, how we should act on dates, and men and women in general. But reality may tell a different story. Maybe the person lost his phone and didn't have your number. Maybe she had a really tough week or had to deal with a family crisis.

Yet instead of looking at these logical ideas, we start to create "meaning" around the events. The meaning-making machine in our heads is constantly creating meaning about the events that we observe in our lives—particularly when they involve people we are seeking love or attention from.

Have you ever created meaning in your head about someone's attitude or feelings toward you because of something they do? That's the meaning-making machine in action.

You might already be tuning in to how some of the Brules in your life have been installed. Can you think of authority figures who had a lot of influence over you? Do you have a memory of doing something you disliked just to follow the herd? Did you behave according to rules that would help you fit in?

No judgment here. Remember, this is part of how humans learn. It's how all the information of past generations gets provided to us—including good stuff like how to make fire, fashion a wheel, tell a knock-knock joke, barbecue some meat, perform CPR, and decorate a Christmas tree. It's not all bad; it's just that many of us need help realizing that it's not all good, either. Some rules aren't useful anymore or were never true to begin with. It's time to uninstall what isn't working.

HOW TO MAKE A DENT IN THE UNIVERSE

Our culturescape is filled with many ideas that are powerful because of the sheer number of people who believe in them. Think of ideas like nation-states, money, transportation, our education system, and more. But every now and then a rebel comes along and decides that some of these colossal constructs are nothing more than Brules. Most of these rebels talk about changing things and are labeled idealists at best, or nut jobs at worst, but once in a while, a rebel grabs reality by the horns and, slowly yet decisively, shifts things.

The drawing below illustrates this point. The circle is the culturescape. The mass of dots in the middle represents most folks. At first a certain person, perhaps you, decides to move away from viewing the world like everyone else. You get labeled a misfit, a rebel, a troublemaker.

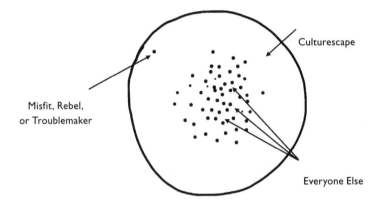

But then you do something original and wild. Perhaps you write a new type of children's book, as J. K. Rowling did with the Harry Potter books. Or, like the Beatles, you decide to move away from traditional sounds and create an original type of music. Or, like entrepreneur Elon Musk, you decide to popularize the electric car. Some misfits will fail. But some will succeed, and when they do, they make a dent in a culturescape.

And that's when the misfit is labeled a visionary.

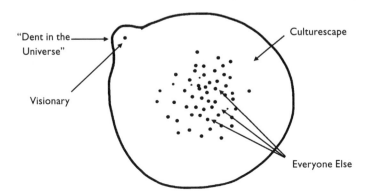

One such visionary is Dean Kamen. I got to visit Dean in 2015 and hear him tell me one of the most incredible stories of Brule-breaking I've ever heard.

Dean Kamen is a modern-day Edison. He holds more than 440 patents. He revolutionized wheelchair technology with the iBOT mobility device, spearheaded development of the leading home dialysis system, and became an icon of engineering with his invention of the Segway Human Transporter. He is a recipient of the National Medal of Technology and a member of the National Inventors Hall of Fame. With the Segway, Dean questioned the Brule of transportation: Could cities be designed without the need for cars? But personally, I'm more impressed by Dean's questioning of the Brule of the nation-state. You see, frustrated by government, Dean started his own nation. He is, by his own fiat, Lord Dumpling, president of North Dumpling Island—a tiny island nation in Long Island Sound that he turned into his own country—only the third country in North America after the United States and Canada.

Dean Kamen was never one to follow dumb rules. As one of America's greatest inventors, he had a strict anti-bureaucracy attitude. A healthy disregard for senseless rules and the mind of an innovator can be explosive when combined. And as he explained to me and a small group of others invited to visit him in May 2015, a giant wind turbine sparked it all.

It started out as what you could call a practical joke, but it became something much more. As a great proponent of alternative energy, Dean wanted to build a wind turbine on North Dumpling Island, his home a few miles off the coast of Connecticut, to help power his house. But New York bureaucrats (even though it's close to Connecticut, the island is actually part of New York's jurisdiction) said the proposed turbine was too big, and the noise would disturb the neighbors. "It's an *island*," said Dean. "There *are* no neighbors!" The bureaucrats wouldn't budge. It was a stalemate.

Dean Kamen is not a man who backs down. As he told us, he was seriously bothered that New York State, which was miles away from North Dumpling, had the power to tell him how to run his island. So Dean decided that he would take no more. Speaking to a friend of his at Harvard who was an expert on constitutional law, Dean found a loophole that allowed him to secede—not just from New York but from the entire United States. And so on April 22, 1988, the *New York Times* carried an article: "From Long Island Sound, A New Nation Asserts Itself."

Dean didn't just create his own island nation. He created North Dumpling's own constitution, anthem, and currency called (what else?) the dumpling.

How's that for bending the Brules? Few of us grow up thinking about starting our own nation. Or currency. Dean, however, is not an ordinary person. Perhaps it was that same inquisitive mind that led him to question the Brules of transportation and invent the Segway. He had now questioned the idea of nationhood itself. But Dean wasn't done yet.

New York didn't relent. Its bureaucrats continued sending warning letters to Dean about the wind turbine. Dean simply sent those letters to the New York press with a statement: "See how disrespectful New York bureaucrats can be—they dare threaten the head of an independent nation-state." The warning letters stopped.

A few months later while visiting the White House (Dean has friends in high places), Dean jokingly got President George H. W. Bush to sign a nonaggression pact with North Dumpling.

As you can imagine, all of this caused tremendous publicity. A local morning talk show decided to visit North Dumpling to do a broadcast from the island. During the filming, Dean explained, he asked one of the talk show hosts if he'd like to convert his US dollars to dumplings. The host scoffed, asking if dumplings were real currency. Dean replied that US dollars are the currency that should really be questioned. After all, the dollar had been taken off the gold standard decades ago and was now backed by thin air. The dumpling, on the other hand, was backed by Ben & Jerry's ice cream. (Seriously. Dean knows the founders.) And, as Dean pointed out, since ice cream is frozen to 32°F (0°C), it had "rock-solid backing."

As I explored Dean's home, I found on one wall what struck me as the most important document of all. It was a framed "Foreign Aid National Treasure Bond" to President Bush in which North Dumpling Island actually gave foreign aid to the United States—in the sum of $100.

I asked Dean for the story behind the picture. He told me that North Dumpling had become the first nation in the world to provide foreign aid to the United States. And here's why, according to the certificate:

> Once the technological leaders of the world, America's Citizens have been slipping into Woeful Ignorance of and Dismaying Indifference to the wonders of science and technology. This threatens the United States with Dire Descent into scientific and technological

illiteracy. . . . The Nation of North Dumpling Island hereby commits itself to helping rescue its neighbor Nation from such fate by supporting the efforts of the Foundation for Inspiration and Recognition of Science and Technology in promoting excellence in and appreciation of these disciplines among the peoples of the United States of America. . . ."

Dean wasn't giving $100 to a superpower as a joke. He was about to pull off yet another Brule-busting move using his newly formed role as an independent nation to do it. He was seeking to change the global education system to bring more attention to science and engineering.

Dean's donation to the United States was for establishing *FIRST* (For Inspiration and Recognition of Science and Technology), an organization with a mission: "To transform our culture by creating a world where science and technology are celebrated and where young people dream of becoming science and technology leaders." *FIRST* does this through huge competitions where kids build robots of all kinds that compete in Olympic-like settings.

When I attended the *FIRST* robotics challenge in St. Louis, Missouri, in 2015, some 37,000 teams from high schools around the world had competed to get their robots to the finals. It was fantastic to see what those kids could build.

Dean said that he thinks one of the problems in the world today is that kids grow up idolizing sports superstars, and while there's nothing wrong with idolizing athletic power, we also need to idolize brainpower—the engineers, the scientists, the people who are moving humanity forward through innovation. That's what he did with *FIRST*. And North Dumpling Island certainly helped fuel publicity for the organization.

Whether North Dumpling Island is really a nation is beside the point. What's important is that Dean is a guy who plays at a different level from most people. He is constantly bending and breaking the rules in pursuit of a better way to live, hacking beliefs and cultural norms that most of us accept without questioning:

■ With his invention of the Segway, he redefined accepted models of transportation.

- With North Dumpling Island, he playfully redefined the idea of the nation-state.

- With *FIRST*, he redefined the idea of science education being as cool to teens as sports.

Extraordinary people think differently, and they don't let their society's Brules stop them from advocating for a better world for themselves. Neither should you. All of us have both the ability and responsibility to toss out the Brules that are preventing us from pursuing our dreams. It all starts with one thing: questioning your inherited beliefs.

You can use the same amazing brain that took those Brules onboard to uninstall them and replace them with beliefs that truly empower you. This idea alone can be hugely liberating. Which leads us to Law 2.

Law 2: Question the Brules.

Extraordinary minds question the Brules when they feel those Brules are out of alignment with their dreams and desires. They recognize that much of the way the world works is due to people blindly following Brules that have long passed their expiration date.

TAKING THE BRULES BY THE HORNS

We have to push our systems—internally and externally, personally and institutionally—to catch up. We do that by making the first move to uninstall Brules in our own minds and then exerting upward pressure on our social systems to evolve. It can feel a little like free fall when you first start—and it is, because you're taking your life off of autopilot. Sometimes things feel chaotic while you take over the controls but have faith in yourself. You were born to do this. The great gift of being human is our capacity to see the world anew, invent new solutions—and then use what we know to transform our lives and change our world. Culture isn't static. It lives and breathes, made by us in real time in the flow of life, meant to change as our world changes. So, let's do it! It starts at home, with you. Your life, on your terms.

Exercise: The Brule Test

So, what might your Brules look like? I'm not talking here about getting rid of moral and ethical standards that uphold the Golden Rule. But certain rules that lock us into long-held habits and irrational self-judgment could be worth a look (for example: *I should work to the point of exhaustion every week or I'm not working hard enough . . . I should call my parents every day or I'm not being a good daughter/son . . . I should observe my religion the way my family does or I'm not a spiritual person . . . I should behave a certain way toward my mate or I'm not a good spouse . . .*) to see if a Brule is coming to call. Apply the five-question Brule Test for a reality check, and decide whether it's a rule you want to live by or a Brule you want to bust.

Question 1: Is it based on trust and hope in humanity?

Is the rule based on the idea that human beings are primarily good or primarily bad? If a rule is based on negative assumptions about humanity, I tend to question it.

For example, in the world today there's a huge amount of guilt and shame about sex, and many rules around it. India recently tried to ban access to all pornography websites—but there was so much public outcry, the ban was ended four days later. That's an example of a Brule based on the idea that humanity is primarily bad: Give people freedom to access porn online, and they'll go berserk and become sexual deviants.

The Christian idea of original sin is another example of fundamental mistrust of humanity. It has caused so much guilt and shame for so many people who feel undeserving of success and good things in life. Original sin is an example of a relative truth. It's held by one particular segment of the world population; i.e., it is not universally held across cultures. There's no scientific evidence that we are born sinners, so it isn't absolute truth. Yet it negatively affects millions.

Always have faith and trust in humanity. I like to remember Gandhi's words: "You must not lose faith in humanity. Humanity is an ocean; if a few drops of the ocean are dirty, the ocean does not become dirty."

Question 2: Does it violate the Golden Rule?

The Golden Rule is to do unto others as you would want them to do unto you. Rules that elevate some while devaluing others are suspect as Brules—

such as rules that grant or restrict opportunities based on skin color, sexual orientation, religion, nationality, whether a person has a penis or a vagina, or any other arbitrary or subjective criteria.

Question 3: Did I take it on from culture or religion?

Is this a rule or a belief that the majority of human beings weren't born into believing? Is it a belief in a particular way of life or a rule about a very particular habit, such as a way of eating or dressing? If so, it's probably a cultural or religious rule. If it bothers you, I believe you don't have to follow it, just as I decided I would enjoy a steak or beef burger when I wanted to. Luckily for me, my family allowed me to question these rules, even though sometimes it might have made them uncomfortable.

You do not have to dress, eat, marry, or worship in a manner that you disagree with just because it's part of the culture you're born into. Culture is meant to be ever-evolving, ever-flowing—in a way, just like water. Water is most beautiful and useful when it's moving—it creates rivers, waterfalls, the waves of the ocean. But when water becomes stagnant, it becomes poisonous. Culture is like water. If it's stagnant, as in the case of dogma or the rules of fundamentalist religion, it can be poisonous. Appreciate your culture, but let it flow and evolve. Don't buy into the dogma that your culture's way of prayer, dress, food, or sexual conduct must stay the same as it was generations ago.

Question 4: Is it based on rational choice or contagion?

Are you following a rule because it was installed in you during childhood? Is it benefiting your life, or have you just never thought about doing things differently? We follow a large number of dangerously unhealthy rules merely because of memetics and social conditioning. Are they holding you back? If so, try to understand them, dissect them, and question them. Do they serve a purpose, or do you take them on merely by imitation? Ask yourself if these rules truly serve you and if you want to pass them down to your children. Or are these ideas—for example, ones about how to dress or traditional ideas of what is moral—stifling and restrictive. If so, let's allow them to die a peaceful death and cut the cord so they do not end up infecting our children.

Question 5: Does it serve my happiness?

Sometimes we follow beliefs that don't serve our happiness, but that feel as if they reflect an accepted and inescapable way of life. It could be following a career path because our family or society tells us it's correct (as happened to me with computer engineering), or marrying a particular person, or living in a certain place or a certain way.

Place your happiness first. Only when you're happy can you truly give your best to others—in society, in relationships, in your family and community.

It's worth remembering these wise words from Steve Jobs when he was asked to address the graduating class at Stanford:

> Your time is limited, so don't waste it living someone else's life. Don't be trapped by dogma—which is living with the results of other people's thinking. Don't let the noise of others' opinions drown out your own inner voice. And most important, have the courage to follow your heart and intuition. They somehow already know what you truly want to become. Everything else is secondary.

IT'S TIME TO START QUESTIONING

What are some beliefs in your life you want to question? Pick a few and try applying the Brule Test. Then try a few more. Don't rush, and don't expect to wake up tomorrow free of all of your Brules just because you've figured out what they are. Brules are powerful, and it can be hard to look squarely at the ones that have had the most influence over you. Throughout this book I'll be sharing strategies for throwing out your Brules and replacing them with new blueprints that will inspire greater happiness, connection, and success. But before you leap forward into a new life, you have to untangle yourself from the old one. I like to recall the words of L. P. Hartley from the 1953 novel *The Go-Between:* "The past is a foreign country: They do things differently there." If so, this is your chance to cross the border, visit some place new and exciting, and discover a whole new way of life.

As you pursue this quest to question, know this: Certain people will tell you that you're wrong, that you're being unfaithful to your family, or to your tradition, or to your cultural norms. Or that you're being selfish. Here's what I want you to know. Some say the heart is the most selfish organ in the body because it keeps all the good blood for itself. It takes in all the good blood, the most oxygenated blood, and then distributes the rest to every other organ. So, in a sense maybe the heart is selfish.

But if the heart didn't keep the good blood for itself, the heart would die. And if the heart died, it would take every other organ with it. The liver. The kidneys. The brain. The heart, in a way, has to be selfish for its own preservation. So, don't let people tell you that you're selfish and wrong to follow your own heart. I urge you, I give you permission, to break the rules, to think outside the norms of traditional society. The Brules of the father should not be passed on to the son.

LIFE BEYOND THE BRULES

When you start hacking your life in this way, you gain a new sense of power and control. With it comes accountability and responsibility for your actions. Since you're deciding what rules you'll follow, your life is up to you. You can't hide behind excuses about who or what is holding you back. It's also up to you to hack responsibly, applying the Brules Test to make sure you aren't violating the Golden Rule as you go.

It takes a certain amount of courage to live in this way. When you hit a certain pain point with a Brule and realize that you cannot continue to live with it, part of abandoning it could feel like abandonment of an important social structure in your life. Life beyond the Brules can be scary and surprising and exhilarating—often all at once. People might push back or hassle you, but you must be prepared to stand firm in your pursuit of your own happiness.

I like to remember the advice from my friend Psalm Isadora, an actress and well-known tantra teacher: "The people making you feel guilty for going your own way and choosing your own life are simply saying, 'Look at me. I'm better than you because my *chains* are bigger.' It takes courage to break those chains and define your own life."

So dare to live your precious days on Earth to their fullest, true to yourself, with open heart and thoughtful mind, and with the courage to change what doesn't work and accept the consequences. You may find that you can fly farther than you ever imagined.

> "What if . . . all the rules and ways we lay down in our heads, don't even exist at all? What if we only believe that they're there, because we want to think that they're there? All the

formalities of morality and the decisions that we see ourselves making in order to be better (or the best) . . . what if we think we've got it all under control—but we don't? What if the path for you is one that you would never dare take because you never saw yourself going that way? And then what if you realized that one day, would you take the path for you? Or would you choose to believe in your rules and your reasons? Your moralities and your hopes? What if your own hope, and your own morality, are going the other way?"

—C. JOYBELL C.

PART II

THE AWAKENING

THE POWER TO CHOOSE YOUR VERSION OF THE WORLD

When I was a kid, my dad enrolled me in Tae Kwan Do classes. Tae Kwan Do is a form of Korean karate that builds discipline and self-defense. I loved it. Every year, we'd strive to perfect our moves so we could achieve the next belt level. I started as a white belt and slowly ascended to yellow, green, blue, brown, and eventually the much-coveted black belt.

The belts were an elegant system dating back centuries that allowed students to rise to mastery level in attainable stages. It made growth easier and motivated students far more than a vague goal such as "become a master." Each belt was a treasured validation of our hard work and progress.

This book is layered like belts for consciousness. As you move from Part I to Part II, you will ascend to the next belt level in awareness. Humanity today is largely operating within the culturescape, or Level 1—trapped by Brules from generations past.

Once you start to see the culturescape for what it is, something within you will begin to change. Rather than follow the status quo, you will start to make your own rules. You will start to question. And the more you question, the more your awareness will expand. The more your awareness expands, the more you will grow. And the more you grow, the more extraordinary your life will become.

At this point you've ascended to Level II: The Awakening. If I were to draw this on a napkin, it would look like this:

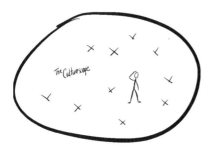 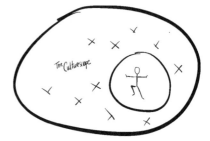

Level I:	Level II:
Life within the culturescape.	You learn to create your own version
The Xs represent potential Brules.	of the world within the culturescape.
	Within your world (the bubble around
	you), you can choose to eliminate
	and filter incoming Brules.

Think of the little Xs as the Brules of the culturescape. You're rising beyond it by creating your own bubble within the culturescape where YOU make the rules.

At this higher level, your tool for influencing the world and creating your own growth is a practice I call consciousness engineering. Think of it as the interface between you and the culturescape around you. You decide what to let in or reject. You're engineering how your consciousness is shaped and influenced.

What ideas and values (we'll call these your models of reality) do you choose to believe? How do you choose to live, learn, and grow (we'll call those your systems for living)? In the chapters that follow, you'll select the models and systems that will advance your journey toward an extraordinary life.

CHAPTER 3

PRACTICE CONSCIOUSNESS ENGINEERING

Where We Learn How to Accelerate Our Growth by Consciously Choosing What to Accept or Reject from the Culturescape

> If you want to teach people a new way of thinking, don't bother trying to teach them. Instead, give them a tool, the use of which will lead to new ways of thinking.
>
> **—BUCKMINSTER FULLER**

FROM COMPUTER ENGINEERING TO CONSCIOUSNESS ENGINEERING

Miserable as I was as a computer engineer, the training did give me one edge: a way of thinking that turns out to be perfect for challenging the Brules of the culturescape. It's called computational thinking.

Computational thinking trains you to look at problems from all angles—to break down problems into processes and parts (decomposition), spot patterns (pattern recognition), and solve them in a very logical, linear fashion (algorithms). The goal is to come up not only with a solution but also with one that's replicable, meaning that anyone—a man, woman, or child from India, Malaysia, or North America—could get the same results. Computational thinking makes you highly logical—and a very good problem solver. It's what gives programmers and hackers their edge.

From the day I busted the beef Brule at the age of nine, I've wanted to hack everything about how I live. With my parents' permission to question, I began looking at everything about life from the context of, "Why do we do this?"

But I never thought I'd be applying it to the human mind.

FROM BROKE FAILURE TO SUPER PERFORMER IN TEN MONTHS

To explain how I found the tools for extraordinary living that you'll learn about in this and later chapters, I have to take you back to some lean years in my life.

I got into personal growth because I was going through a tough period. In 2001, fresh out of college, I moved to Silicon Valley to launch a start-up. I was twenty-five. This was a time before Y-Combinator, 500 Startups, or any of the other dozen or so programs that fund aspiring young engineers and their dot-com dreams. Money, especially for twenty-five-year-olds, wasn't easy to come by. I took what savings I had, borrowed some money from my dad, and went out to try my luck.

My timing, in a word, sucked. A few months after moving to Silicon Valley, the dot-com bubble burst. I remember reading that 14,000 people had been laid off in April 2001. Pink slip parties—where the jobless go to network and drink themselves into comfort—became the norm. Broke and desperate, I sent my résumé to every job I could find on craigslist.org but got zero replies. Funds were so low I couldn't afford to rent a room, much less an apartment. So I rented a couch.

And it wasn't even a three-seater couch. It was a two-seater, so my legs dangled off at night when I went to bed. I was renting it from a Berkeley college student who was trying to optimize his finances by renting out his least-favorite piece of furniture. On that couch in Berkeley, and on the radiator beside it, lay my entire life. All my clothes, my books, my laptop, and my shattered dreams. It was humbling to be living in a college town as a graduate with a computer engineering degree and realizing that most of the college students there were living in better conditions than I was.

Finally, one day, after another mind-numbing bout of sending my résumé to jobs on craigslist, I got a reply. It was from a company looking for people who would call law firms to sell case management software. It was a dialing-for-dollars job. And it was straight commission: If I didn't sell, I didn't eat. The economy was so bad that startups could get away with paying no base salary.

I knew nothing about sales and marketing, but it was the only job I could get, so I took it.

On my first week in the office, we were assigned territories to cover. Mine was San Antonio, Texas.

Work looked like this: I'd have to go to the San Francisco Public Library, get a copy of the San Antonio Yellow Pages, look up law firms, and start dialing every attorney from A to Z to find one bored enough to listen to my pitch without hanging up on me. Since my boss doubted that any lawyer in Texas would be able to pronounce the name Vishen, I became Mr. Vincent Lakhiani for convenience.

My first few months on the job, I earned around $2,500 a month in commissions—hardly enough to survive on in the Bay Area.

But it's often when we're feeling down that we end up taking a step toward our next level of personal growth. Remember the drawing from Chapter 1 on how extraordinary lives are meant to be bumpy? I was in for another bump that would help me grow and learn.

Bored and mildly depressed, I began searching online for classes to take to help get my mind off the drudgery of my job. I can't remember exactly what I typed into Google—maybe "hope," maybe "success," or maybe "why does life have to suck so bad." And that's when I saw it.

I noticed a class on meditation and intuition. It was in Los Angeles and seemed interesting, especially since the lecturer was in pharma sales and spoke about how these methods had allowed her to rapidly expand her sales volume. Sold! I rather impulsively decided to fly down and take the class. When I showed up, I was the only student there (meditation wasn't as popular then as it is now). I completed the entire two-day class in one day and flew back to San Francisco that night.

Immediately I began applying some of the techniques I'd learned, one of which was a simple technique to meditate and get myself into the alpha state of mind. Alpha is a brain wave frequency common in meditation where you're in a relaxed state. People who advocate this type of meditation say that alpha puts you highly in tune with your intuition, your creativity, and your problem-solving abilities. A key part of what I had learned was listening to my inner voice or intuition. I practiced this when making my phone calls. I stopped calling every lawyer from A to Z in the Yellow Pages, as my coworkers were doing. Instead, I'd go into a relaxed, meditative level of mind, run my finger down the listings, and call the ones where I felt an *impulse*. The impulse often felt like guessing, but I heeded it. I realize this makes no logical sense. But I discovered that listening to my impulse somehow caused me to call lawyers more likely to buy. My closing rate started rising rapidly.

How much of a change can you expect from studying meditation? I certainly didn't expect much, other than learning to relax and destress better. But by the end of the first week after flying back from L.A., I had my best-ever sales week. I assumed it was an aberration and that it wouldn't last. But I closed two deals the next week. And the next. And it got better. A month later, I leveled up to closing three deals. Listening to my intuition seemed to triple the odds of my calling a receptive lawyer.

Other things improved, too. I started feeling happier and more positive about my days. My confidence and my rapport with people at work improved. I credit these to the fact that I was now meditating for about fifteen to thirty minutes every day, listening to my intuition and visualizing myself closing deals with ease.

Then I started using another technique I'd learned from another class: a simple empathy technique for connecting more effectively with people. Before speaking to a lawyer, I'd tell myself that I'd be able to connect with my potential client at a subconscious level, have empathy for his or her needs, know the right things to say at the right moment, and then—only if this was a software that would genuinely benefit the lawyer's firm—close the sale. While in meditation, I would visualize the lawyer in front of me and imagine beaming genuine kindness and compassion toward him or her. I'd end the three-minute visualization with a mental affirmation that we'd close the deal if it was in the best interest of all the parties involved.

Again I saw a massive boost in my sales. Soon I was closing more than anyone in the company. And so, twenty-six-years-old and with no prior sales experience, I got promoted three times in the next four months and was made director of sales. In September of 2002, just nine months after I joined the company, my boss sent me to New York City to head up the company's New York office.

I continued to grow within the company. I also continued experimenting, adjusting, and refining my meditation practice. And with each refinement, my abilities at work seemed to grow. Soon I was doing the jobs of two people—business development manager (managing the company's advertising spend on Google AdWords) *and* heading the New York office—excelling in both roles. My salary had tripled in a few short months.

At the time, I couldn't explain why all of this success was happening. I just knew that what I was doing worked.

COMPUTATIONAL THINKING MEETS PERSONAL GROWTH

My rapid success in the world of sales sparked my fascination with decoding the human mind. I realized that we can improve our performance in logical ways—by, say, reading a book on sales—and there's nothing wrong with that. But there are also techniques that can dramatically accelerate our performance. The ones I learned changed my life in just *one week*.

My computational thinking training kicked in, big-time. I wanted to break down human behavior—which at first glance appears like a huge, tangled knot of thoughts, actions, responses, emotions, impulses, drives, cravings, habits, and God knows what else—and crack the code for how we humans work.

As I got better at meditation and other conscious practices, it started to bother me that I'd been the only person in that class in Los Angeles. There was a lot more to learn. I wanted to teach others what had worked so awesomely for me. So I quit my software sales job and started a small e-commerce store. I called it Mindvalley. Our first products were nothing more than meditation CDs I sourced from established publishers. As Mindvalley grew, I launched as many companies as I could, teaching people mindfulness, meditation, contemplative practices, how to have better relationships, nutrition, health, wellness—basically, the knowledge that we truly need in order to have richer, healthier, more meaningful lives—knowledge that our industrial-age education system had failed to teach us. Soon we were publishing many of America's leading thinkers in health, wellness and consciousness from Ken Wilber to JJ Virgin to Michael Beckwith. I started Mindvalley with nothing more than $700 in 2003. Twelve years later, with not a single bank loan and no venture capital money, the company had grown to 200 employees and more than 500,000 paying students.

In that time I got to know at a deep personal level many of America's top minds in human development. I spent nine days at the invitation of author and motivational speaker Tony Robbins on his Fiji estate. I hooked my brain to electrodes with famed biohacker Dave Asprey to study different levels of consciousness. I met masters and gurus from India, billionaires at the peak of their game, and legends in business and society. And with every meeting, interview, and experience, I began dissecting, assimilating, and assembling the framework that helped create this book.

Today, I obsessively seek out new models and systems for how we can best understand ourselves and reach levels of potential we've only dreamed about. My hacker mentality pushes me to always be looking for the most effective solution that is replicable—that brings extraordinary results within reach of the greatest number of people. This is how I developed the model I'm about to share with you: consciousness engineering.

AN OPERATING SYSTEM FOR HUMAN CONSCIOUSNESS

If you have a computer, you've probably had to install a new operating system from time to time. Windows 95 gave way to Windows 8 over the last two decades. And the boring 1996 Macintosh computers I used as a freshman at the University of Michigan gave way to the gorgeous Mac OS we see powering MacBooks today. Every few years, we upgrade our operating systems on our machines to make our computers run faster, better, and take on increasingly complex tasks with ease.

But how many of us even think about doing the same for ourselves? Consciousness engineering is an operating system for the human mind. And the beauty of it is that—like the best hacks—it's really simple. It all boils down to just two things.

I. Your Models of Reality (Your Hardware)

Your models of reality are your beliefs about the world. In Chapter 2, we talked about how most of the rules we accept as true exist inside our heads and were put there, as Steve Jobs said, "by people no smarter than you." Human society today runs on the accumulated beliefs of our forefathers: Our economic systems, definitions of marriage, the food we eat, our methods of schooling and work—these structures were created long ago by people in very different settings than what we live in today.

Some of us were raised with empowering beliefs about ourselves and the world. Yet most of us also have at least a few sickly, disempowering beliefs that hold us back. The important thing to realize is that no matter what these beliefs are, they became true because we act and think in accordance with them. Thus, our beliefs truly do shape our world in a very real sense.

But while your beliefs make you, your beliefs are NOT you. You can use consciousness engineering to swap out old beliefs, swap in new ones, and take on new understandings of the world that might serve you better.

Using our computer analogy, think of your models of reality as your hardware. Want a faster machine or a better resolution monitor? Just swap the older model and replace it with the latest model. Need more space? Replace your 250 terabyte hard drive with a 500 terabyte drive. Beliefs are like that, too. When an old belief no longer serves you, you have every right to swap it out. Yet we don't. When you use the Brule Test to challenge your Brules and swap out obsolete Brules for rules that work better, you're upgrading your hardware so your operating system works optimally. In people-speak, that means you're choosing what to believe, and your life is yours to control.

Replacing outdated models of reality is essential. Our models of reality do more than just create our feelings around an event or life in general. To an astonishing extent, they seem to influence the reality of the world that we experience every single day.

What You Think Is What You Get

Our models of reality make us who we are. The problem is, as we saw in Chapter 2, that many of them weren't taken on by rational choice but rather by imitation. Our beliefs about life, love, work, parenting, our bodies, our self-worth—are often a result of our innate tendency to imitate the people and practices around us. What you think and believe about the world shapes who you are and your experience of the world around you. Change your accepted models of reality, and dramatic changes will happen in your world.

For example, researchers Ellen Langer, PhD, and Alia J. Crum, PhD, set up a study, reported in 2007 in *Psychological Science*, in which they asked 84 hotel maids how much they exercised. You'd think that with all the physical work involved with cleaning hotel rooms, they would have answered, "A helluva lot!" But although they cleaned about fifteen rooms a day, one-third said they didn't get any exercise, and the other two-thirds said they didn't exercise on a regular basis. Now, as anyone who has just completed a weekend of housecleaning can tell you, cleaning a room, changing sheets, vacuuming, and so on is a lot of work. Yet according to their model of reality, the maids didn't consider their work activities to be "exercise." That seemed to be borne out when the researchers assessed the women and found that they seemed about as fit as sedentary folks.

Here's where it gets interesting. The researchers implanted a new model of reality in the maid's minds. They informed forty-four of the maids that their daily duties met the Centers for Disease Control's (CDC) activity guidelines and surpassed the Surgeon General's guidelines. They also gave the maids a rundown of calorie counts for various cleaning activities and put similar information where the maids could see it at work. In short, they flipped a belief switch. They gave the maids new information about their existing habits that showed how the work they did was, in fact, exercise.

A month passes. The researchers follow up. Incredibly, the maids who'd been given the fitness information had, on average, lost two pounds, had lower blood pressures, and overall "were significantly healthier" based on measurements of their body fat, body mass index (BMI), and waist-to-hip ratio. And guess what? The maids told the researchers of no changes in their actions. The only change was in the information they'd been given— the truth the researchers had provided. The researchers had successfully swapped out an old model of reality and implanted a new one. They made the maids view their work as "exercise." And the results caused actual physical changes in the bodies of the maids.

The researchers concluded that what's become known as the placebo effect—results that appear to come purely from a person's mind-set instead of from a specific medication or medical treatment—plays a role when it comes to exercise.

Amazing, isn't it? Measurable positive change—just from installing a new belief that their work was actually healthy work. Imagine the implications this could have for how we encourage employees to be more engaged in their work or how we encourage people to lose weight. If the mind is so powerful that it can actually change health based on a changed perspective, imagine what that could mean about the mind's power to control our mood, our self-confidence, our happiness, and everything else that determines the quality of our time here on Earth.

As the hotel maids' study vividly shows, while your models of reality are not you, they make you who you are. When you realize that, you can swap out a bad or outdated model, swap in a healthier one, and gain incredible power to shift your world. Let's return for a moment to our computer hardware analogy. If your computer hardware can't handle the tasks you need it to do, you get a faster, more powerful computer, a higher-quality monitor, a better mouse. Look how sleek and efficient our computers have become in the last thirty years. Wouldn't it be great to think with that same level of elegance, speed, and efficiency? Yet when it comes to updating our models of reality, most us are stuck with the 1980s Macintosh rather than the new MacBook. We hold on to our old models and deny ourselves an upgrade.

The hotel maids in the study lost weight and got healthier simply because a new belief was installed in them. What would happen to you if you swapped in new beliefs about your love life? Your work? Your body? Your ability to make money? We'll explore how to do this in the next chapter.

As I've learned about the power of beliefs, I've chosen specific models of reality to help me stay healthier and younger. I've decided I'm going to live to be one hundred. I've chosen a model where seven minutes of early-morning exercise gets me the same results as hours in a gym. As a result, I've been able to get fitter and develop a better body in my forties than I had in my twenties. I've also decided on a belief that work is one of the most pleasurable things in life—so I enjoy what I do on a daily basis. All of us have this ability to decide what models of reality we'll adopt. You get to choose.

Thus the single most effective model of reality you can adopt right now is the idea that your models of reality are swappable. You do not have to continue believing and seeing the world through the lens installed within you in your younger years. I'll show you how to swap in a new, optimal set of beliefs in the next chapter. But first there's another important part of the picture to look at.

2. Your Systems for Living (Your Software)

Your habits, or systems for living, are how you put your models of reality into practice. If models of reality are the hardware of the human "machine," systems for living are the software. They're your activities and daily habits—for example, how you eat (based on your beliefs about nutrition), how you work (based on your beliefs about what kind of career and work behaviors are acceptable), and how you deal with money (based on your beliefs about the ease of acquiring money or the guilt or honor of having lots of it). There are many others, from how you raise your kids to how you make love, make friends, work out, solve problems, finish a project at work, make a difference in the world, and have fun.

Systems of living are easy to acquire. You can always learn new ones. The problem is that our Industrial Age school system hasn't done a very good job of keeping us up to date with the best systems for functioning in the world. Nobody taught us optimal ways to exercise, love, parent, eat, or even to speed-read or improve longevity. I think of them like apps you can easily download and update, intended for specific purposes or to solve specific problems. Not working? Download the new version that fixes old bugs. Found a better one? DELETE. The trick is recognizing what systems you're running and doing enough self-checks to quickly identify the ones you need to upgrade.

All of this now brings us to Law 3.

Law 3: Practice consciousness engineering.

Extraordinary minds understand that their growth depends on two things: their models of reality and their systems for living. They carefully curate the most empowering models and systems and frequently update themselves.

THE LIMITATIONS OF TODAY'S MODELS OF REALITY AND SYSTEMS FOR LIVING

Our current models and systems have three limitations:

1. Our models of reality are programmed by the world we grew up in.

2. Our models of reality (good or bad) determine our systems for living. In short, bad beliefs create bad habits.

3. Our modern models and systems are lacking in conscious practices—we're only just beginning to realize the power of our minds.

To understand these three limitations, we need to look at our current world from the outside in. Getting outside our culturescape is easier said than done. That's why, in order to understand how we can improve our models and systems, I decided to journey to visit a culture far removed from the modern Western world.

Strange Lessons from the Amazon Rain Forest

Kristina and I arrived in the deep Ecuadorian Amazon just before sunset. Our small plane took off from a run-down town called Puyo on the border of the jungle and flew over a sea of green before landing on a dirt airstrip smack in the center of the rain forest. A boat ride, a hike, and several hours later, we were at Tingkias, a village belonging to a family of the Achuar tribe. The nearest "civilized" town was more than one hundred miles away. Around us was nothing but green, humid jungle and the sounds of countless birds and animals. Here we would spend the next five days, living life in a radically different culture where many of the norms of human civilization—from how we sleep to how we care for our bodies to how we drink water or worship a higher power—were completely challenged.

The Achuar people of the Amazon rain forest in Ecuador evolved for generations with little contact with the wider outside world. They only became known to the Western world in 1977, so being with them is about as close as you can get to visiting a culture relatively untouched by modern human beings. With minimal exposure to the modern culturescape, their models of reality are dramatically different from ours. I'm not talking about conventional things that we expect other cultures to do differently—like food, dress, music, and dance. I'm talking about things so different that if we were to read about them in a historical text, we would find it hard to believe that these were normal human beings alive on the planet today.

Many truths that we assume to be absolute, such as "drink water" or "eat breakfast," are meaningless to them. Living with the Achuar was eye-opening. What I saw there profoundly shifted my thinking about what I believe to be acceptable truths.

Lesson 1: Our Models of Reality Are Programmed by the World We Grew Up In

By the time you arrive at the village, you're ready for a bath and a long drink of water. You can bathe in the pond nearby. But if you want a drink of water, you're out of luck. Because the water you bathed in—where everyone in the tribe bathes and swims, too—is the only water around. And it's filled with bacteria that would not be wise to ingest.

We assume that all human beings drink water. You might even consider that it's an absolute truth, as we discussed in Chapter 1. But the Achuar have evolved a brilliant hack for the fact that there's no clean water in the Amazon. The women harvest, boil, and mash yucca roots and then repeatedly chew and spit the chewed-up root into a bowl. They mix this combo of yucca and saliva with pond water and leave it for several days. The mixture ferments, yielding alcohol, which kills the bacteria. What you end up with isn't water, but *chicha*, a beer of sorts, made from the fermented spit of the tribeswomen. Every woman has her own brew, which she makes for her husband (men can have more than one wife) and children. Every woman's brew tastes different, based on the taste of her saliva. The women spend hours each day chewing and spitting to make *chicha* while the men go hunting. It's a big job, since this is all that the tribe drinks.

How does *chicha* taste? Well, to me, really awful, only because I haven't been trained to appreciate it. To the Achuar, it tastes delicious, and the men come home from a long hunt craving it. It sounds weird to us, but it's totally normal for them, and it's how they survive in one of the most challenging places on Earth to live.

Is drinking water normal? It is to most of humanity. But to the Achuar, drinking water is unusual and distasteful. Our definition of what is normal is nothing more than what is programmed into us.

What we see as our culture is really nothing more than a quirk of history. It's not necessarily right or wrong. Just like the Achuar way of living isn't right or wrong. Our culture is the result of thousands of years of ideas emerging, clashing, and dissolving, battling for dominance. But I can assure you of one thing: Our culture wasn't created by pure rational choice. In many ways it took form merely by imitation and chance. Yet we cling to our culture, both the good and the bad, as if it's the only way of living. When you look at the Achuar and you look at us, you see that pretty much every aspect of human culture—of life as we live it day to day—is malleable, up for grabs, within our control, and open for questioning.

Lesson 2: Our Models of Reality (Good or Bad) Determine Our Systems for Living

The Achuar don't have a model of reality for God in the way that most humans beings do. Instead, they believe that animals and plants possess human souls and that these souls have the ability to communicate through language and signs. To communicate with this world, they drink *ayahuasca* (a natural plant-based drug) that induces vivid visions and metaphysical experiences.

I decided to experience the *ayahuasca* ceremony with a visiting shaman who was stopping by our village. I knelt on a platform before him. In the darkness I could not see his face, only the flicker of light from the tobacco leaves he smoked. It was a surreal moment, like stepping back centuries in time to an ancient culture. The shaman mumbled some words, blew smoke in my face, tapped me with a branch, and then gave me a tiny taste of the precious *ayahuasca*.

Everything seemed fine for a moment. Then suddenly: unbearable pain in my stomach. I fell to my knees as the pain hit, hung my head over the edge of the platform, and started vomiting violently as my guides held my arms and legs to prevent me from falling off the platform onto the jungle floor. After four to five minutes I stopped vomiting but was so weak I could barely walk. I was helped to a hammock. As soon as I closed my eyes, all I could see were fractals. It was as if the world were a series of interlocking triangles of all different colors spinning, pivoting, and merging.

When I opened my eyes and turned on my side to stare out at the jungle, the trees looked like huge, friendly monsters of the type you'd see in the book *Where the Wild Things Are* by Maurice Sendak. It was as if Sendak's famous line: "Let the wild rumpus start!" had somehow been signaled in my brain. I don't know how long I stared at the tree monsters before I felt the urge to fall asleep, but closing my eyes thrust me into that mesmerizing world of dancing fractals forming random shapes.

I felt scared at first, but the fear turned into a sense of sublime peace. I felt a oneness with the forest, the trees, the humidity, and the sky. It was a beautiful feeling of being completely in the now with no regard for the past or future. It felt good to be alive. Eventually I fell asleep and woke later as dawn broke, when I joined the rest of the group to eat and discuss our experiences.

The beliefs of the Achuar in the spirit of the forest led to their system for experiencing the divine through *ayahuasca*. Similarly many of our systems for living evolved as our culture did—in response to certain beliefs of the time. But in modern times they evolve into habits because of, well, just habit. We've done them for so long we don't even know how we got started. We accept our current systems as "just the way things are," but look deeper and you'll see that these systems stem from beliefs from the past that you may have absorbed through the culture you were raised in.

Lesson 3: Our Modern Models and Systems Are Lacking in Conscious Practices

Many of our models and systems are rooted in the purely physical aspects of life—what we eat, how we take care of our bodies, beauty regimens, and so on. But until recently, there's been almost no innovation in the systems that improve the way our minds and spirits function.

The Achuar wake up each day at 4:00 a.m. and assemble as a tribe around a fire to drink a certain type of tea called *wayusa*. While drinking their tea, they also share life experiences, problems, worries, and dreams from the previous night. Most of us don't remember our dreams without effort. We tend to see them as fleeting images, soon forgotten in the serious business of the day. But the Achuar view their experiences during the day and at night as equally important and seem to simultaneously live in the waking and dream states. In the blending of these worlds, they solve problems, have adventures, and communicate with one another and with the spirit realm. They share these events while drinking their tea, and the elders listen and advise. The morning tea is a ritual for mental and spiritual cleansing.

Are the Achuar simply gifted at remembering dreams? Perhaps. But there might be more to it. We had journeyed into the jungle with the celebrated philanthropist and aid worker Lynne Twist. Lynne told me how she had come in contact with the Achuar. She'd repeated dreams of indigenous people with distinctive red markings on their faces. They seemed to be calling to her for help. When she described these visions to friends, one remarked that the faces she described looked much like the Achuar. That's how Lynne came to Ecuador to meet the tribe. The Achuar are facing eviction from their centuries-old home due to logging and oil and gas companies cutting large swaths of the Amazon. Lynne, working with the Ecuadorian government and the Achuar, has helped create laws to protect as much as four million acres of rainforest.

And it all started with visitors who seemed to enter her dreams calling for her to help. Are dreams more than what we in the modern world make them out to be? Perhaps there's something to the Achuar early-morning commitment to exploring the dream world.

Just how much of these spiritual experiences and abilities are we lacking in our modern world? Perhaps similar to the Himba tribespeople who have difficulty seeing the color blue, are we blind to certain spiritual experiences?

We're physical beings, and we evolve our physical systems very fast. Think of all the new diet and exercise routines you've heard or read about in just the past year or so. Yet our spiritual evolution is stuck in the past. Many of us are dissatisfied with the dogma of conventional religion; that's not new. But it's only been fairly recently that we've come to realize that the spiritual landscape is vast and varied and offers many options besides participating in your family's religion. I believe our spiritual systems need a major leveling up. That's why I was so struck by the Achuar morning ritual of sharing their dreams and cleansing their minds while drinking the morning tea that cleanses their bodies.

In the next two chapters, we'll talk about new models and systems that are evolving to help our minds catch up with our bodies.

THE ODDITY OF CULTURE

We might consider their lives bizarre, but to the Achuar, *we* seem bizarre. We run off to stressful jobs, leaving our kids in the care of others. We sit and stare at a lit-up screen for most of the day. Then we exercise like maniacs to burn off the calories we consumed the day before. We pack our elders into communal homes and then worry about how to care for them. We take pills to keep from feeling fear and other emotions we believe are negative. We drink potions to stay awake. Then we take pills to put ourselves to sleep. We eat and drink too much, partly because we have more than we need and partly because we're stressed out. Every tribe has its troubles. But the Achuar taught me that what we consider real, what we define as culture, what we believe is true about life—the nine-to-five, marriage, the way we raise our kids, how we treat our elders, what we do all day—are just collections of beliefs and practices that we put together because, well, they seemed like good ideas *at the time*. When you become aware of this fact, you also gain the ability to transcend and evolve these cultural practices.

LEVELING UP OUR INNER GAME

I once got to meet a man who many say is one of the most brilliant minds alive today. Ken Wilber is the most widely translated academic writer in America, with twenty-five books translated into some thirty foreign languages. Wilber is the originator of an extremely comprehensive philosophy called Integral Theory, which is a sort of theory of everything that unifies the disciplines of cultural studies, anthropology, systems theory, developmental psychology, biology, and spirituality, to name just a few. Ken has been quoted by everyone from Bill Clinton to Kermit the Frog, and Integral Theory has been applied in fields as diverse as ecology, sustainability, psychotherapy, psychiatry, education, business, medicine, politics, sports, and art. As part of the research for this book, I spent five hours interviewing Wilber about human development models and how consciousness evolves.

One of the questions I asked Ken was "what's your vision of an ideal education curriculum for children?" This is what Ken told me:

> Humanity is flying way under its full potential simply because we do not educate for the whole or complete human being. We educate for just a small part, a slice, a fragment of just what's possible for us. . . . Because according to the great wisdom traditions around the world—not only do humans possess typical states of consciousness like waking, dreaming, or deep sleep, they also possess profoundly high states of consciousness like enlightenment or awakening—and none of our education systems teach ANY of that. Now, all of these factors I've mentioned . . . none of these are rare, isolated, esoteric, far-out, strange, or occult. They are all some of the very most basic and most fundamental potentials of a human being everywhere. They are simply human 101. Yet we don't educate human 101. We educate something like human 1/10. So yes, I firmly believe that we can bring about health on this planet for the planet and the humans on it if we started educating the whole person with all their fundamental potentials and capacities and skills and stopped this fragmented, partial, broken system that we have now.

Consciousness engineering isn't just about being happy—though happiness is a wonderful by-product. It's about getting to human 101 and beyond and striving to be at the highest level of human development we can be, so we can fulfill our highest potential and, as the saying goes, leave this world a little better for our having been in it.

While there are many ways to get beyond human 101, I've found the framework of consciousness engineering to be the most powerful tool, since all growth comes from changing your models of reality or upgrading a system for living.

Changing a model of reality is a form of growth that often comes from epiphany or insight. It's a sudden awakening or revelation that shifts a belief. Once you adopt a new model of reality that is superior to an older model, you can't go back. It's what happened to me when I moved from seeing work as a job to seeing my work as my calling. Or when someone moves from following a religion to discovering spirituality.

Changing a system for living, on the other hand, is a process change. It's a step-by-step upgrade of a given process—as when you learn to go from riding a bicycle to driving a car as a means for mobility.

Once you understand the consciousness engineering approach, you can view yourself as a highly tuned operating system ready to install new hardware (models of reality) or new apps (systems for living) when needed. You never get attached to the ones you have because you know newer, better ones are always being discovered.

In short, you view yourself as always ready for change and growth.

How We Grow

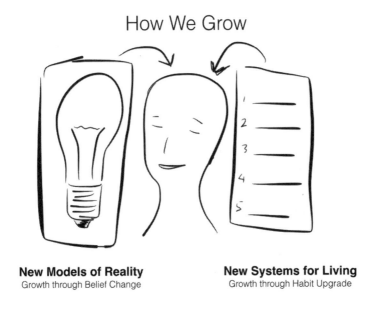

New Models of Reality
Growth through Belief Change

New Systems for Living
Growth through Habit Upgrade

How to Speed Up Your Learning Rate

Consciousness engineering primes you to learn and grow much faster than before because it creates a mental map in your brain.

Elon Musk was once asked in a Reddit.com Q&A: "How do you learn so fast?"

He replied: "It is important to view knowledge as sort of a semantic tree—make sure you understand the fundamental principles, i.e. the trunk and big branches, before you get into the leaves/details or there is nothing for them to hang on to."

As you think of your personal growth, think of consciousness engineering as that trunk. The two big branches are models of reality and systems for living. Everything you study in personal growth will either be a model (a new belief about money, for example) or a system (say, a new exercise or diet routine). These things cling to the two big branches.

I've found that by keeping this idea in mind, I can learn and grow faster than ever before. Once you internalize consciousness engineering, every time you pick up a book to read on personal growth or health, or an autobiography of a great leader, you start to look for model upgrades that you can swap in and new systems you can adopt.

In the next two chapters we'll refine this learning process by showing you exactly HOW to upgrade your models and systems in the best way possible.

Each of us has so much untapped capability. We're reminded of it every time we hear stories of triumphs of will and ingenuity—whether it's an innovation by someone like Dean Kamen, one of America's greatest inventors, or a citizen standing up for honor in the community. We call it all kinds of things—courage, brilliance, vision, even miracle. But consciousness engineering on a regular basis catapults us into becoming our best, most extraordinary selves. And that, my fellow hackers, is within reach of every one of us.

Here's an important exercise. Consciousness engineering works best when applied in a holistic way across our lives. In order to do that, we need to understand two things: First, we need to identify the key areas of our lives where we can apply consciousness engineering, and second, we need to pinpoint which of those areas could use some rebalancing.

Exercise: The Twelve Areas of Balance

My friend Jon Butcher is the owner of Precious Moments, the famous American catalog order company that sells giftware in the form of cute porcelain dolls. He's one of the most successful entrepreneurs in America today, but what is really unique about Jon is how superbly well balanced his life is. He seems to have it all—wealth, success, a perfect marriage, great kids, and a life filled with adventure. For example, Jon's a grandfather, but he's in such great health, you'd mistake him for a forty-year-old.

Jon's secret, he claims, is how he sets his goals in life.

Jon divided his life into twelve categories, and for each category he mapped out his beliefs, his vision, his strategy, and his purpose. It's goal setting at the deepest level. When Jon's friends asked him what his secret was, he would teach them his system. It eventually evolved into Lifebook, a personal growth seminar you can take in Chicago, where you spend four days diving deep into different aspects of your life to create a detailed life plan.

The idea I'm sharing here is partially inspired by Jon Butcher's Lifebook seminar, which I attended in 2010. I've adapted the categories (my own twelve are different from Jon's) for this exercise to help you discover the models and systems you're applying in your life so that you can begin to consider where you need to upgrade. I call them the Twelve Areas of Balance. Each area influences and shapes you in an important way. This exercise will help you elevate yourself on every level, leaving no part of your life behind.

Ready to start your adventure in consciousness engineering? Here goes:

When you think of your life and where you want to grow, think holistically. Too many people live lives lacking in balance. They may have great wealth but lousy relationships with their family. Or they may be incredibly fit and healthy but struggle with debt. Or they may have a career filled with achievements but feel heartbroken and lonely. An extraordinary life is balanced on all levels. Thinking holistically will help you make sure you don't end up winning in one area but losing in another. I use the Twelve Areas of Balance to help keep an even keel, and now it's your turn.

For each category below, rate your life on a scale of 1 to 10, with 1 being "very weak" and 10 being "extraordinary." If you have a pen handy, write your rating next to each category now. Don't think about each item for too long. Often the first impulse—your gut check—is the most accurate.

1. **YOUR LOVE RELATIONSHIP.** This is the measure of how happy you are in your current state of relationship—whether you're single and loving it, in a relationship, or desiring one. Your rating: __2__

2. **YOUR FRIENDSHIPS.** This is the measure of how strong a support network you have. Do you have at least five people who you know have your back and whom you love being around? Your rating: __7__

3. **YOUR ADVENTURES.** How much time do you get to travel, experience the world, and do things that open you to new experiences and excitement? Your rating: __3__

4. **YOUR ENVIRONMENT.** This is the quality of your home, your car, your work, and in general the spaces where you spend your time—even when traveling. Your rating: ___5___

5. **YOUR HEALTH AND FITNESS.** How would you rate your health, given your age, and any physical conditions? Your rating: ___8___

6. **YOUR INTELLECTUAL LIFE.** How much and how fast are you growing and learning? How many books do you read? How many seminars or courses do you take yearly? Education should not stop after you graduate from college. Your rating: ___7___

7. **YOUR SKILLS.** How fast are you improving the skills you have that make you unique and help you build a successful career? Are you growing toward mastery or are you stagnating? Your rating: ___7___

8. **YOUR SPIRITUAL LIFE.** How much time do you devote to spiritual, meditative, or contemplative practices that keep you feeling connected, balanced, and peaceful? Your rating: ___7___

9. **YOUR CAREER.** Are you growing, climbing the ladder, and excelling? Or do you feel you're stuck in a rut? If you have a business, is it thriving or stagnating? Your rating: ___3___

10. **YOUR CREATIVE LIFE.** Do you paint, write, play musical instruments, or engage in any other activity that helps you channel your creativity? Or are you more of a consumer than a creator? Your rating: ___3___

11. **YOUR FAMILY LIFE.** Do you love coming home to your family after a hard day's work? If you're not married or a parent, define your family as your parents and siblings. Your rating: ___8___

12. **YOUR COMMUNITY LIFE.** Are you giving, contributing, and playing a definite role in your community? Your rating: ___4___

Are you already seeing some areas where you'd like to improve? That's just the point—now you have a clear baseline from which to begin your journey toward the extraordinary. For the moment, just think about how you'd currently rate yourself in each category. In the next few chapters we'll return to these Twelve Areas of Balance to help you identify where you want to focus your attention to improve your models of reality and your systems for living.

CHAPTER 4

REWRITE YOUR MODELS OF REALITY

Where We Learn to Choose and Upgrade
Our Beliefs

Our beliefs are like unquestioned commands, telling us how things are, what's possible and impossible and what we can and cannot do. They shape every action, every thought, and every feeling that we experience. As a result, changing our belief systems is central to making any real and lasting change in our lives.

—TONY ROBBINS

ADVICE FROM A MONK IN A HOT TUB

"Do you have time right now?" the young monk asks me. "Let's go talk."

Did I have time? It was our last night in Fiji. We were sitting around a large table, enjoying one of the grandest meals I've ever seen. It was 2009 and my then business partner, Mike, and I were guests at a nine-day advanced meditation retreat at Namale, a magnificent resort owned by author and world-famous trainer Tony Robbins. Our group was an interesting assortment that included Hollywood actors, a stock market prodigy, and a former Miss America—plus the monks from India who led the retreat. I was honored that Tony and his wife had invited me to join this group and experience their beautiful island home.

It was a celebratory close to nine days of intensive self-exploration, during which we tried to truly understand ourselves and our potential. And on the final day, we were told we would have a private consultation with a monk who would give us a "revelation."

For reasons I'll never know, my monk decided to have his consultation with me in the middle of this sumptuous dinner, just after my third glass of wine.

But when your monk calls, you listen. "Where would you like to go?" I ask.

"Let's go to the hot tub," he says.

Naturally.

We go to the open-air hot tub under the starry Fijian sky. I climb in. He sits on the edge, dipping his feet into the water. He looks at me and says:

"You know what your problem is?

"No," I respond, surprised and, to be honest, mildly annoyed, "What is my problem?

"You have low self-esteem."

What the . . . ?

"I don't think so," I reply, as reasonably as I can, trying to hide my growing irritation. "I think I'm pretty confident. I run a business. I'm thrilled with my life—"

"No no no no no." He cuts me off. "You have low self-esteem. This is the cause of all your problems. I've observed you. When you're brainstorming with your partner and he shoots down one of your ideas, you get agitated and defensive. I bet you have issues with your wife, and I bet you have issues with others. You cannot take criticism. It's all because of one thing: You have low self-esteem."

It was like a smack in the face. The warm water in the hot tub no longer felt so comforting. The monk was dead-on. And after nine days of meditation and self-reflection, I was more open to this sort of insight, even if it was painful to hear.

I was overly defensive in brainstorming meetings, especially with my business partner. I did often feel hurt or misunderstood in family situations. But the real problem wasn't that someone was shooting down my idea, not listening to me, or misunderstanding me. It all boiled down to a deeply buried belief that I, by myself, was *not enough.*

It was why I got defensive in meetings. I felt the dismissal of my ideas as a dismissal of *me*.

It's why I became an entrepreneur. To prove I was worthy and enough.

It's why I built the most beautiful office in my city. To prove I could do it.

It was why I became wealthy. To prove something.

I could see how this belief that I needed to prove that I was enough—this model of reality I'd held for so long—had driven me into the arms of success. But I could also see how the idea that I had to prove myself had caused great pain in my life. Was it possible that without this limiting belief, I might be even more successful in my work and relationships—without paying such a high personal price?

What might happen if I developed a belief that I was enough and had nothing to prove?

Our models of reality are often unknown to us. Some models we know we have. For example, I know I believe in the importance of having a calling, in the power of gratitude, and in being

> **LESSON 1:** Our models of reality lie below the surface. Often we do not realize we have them until some intervention or contemplative practice makes us aware.

kind to the people I work with. But we also have models of reality embedded deep within that we're mostly unaware of. What you know you believe is much smaller than what you don't know you believe.

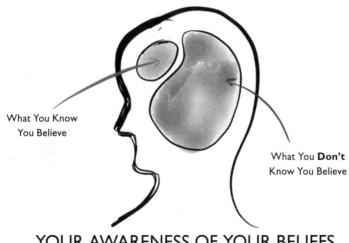

What You Know
You Believe

What You **Don't**
Know You Believe

YOUR AWARENESS OF YOUR BELIEFS

Much of growing wiser and moving toward the extraordinary is really about becoming aware of the models of reality that you carry with you without realizing it.

I was unaware I had a belief that I was not enough. Identifying it and learning to resolve it made a huge impact on the quality of my life and how I behaved as a friend, colleague, and lover.

In this chapter we'll explore how the world of our past infused us with certain beliefs—and how these beliefs now shape the world of our present and future. We'll also explore how we can become more aware of our hidden models and then how to swap the unhealthy ones with updated models. The first step is to discover how we take on these models.

THE GIRL AT THE DANCE

Where does this belief of "I am not enough" and other limiting models of reality come from? For most of us, they come from our childhood.

I grew up in Kuala Lumpur, Malaysia, but was of northern Indian origin, so I looked different from the other kids at my school, who were of Chinese or Southeast Asian origin. I had skin of a different color, a bigger nose, more body hair. It was tough being a minority kid. I was ridiculed and called names in elementary school, including Gorilla Boy because I had hair on my legs and Hook Nose because of my large Roman nose. As a result, I grew up believing I was different. I hated my long nose and my "gorilla" legs.

When I turned thirteen, my father enrolled me in a private school for expat children. Surrounded by diversity, with kids from some fifteen countries in my class, I felt somewhat normal. But adolescence had other challenges. I developed severe chronic acne that landed me in dermatologists' offices, and I was on frequent acne medication by age sixteen. That earned me yet another name at school: Pimple Face. It got worse. By my teen years, my eyes had deteriorated to the point where I had to wear glasses with superthick lenses. They broke frequently, and I'd patch them with tape, making me a walking stereotype of the nerd with tape on his glasses. As you can imagine, teenage life for me was not particularly easy.

My negative beliefs about my appearance wrecked my confidence for the first decades of my life. I was socially awkward. I hardly went out with friends. I had crushes on girls but never had the guts to ask anyone out.

In college at the University of Michigan, I saw myself as the engineering geek, the guy girls might want as a friend but no one wanted to date. Thus I found myself at twenty-two, a college junior, never having had a girlfriend.

Then something changed. And it started with a kiss.

It happened at a college dance. I'd had one too many beers, which is probably the only reason I was dancing with the prettiest girl in the room. Her name was Mary. I'd known her for years and had always admired her, but she was way out of my league.

To this day I don't know what came over me, but while we were dancing, I leaned in and kissed her. Immediately I pulled back, babbling something like, "I'm so sorry—I didn't mean to do that." I expected Mary to be offended.

Instead, she looked at me and said, "Are you kidding? You're f**king hot." Then the prettiest girl in the room grabbed me and locked her lips with mine. One thing led to another, and that ended up being one of the most amazing nights of my college life.

When a model of reality changes, the way you operate in the world changes, too. I woke the next day feeling as if I'd awakened in a whole new reality. If Mary, the prettiest girl in the room, thought I was hot, maybe I wasn't so unattractive, and maybe other women could think so, too.

That single realization ended my belief that I was invisible to women. It radically transformed my ability to communicate with the opposite sex. Thanks to Mary, my dating life took off. Nothing about my appearance had changed. But armed with a new model of reality about my attractiveness, I suddenly seemed to be a magnet for female attention. It was amazing how a belief, when shifted, could create such a dramatic turnaround in my world.

Shortly thereafter, I met up with another beautiful woman, Kristina, whom I'd had a crush on for a long time. I'd known her for years as a friend and always considered her the dream woman. Beautiful, bold, highly intelligent. And a redhead. I loved redheads.

But this time, with my new model of reality, I approached Kristina differently. We started dating. Three years later, I proposed. Today, fifteen years later, we're still together, with two wonderful kids.

Now I go on stage without feeling awkward. I go on camera without fearing how I look. All because one girl I had great admiration for helped me turn around a long-held model of reality. I had a lot more damaging beliefs to heal, but it was proof that with the right force, even entrenched childhood models of reality can be completely disrupted. And when it happens, the rewards can be amazing.

THE HYPNOTIST IN THE HOTEL ROOM

In 2015 I had an experience that helped me knock down another model of reality that was having an incredibly limiting impact on my life: I could not hold onto money. My business was doing well, but I was extremely uncomfortable taking ownership of the financial gains. My festival-like event, A-Fest, for example, was profitable, but I was giving away 100 percent of the profits to good causes without actually keeping anything as a reward. I was the coauthor of several personal development courses, but I'd never negotiated for the higher royalty I felt I deserved. This detachment from material wealth wasn't a totally bad thing. But I also felt it had a downside, as it could limit the growth of my businesses and projects.

In 2015 I was wrapping up another great A-Fest, a festival I had founded in 2010, this time in Dubrovnik, Croatia. The event had just ended, and hundreds of participants were heading home. Walking into the restaurant overlooking the Adriatic Sea, I saw hypnotherapist Marisa Peer and her husband, British entrepreneur John Davy, having breakfast.

Marisa is an extraordinary individual who has helped people with serious problems have profound breakthroughs in personal growth very quickly. Marisa is one of the most powerful transformers of human belief systems I had ever come across; her work and her results are legendary. She counts the British royal family and a Who's Who list of Hollywood celebs among her clientele.

Marisa's speech at that A-Fest had commanded a standing ovation and was voted the best presentation of the event. In her speech, Marisa explained that the biggest ailment afflicting human beings is the idea of "I am not enough." This childhood belief carries well into adulthood and becomes the root cause of a lot of our problems.

As we had breakfast and discussed her work, I asked Marisa if she could hypnotize me. I'd never had hypnotherapy and was curious about the effects.

A few hours later, Marisa came to my hotel suite, and we talked about my goals for the session. My aim was this: I wanted to understand my attitude about money. I wondered if it connected with some models of reality I might need to get rid of.

Marisa guided me into a regression, sifting through memories and images from my life. I felt as if I was drifting off into a light nap as she guided me with her voice. "Go back to a moment in your past when you first developed this belief," she said.

Suddenly, I saw Mr. John, a teacher I'd had as a teenager. I adored him, and he was an incredible teacher. But while everyone in the class liked him, we all felt sorry for him. He always seemed so lonely. We knew his wife had left him. We knew he lived in a small apartment and didn't have much money. But we loved him; we spent a lot of time talking about what a great guy he was and what a shame it was that he was in that situation.

"Can you see a thought pattern that you may have developed from this moment?" Marisa asked. And I realized that the Brule I'd internalized was:

To be a great teacher, you have to suffer.

I saw myself as a teacher because I run an education company and speak and write on personal growth. And I had an unconscious belief that I had to suffer in order to be a great teacher—which in my case manifested as having to be broke.

But Marisa didn't stop there. She made me regress to another moment. I saw myself in the back seat of my parents' car. It was my birthday. I was maybe nine or ten. My parents were driving me to a store to buy me a birthday gift. I was pretending to be asleep, but I could hear them talking in a worried way about money. At the time my parents were not wealthy, but they had enough. My mom was a public school teacher and my dad was a small entrepreneur. I remembered a feeling of guilt washing over me about my birthday gift. At the store, I picked out a book. "That's all?" my mom asked. "You can pick out something more." So I picked up a hockey stick. She said, "It's your birthday. You can have more." But I didn't want to burden my parents with any more expenses. That memory crystallized another model of reality I'd been carrying around:

*Don't ask for too much because someone will get hurt
if you do.*

We kept going. I regressed to another moment. I was sixteen, standing in the hot sun on a basketball court. The head of my school, a burly former weight lifter who, for whatever reason, seemed to despise me, even though I was a top student, was punishing me. That day, I'd forgotten my shorts for physical education class. He punished me for this small infraction by making me stand in the sun for two hours. Then, because I didn't seem afraid, he amped up the punishment by phoning my father in front of me and saying to me, "You're expelled from the school." Then he walked away.

When my father arrived at the school, the headmaster told him, "I'm not really expelling your son. I'm just trying to scare him to teach him a lesson." My father was livid and confronted him about this extreme behavior in response to such a minor infraction.

I had tolerated being treated in this way.

"Now that you're an adult, can you see why he did this to you?" Marisa asked. In my mind another Brule surfaced:

Do not stand out. It's not safe to stand out.

I immediately saw how these three childhood models of reality were holding me back in numerous ways. My beliefs that it was dangerous to stand out, that being a good teacher meant not having wealth, and that I'd hurt or disappoint others if I asked for more, all were undermining me. I had never even realized I *held* those beliefs. When the beliefs were removed, massive changes occurred in my life.

What happened in the months afterward was incredible. Because my belief about standing out disappeared, I started speaking more. Almost immediately I got two major speaking engagements and my biggest speaking payment yet. I got on camera more and hired my first PR firm. It seemed as if requests for interviews and appearances came out of nowhere. I made the cover of three magazines, was more active on social media, and saw massive rises in the number of followers I had on Facebook.

I also decided I wouldn't be a suffering teacher anymore. I gave myself the first raise I'd had in five years.

The result? In just four months, I doubled my income. My business began to grow, too. We hit new revenue milestones. It turned out that not only had my beliefs held me back but they had also been holding back my business and everyone who worked for me. These experiences proved to me how erasing old models of reality can have a profound impact on our lives.

> **LESSON 3**: When you replace disempowering models of reality with empowering ones, tremendous changes can occur in your life at a very rapid pace.

THE MEANING-MAKING MACHINE IN YOUR HEAD

Most of us have our own versions of disempowering beliefs. Beliefs about the way we look, about our relationship with money, about our self-worth. These beliefs can come from unexpected sources: a bullying teacher, overhearing a conversation between parents or other authority figures, or the attention (or lack thereof) from people we're attracted to.

As we believe these things to be true, they *become* true. All of us view the world through our own lens, colored by the experiences, meanings, and beliefs we've accumulated over the years.

It's as if we have a meaning-making machine in our minds that kicks in and creates Brules about every experience we have. So, the kids tease me and call me names. This means I must be ugly. Never mind the fact that a more likely explanation is that those kids were simply being kids, and children sometimes make fun of others. But as a kid I wasn't mature enough to understand this, so instead I installed the model of reality that I was unattractive.

The meaning-making machine never sleeps. It runs during childhood and in adulthood, too: while on a date, dealing with your mate and your kids, interacting with your boss, trying to close a business deal, getting a raise (or not), and much more.

We add meanings to every situation we see and then carry these meanings around as simplistic and often distorted and dangerous models of reality about our world. We then act as if these models are laws. The experiences I've just described proved it to me personally, but scientists are beginning to study this phenomenon, and the results are astonishing. While the bad news is that our models of reality can cause stress, sadness, loneliness, and worry, the good news is that we can upgrade them. When we swap in optimized models that work better, we dramatically improve our lives.

Here are just a few of the amazing studies that speak to the power of our beliefs.

HOW OUR BELIEFS AFFECT OUR LOOKS AND OUR HEALTH

A simple suggestion can change what we think about ourselves and even our bodies, inside and out. In their report in *Psychological Science* on the famous study of the hotel maids, the researchers noted that just by being "told that the work they do (cleaning hotel rooms) is good exercise and satisfies the Surgeon General's recommendations for an active lifestyle," the women "perceived themselves to be getting significantly more exercise than before" and "showed a decrease in weight, blood pressure, body fat, waist-to-hip ratio, and body mass index" compared to those who weren't told this.

Weirder still, in a 1994 study, ten men with knee pain agreed to take part in a surgical procedure to relieve them of their pain. They were going to go through arthroscopic surgery—or so they thought. In reality, not all ten were going to actually receive the full surgery—instead, they were part of an intriguing experiment. J. Bruce Moseley, MD, was about to test an idea that the placebo effect so common with simple pills might actually extend to more serious conditions including those that required surgery. The men were going to be fully prepped for surgery, and they were going to leave the hospital with crutches and pain pills. But Dr. Moseley performed the full surgery on only two. On three others, he performed only one part of the procedure. On the knees of the remaining five, he made just three incisions so the patients would have the sight and sensation of incisions and then scars, but he performed no actual surgery. Even Dr. Moseley didn't know which procedure each patient would receive until just before he performed the surgery, so that he would not unconsciously tip off the patients in any way. When all ten men left the hospital, all of them *believed* that they might have had the surgery to alleviate their condition.

Six months later, none of the men knew who had gotten the full surgery and who had gotten the sham. Yet *all ten* said their pain was greatly reduced.

Imagine that! Marked improvement from a serious medical ailment for which surgery is performed—yet no surgery was performed.

The placebo effect, as it's generally known, can be so powerful that all modern drugs have to be tested against a placebo before they are released to the public. According to *Wired* magazine, "half of all drugs that fail in late-stage trials drop out of the pipeline due to their inability to beat" placebos. Dr. Moseley's work rocked the medical establishment by showing that the placebo effect could apply to ailments for which they were performing surgery. Our beliefs about our bodies seem to have an uncanny impact on how we experience our bodies—for good or bad.

HOW OUR BELIEFS INFLUENCE OTHERS

If our beliefs can influence our bodies to such a dramatic degree, what else can they do? Can our beliefs influence the people around us?

The landmark studies by Robert Rosenthal, PhD, on the *expectation effect* prove just how much our lives are affected by other people's models of reality, however true or false they might be. After discovering that even lab rats navigated mazes better or worse depending on the expectations of the researchers doing the training (the researchers were basically told that they had either smarter or dumber rats, when in fact all the rats were, well, just rats), Dr. Rosenthal took the inquiry into the classroom. First, he administered an IQ test to the students. Then teachers were told that five particular students had extra-high scores and were likely to outperform the others. In fact, the kids were randomly selected. But guess what? While the IQ of all of the kids had increased over the school year, those five had much better scores. The now-famous findings, published in 1968, were called the Pygmalion Effect, after the myth about Pygmalion, who fell in love with his sculpture of a gorgeous woman who came alive—much as the teachers' expectations of those five students became reality.

Dr. Rosenthal and his colleagues spent the next thirty years verifying the effect and learning how it happens. It has also been found in business settings, the courtroom, and nursing homes. Bottom line: Your beliefs can influence both you and the people around you. What you expect, you get.

We create models of reality about the behaviors of our spouses, lovers, bosses, employees, children—but as the research shows, our beliefs influence how others respond to us. How much of the irritating or negative characteristics you see in others is really a belief you're projecting onto them?

This brings us to Law 4.

Law 4: Rewrite your models of reality.

Extraordinary minds have models of reality that empower them to feel good about themselves and powerful in shifting the world to match the visions in their minds.

HEALTHIER MODELS FOR OURSELVES AND OUR CHILDREN

Each disempowering model of reality we have is really nothing more than a Brule we've set up for ourselves—and, like any Brule, it should be questioned.

The monk in the hot tub helped me see past a Brule that I had to keep proving myself to validate my own self-worth. Mary's kiss shattered my Brule that I was unattractive to women. My session with Marisa shattered my Brules that only those who suffer make good teachers and that my visibility and success could hurt me or others.

What's the primary source of these Brules?

It's got to do with how we were raised as children.

In Chapter 2, I quoted historian Yuval Noah Harari, PhD, who compared children to molten glass when they're born. Kids are incredibly malleable, taking a huge number of beliefs onboard as they grow up and make meaning of the world around them. Under the age of nine, we're particularly susceptible to making false meanings and then clinging to them as disempowering models of reality.

While we work to clear our own limiting models, it's crucial to also make sure that we're not saddling our children with models that are disempowering. Incidentally, the ideas below can be applied to interacting with adults, too. Remember, our meaning-making machine never turns off—it doesn't stop just because we aren't kids anymore. There are always opportunities to help others develop new beliefs and get rid of old, destructive ones.

How We Form Beliefs as Children

Author Shelly Lefkoe and her late husband, Morty—who passed away just as I was writing this book—developed an incredible understanding of how beliefs influence our lives. I once asked Shelly, "What's the single biggest piece of advice you could give a parent?"

Shelly said this: "No matter what you do, in any situation with your child, ask yourself, *What beliefs is my child going to take away from this encounter?* Will your child walk away thinking: *I just made a mistake and I learned something great* or *I'm insignificant?*"

There are many opportunities to practice this wise advice.

Suppose you're at the dinner table with your kids and your son drops his fork on the floor. You might say, "Billy, don't do that." Now he throws his spoon on the ground. You say, "Billy, I TOLD YOU not to do that. You need to go stand in the corner for ten minutes and think about what you've done."

Now, you might believe this is an okay way to handle things. You were calm. You simply sent Billy to a corner. But we're losing the chance to influence the beliefs Billy might be developing from what's happened. Remember to ask yourself: *What are the beliefs my child is going to take away from this encounter?*

Maybe Billy dropped his fork by accident, so when you reprimand him, he's confused: *Why doesn't Mom trust me?*

He drops the spoon to validate that belief, and sure enough, Mom gets angry and puts him in a corner. Now he forms a new belief: *Mom doesn't trust me, and I bother her.* In the corner, Billy forms yet another belief: *I am not worthy* and *I don't have a right to speak my mind.*

See how the meaning-making machine amps up?

Shelly's advice is, at the end of any situation like that, ask your child, "Billy, what happened? What was the consequence? What can you learn from this?"

Shelly makes it very clear. Don't ask Billy, "Why did you do that?" *Why* questions corner a child and put the child on the defensive. For one thing, the child is emotional, and even many adults can't answer why in the grip of emotion. For another, it's not appropriate to expect a young child to be psychologically savvy enough to dive into his own mind and accurately answer why he did what he did.

Instead, ask *what* questions: "Billy, what happened that made you drop that spoon?" This allows him to look within and think. He might answer, "I dropped it because I thought you weren't listening to me." *What* questions allow you to get to the root of the problem and work to heal it faster.

Shelly notes that *why* has to do with meaning, and meaning is always made up—a mental construct from the world of relative truth. Even if Billy did know why he dropped the spoon, it wouldn't be empowering. Getting to the bottom of the situation itself—figuring out the what—allows you to work with your child to do something about it. Bottom line, Shelly suggests that when you walk away from an interaction with your child, ask yourself: *What did my child just conclude about that interaction?* Did your child walk away thinking: *I'm a winner* or *I'm a loser? I made a mistake and learned something new* or *I'm an idiot?*

Now, even if you're not a parent, the idea here is quite profound. Imagine all the dangerous beliefs you may have taken on about the world even when the people around you were well-meaning, not to mention what happened when people's intentions weren't always the best.

NIGHTTIME EXERCISES TO REWIRE BELIEFS

Realizing just how much we absorb as children has made me extra careful about what I say to my kids. Over time I developed this simple hack to help remove negative beliefs in my children before they fester too long.

Every evening after work, I try to spend some time with my son, Hayden. We call this Dad and Hayden time. After playing with Legos or reading books, I tuck Hayden into bed. As I do so, I ask him two simple questions that I hope will end his day with positivity. First, I ask him to think of one thing he was grateful for that day. It could be the soft sheets he's sleeping on, a friend he played with, a conversation we had, or a book he read. I show him that he can be grateful for anything. Second, I ask, "Hayden, what did you love about yourself today?" I ask him to talk about something he did. Maybe it was an act of kindness—he helped another kid at school. Or a demonstration of intelligence—something he figured out or something smart that he said. Maybe it was being helpful—the way he took care of his baby sister. If he can't think of anything, then I tell him something I love about him. As we play before bedtime, I try to notice little things about him. As I tuck him in, I tell him what I saw. Last week it was, "I love the questions you ask about science. I think you have a great mind for solving problems." If you can do this for your children, you end up raising children who are far more resistant to Brules, because inside, they are a lot more secure.

Instilling this habit into Hayden's life is my way of trying to keep his models of reality clear of Brules before they form—but it's never too late to start. I encourage you to integrate these exercises into your own evening routine so that you, too, will have a way of rooting out any damaging models of reality before they take hold. These two exercises work just as well for adults as they do for kids. Try it on your kids—or yourself—each night before going to bed.

Exercise: The Gratitude Exercise

Take a few minutes and think of three to five things you're grateful for today:

- Perhaps it's how the sun felt on your face when you left the house this morning.
- Or the music you listened to on your way to work.
- Was it the smile and thank you that you exchanged with a store clerk?
- Or a laugh you shared with some people at work?
- Maybe it was that special look your partner, best friend, child, or pet gave you.
- Or the good workout tips you got from the trainer at the gym.
- Or was it just how great it feels to get home, kick off your shoes, and call it a day?

Exercise: The "What I Love about Myself" Exercise

Think about a quality or an action of yours that made you proud today. Maybe nobody else told you that they appreciated it, but it's time that you affirmed it for yourself. Think about what it is about you as a human being that you can love. Is it your unique style? Did you solve a complex problem at work? Is it your way with animals? Your dance moves? Your jump shot? That awesome meal you cooked last night? The fact that you know the lyrics to every Disney song since *The Little Mermaid*? You can identify qualities that are big or small, but you must pinpoint three to five things every day that make you proud to be who you are.

You can practice this simple self-affirmation in the morning when waking up or just before going to sleep. For me, it's helped me heal much of what the monk in the hot tub pointed out to me.

Marisa Peer suggests that all of us have a child within who never received all the love and appreciation we deserved. We can't go back and fix the past. But we can take responsibility to heal ourselves now by giving ourselves the love and appreciation we once craved. You can help heal your own inner child.

EXTERNAL MODELS OF REALITY

Thus far we've looked at internal models of reality, models that apply to how we perceive ourselves. But external models of reality are just as powerful in our lives. Your external models of reality are the beliefs you have about the world around you.

Below are four of the most powerful new models I've decided to believe are true about the world.

I came to accept these four models as I went through life. They replaced older, less evolved models and added immense value to my life. Read with an open mind.

I. We all possess human intuition.

This model of reality replaced an earlier model that all "knowing" comes purely from hard facts and data. Today I strongly believe in intuition and use it in my daily life. It helps me make better decisions, know whom to hire, and even helps me with creative pursuits like writing this book. Remember how my phone sales career took off when I used intuition as part of my selling strategy? Human beings can function as logical beings *and* as intuitive beings. When we use both capabilities, we're priming ourselves for extraordinary results.

Science is finding that we operate on two levels. One is what we might call instinct, which runs below rational awareness. It's connected with prehistoric brain areas and is lightning fast. The other is the rational side that evolved later, but on which we rely heavily in our lives today.

In one study, scientists gave participants two decks of cards and told them they were going to play a card game for money. Unbeknownst to the players, both decks were stacked: one like a roller-coaster ride—major wins, major losses; the other a smoother ride—few losses, small wins. After drawing fifty cards or so, players suspected one deck promised a smoother ride. By eighty cards or so, they had the whole ruse figured out. But here's the thing: Their sweat glands knew something was up after just *ten* cards. Yup, these glands on the players' palms opened up a little with every reach toward the roller-coaster deck. Not only that, but at about the same time, the players began reaching more often for the smoother-ride deck without even realizing it! Their intuitive selves recognized and somehow drew them to the safer choice.

I believe human intuition is real, and with practice we can get better at tuning into it for decision making. I do not believe you can foretell the future, but I do believe in gut instinct in decision making. I try to listen to my gut on a daily basis. See what happens when you try to do the same.

2. There is power in mind-body healing.

Earlier I talked about the terrible acne I had as a teenager. With little social life to speak of, I spent a lot of time reading. One thing I read about was creative visualization. Creative visualization is a practice of shifting beliefs by meditating and then visualizing your life as you want it to evolve. It's based on the idea that the subconscious mind cannot differentiate between a real and imagined experience. So I started visualizing my skin getting better. I spent just five minutes, three times a day visualizing my skin undergoing healing. I used imagery that felt powerful to me: looking at the sky, reaching out and scooping up some of that radiant blueness, and smoothing it on my face. I saw the blue hardening and then saw it being pulled off, taking the dead skin with it, leaving glowing new skin beneath. Essentially this process trains the subconscious mind to develop a new belief—in my case, *my skin is becoming beautiful.*

In one month of practicing this technique three times a day for five minutes per session, I ended my acne problem. Mind-body healing involves the conscious practice of certain mindfulness or visualization techniques to heal certain aspects of yourself. I'd had acne for five years and seen many doctors, to little avail. Using creative visualization, I healed my skin in four weeks—giving myself a huge boost of confidence and self-worth.

For those of you who'd like to try this practice, I've recorded a video explaining how I worked with creative visualization. I also explain the exact method I used to heal my skin. You can download it as part of the free resources on www.mindvalley.com/extraordinary.

3. Happiness at work is the new productivity.

Most of us are told to work hard. Few of us are encouraged to work happy. In the developed world, we spend close to 70 percent of our waking hours at work—but according to multiple studies, close to 50 percent of us dislike our jobs. That's an unfortunate situation for billions of people today. Unless we're passionate about some aspect of our work, a big part of life will feel unsatisfying.

Work, I believe, should be something that inspires you to jump out of bed each morning. From the start at Mindvalley, we embraced the idea that "happiness is the new productivity." Our unique work culture is designed to ensure that while employees get things done, we have immense fun doing it. We do this through various models and systems designed to boost happiness. These include investing in beautiful, inspiring office design, offering flexible working hours, hosting annual team retreats to paradise islands if we hit our goals, and almost weekly social gatherings and parties to foster friendship and connection.

This culture of happiness at work significantly helps reduce the immense stress of racing to build a fast-growing company. It's helped me keep my sanity while working long hours to hit our goals. It's possible to bring a culture of happiness to any work environment. Whether you're a CEO or a freelancer, an assistant or a manager, it is critically important that you find a way to enjoy your work. Have lunch with someone from your office or someone in your business network once a month, even once a week. Pay someone a compliment about his or her work every day. Or take Richard Branson's advice. He said: "I have always believed that the benefits of letting your staff have the occasional blast at an after-hours get-together is a hugely important ingredient in the mix that makes for a family atmosphere and a fun-loving, free-spirited corporate culture. It also goes a long way to tearing down any semblance of hierarchy when you've seen the CFO doing the limbo with a bottle of beer in her hand."

In short, happiness and work need to go hand in hand.

Want to learn more about my models for bringing happiness to work? I've given several detailed talks on my methods for injecting happiness at work to fuel a company's productivity. You can watch a short TEDx talk or a longer 90-minute training session with information on how to apply these models to your company or business. Both are available on www.mindvalley.com/extraordinary.

4. It is possible to be spiritual but not religious.

The traditional model of reality goes like this: I can only be spiritual if I follow a particular religion. But why not consider that our spiritual self exists apart from religious systems, and that morality is not dependent on religion or belief in God?

Goodness, kindness, and the Golden Rule do not just have to be taught via religion. According to the book *Good without God* by Greg M. Epstein, the humanist chaplain at Harvard University, the fourth biggest life adherence in the world today after Christianity, Islam, and Hinduism is now humanism. Humanism is the idea that we do not need religion in order to be good. It differs from atheism in the sense that humanists believe that there is a "God," but He's certainly not the judgmental, angry being that many religious texts make Him out to be. Instead, to a humanist, "God" might be the universe, or the connectedness of life on Earth, or spirit. Humanism is opening up a new spiritual path for people who want to reject the Brules of religion but who don't embrace atheism. One billion humanists now exist on the planet, and their numbers are growing.

In addition to exploring humanism, you could also try to craft your own religion—rich in tradition and self-discovered experiences, but free of the Brules of organized religion. In the book *A Religion of One's Own* by Thomas Moore, the author suggests that we should all create our own religion. He writes:

> This new kind of religion asks that you move away from being a follower to being a creator. I foresee a new kind of spiritual creativity, in which we no longer decide whether to believe in a given creed and follow a certain tradition blindly. Now we allow ourselves a healthy and even pious skepticism. Most important, we no longer feel pressure to choose one tradition over another but rather are able to appreciate many routes to spiritual richness. This new religion is a blend of individual inspiration and inspiring tradition.

Personally, I struggled when I left religion. I believed in a higher power, so pure atheism did not feel right to me. Then I started exploring models such as humanism and pantheism and found my answer. Today I combine ideas from humanism, pantheism, and spiritual practices like meditation with my family's own beliefs from Hinduism and Christianity, which I pick and choose depending on how empowering these models feel.

Exercise: Examining Your Models of Reality in the Twelve Areas of Balance

Below is a list of the Twelve Areas of Balance from the previous chapter. On your computer or in your journal, write down the models of reality that you have in each of these categories. I've listed a few common ones to get you started. You should notice a correlation with your results from rating these categories in Chapter 3; in other words, the categories where you assigned the lowest rating may also have the most disempowering models of reality.

1. **YOUR LOVE RELATIONSHIP.** How do you define love? What do you expect from a love relationship, both to receive and to give? Do you believe love brings hurt? Do you believe love can endure? Do you believe you have the capacity to love greatly? Do you believe you deserve to be loved and treasured?

2. **YOUR FRIENDSHIPS.** How do you define friendship? Do you believe that friendships can be long lasting? Do you believe your friends take more from you than they give? Do you believe making friends is easy or hard?

3. **YOUR ADVENTURES.** What's your idea of an adventure? Is it about travel? Physical activity? Art and culture? Urban or rural sights and sounds? Seeing how people live in places totally different from yours? Are you making time and space for adventure in your life? Do you believe you need to save for retirement before taking a long trip? Would you feel guilty if you left your job or your family to take a holiday by yourself? Do you think that spending money on experiences (such as skydiving) is frivolous?

4. **YOUR ENVIRONMENT.** Where do you feel happiest? Are you content with where and how you live? How do you define "home"? What aspects of your environment are most important to you (colors, sounds, type of furniture, proximity to nature or culture, neatness, level of convenience/luxury items, etc.)? Do you believe you deserve a gorgeous home, to stay in five-star hotels when you travel, and to work in great environments?

5. **YOUR HEALTH AND FITNESS.** How do you define physical health? How do you define healthy eating? Do you believe you're genetically inclined toward obesity or any other health issues? Do you believe you'll live as long as or longer than your parents? Do you believe you're aging well or poorly?

6. **YOUR INTELLECTUAL LIFE.** How much are you learning? How much are you growing? How much control do you have over your mind and your daily thoughts? Do you believe you have adequate intelligence to accomplish your goals?

7. **YOUR SKILLS.** What do you consider something you're "good" at? And what not so much? Where did those perceptions come from? What holds you back from learning new things? Are there some skills you're ready to let go of? What keeps you from making the change? What special abilities and character traits do you have that you feel are most valuable? What do you feel you "suck" at?

8. **YOUR SPIRITUAL LIFE.** What type of spiritual values do you believe in? How do you practice them and how often? Is spirituality a social or individual experience for you? Are you stuck in models of culture and religion that hold little appeal but that you're afraid to abandon for fear of hurting others?

9. **YOUR CAREER.** What is your definition of work? How do you define a career? How much do you enjoy your career? Do you feel you're being noticed and appreciated in your career? Do you feel you have what it takes to succeed?

10. **YOUR CREATIVE LIFE.** Do you believe that you are creative? Is there a creative person you admire? What do you admire about him or her? What creative pursuits do you engage in? Do you believe you have a talent for a specific creative project?

11. **YOUR FAMILY LIFE.** What do you believe is your main role as a life partner? How about as a son or daughter? Is your family life satisfying to you? What were your values about family growing up? Do you believe a family is a burden or an asset to your happiness?

12. **YOUR COMMUNITY LIFE.** Do you share the values of the communities that you're a part of? What do you believe is the highest purpose of a community? Do you believe you're able to contribute? Do you feel like contributing?

TWO TOOLS TO REWRITE YOUR MODELS OF REALITY

After doing the exercise above, you should have some idea of the models of reality you need to upgrade. You don't need to meet with monks in hot tubs or get hypnotherapy to upgrade your models. (Though wouldn't it be nice if we could all get an instant upgrade with a kiss?) Bad models can evaporate through sudden realizations—sometimes spontaneous ones (such as I had in the hot tub)—or through meditation, inspirational reading, or other mindfulness practices, including just sitting in a room by yourself, reflecting on your life, and asking yourself, *Where did I come up with this particular world view?*

As you progress through this book, you'll gain insights and experience "ah-hahs" that will open you up for letting go of certain disempowering models. There will also be specific exercises that will help you shed models through the awakening these exercises will bring. For now, though, here are two instant techniques you can apply to remove negative models of reality that you might develop on a day-to-day basis. Both are based on the idea of activating your rational mind before you unconsciously adopt a model.

Question 1: Is my model of reality absolute or relative truth?

While some things in the world are absolute truths (they hold true for all human beings across every culture—such as the idea that parents must take care of their children when children can't take care of themselves, or that we all need to eat in order to survive), many things are only relative truth: They're done differently by different cultures, such as particular ways of parenting, eating, spiritual expression, handling a love relationship, and much more.

Is your model of reality absolute truth or relative truth? If you have a model that isn't scientifically validated, feel free to challenge it. This is certainly true of religious beliefs. One reason why as a kid I questioned my culture's rules on eating beef was that I noticed that millions of people all around the world could enjoy eating beef. Why couldn't I?

Is there an aspect of your culture you know is relative truth for the greater part of humanity? If you still enjoy believing it, do so. But if it's harmful or results in your having to dress in a certain way, marry in a certain way, or restrict your diet or life in a way you dislike, you owe it to yourself to abandon it. Brules are made to be broken.

Remember that no single culture or religion dominates the majority of the planet today. No major religion holds sway over the majority of the human population. Know that whatever your culture trained you to believe, the vast majority of human beings probably do not believe. And you can choose to disbelieve, too. The power to choose what we want to believe and what we want to disbelieve is one of the greatest gifts we can give ourselves.

The best advice is often to listen to your heart and intuition. Remember that our models of reality all have expiration dates. Even what we take to be absolute truth today may not always be a truth in the future. This question is wonderful for situations where our models are indoctrinated through our culture and society. But it's important to understand that we ourselves also create models of reality via our meaning-making machine. That's where Question 2 comes in.

Question 2: Does this really mean what I think it means?

Morty and Shelly Lefkoe have an interesting model for hacking beliefs that has to do with turning off your mind's meaning-making machine. According to Morty, we can manufacture as many as 500 different "meanings" a week. But as we learn to ask ourselves, *Is this really true? Am I 100 percent sure that this is what's really going on?*—we start to reduce the number of meanings.

Morty says it's easy to get from 500 to 200 a week if you just do an internal inventory at regular intervals to check whether you're creating meaning where none should exist. Then it's just about practice. Eventually you stop adding meaning to events. You will become less reactive to stress and less upset with others in your life. It helps your marriage, and I can tell you it will help your relationships with your boss and coworkers. As a CEO leading a team of 200 people, I've consistently found that those who had their meaning-making machines under control at work were more effective leaders.

I recorded a longer conversation with Morty on his Lefkoe belief process. This video is very personal to me as it was the last training Morty Lefkoe ever gave before he passed away in November 2015. I feel it is my duty to share his final words of wisdom with you. You can watch the full experience at www.mindvalley.com/extraordinary.

I believe the best thing we can do with outdated models of reality is to let them go gracefully. Turn them into history. Let's celebrate our extraordinary ability to evolve emotionally, mentally, spiritually throughout life, taking on new ideas, thoughts, philosophies, and ways of being and living. When enough people challenge the Brules and adopt optimal models, you have evolutionary progress of the human race. And when enough people optimize their models all at the same time, you have revolutionary change that acts like a slingshot to hurl us to a new order, powered by the impetus of our collective awakening.

> True brilliance is not a function of understanding one's view of the world and finding order, logic, and spirituality in it. True brilliance is understanding that your view of order, logic, and spirituality is what created your world and therefore being forever capable of changing everything.
>
> **—MIKE DOOLEY**

Now that you've taken a closer look at how models of reality take root and identified some of the key models of reality in your life, it's time to connect those insights with the next step in consciousness engineering. In the next chapter, you'll discover how your everyday life—your systems for living—dovetails with your models and learn how to optimize your systems to set the stage for extraordinary growth in all areas of your life.

CHAPTER 5

UPGRADE YOUR SYSTEMS FOR LIVING

Where We Discover How to Get Better at
Life by Constantly Updating Our Daily Systems

> I think it's very important to have a feedback loop, where
> you're constantly thinking about what you've done and how
> you could be doing it better. I think that's the single best
> piece of advice: Constantly think about how you could be
> doing things better and questioning yourself.
>
> **—ELON MUSK**

RICHARD BRANSON'S SECRET SYSTEM

It was a starry evening on Necker Island, the private island owned by Richard Branson, and the beach party had wound down to that lazy lull where you're totally relaxed, sitting there gazing at the stars, and soaking in the beauty all around you. It was my second trip to Branson's beautiful home on Necker Island. I was there with a group of entrepreneurs for a four-day mastermind and adventure trip.

In the quiet, I had a chance to sit with Richard for a while and talk one-on-one about all sorts of things, from life to parenting to personal philosophy. My wife and I were struggling to conceive our second child but had failed for four straight years. Richard was actually giving me advice on what I could do to improve my odds of being a father again. (Getting procreation advice from Branson will always be an interesting memory for me.) It was impressive to see how much he cared and how genuine he was.

That's when it occurred to me that, given that I was sitting in private conversation with one of the world's greatest entrepreneurs, maybe I should stop discussing ways to improve sperm count and instead ask Richard for something a bit more related to his genius zone. So I asked him this: "Richard, you've started eight different companies in eight different industries and taken all of them to a billion dollars. That's huge. If you could summarize in one sentence how you did it, what would you say?"

Richard didn't blink. He answered immediately like a wise, kind sage. Here's what he said:

> It's all about finding and hiring people smarter than you, getting them to join your business and giving them good work, then getting out of the way and trusting them. You have to get out of the way so you can focus on the bigger vision. That's important, but here is the main thing: You must make them see their work as a mission.

This, in Richard's words, is his "system" for starting game-changing companies. His focus is on hiring smart people, giving them freedom and getting out of the way, and continuously thinking of the vision, ensuring that a mission was driving the company.

A system for living is a repeated, optimized pattern for getting things done. How we dress in the morning is a system. How we get through our e-mail is often a system. Our work, our parenting, our exercise routine, how we make love and handle relationships, our methods for creativity—all often fall into specific systems for living.

I compare systems for living to the software that computers use to perform specific operations. They're the things you do to function in the world, from the moment you wake up to your nighttime rituals like putting on your pajamas and reading a book before going to bed. We have societal systems, too, such as our educational system, business structures, and community systems.

Where do our systems come from? As you know from Chapter 3, they come from our beliefs about what's true, right, good, healthy, necessary, appropriate, and effective. After our models of reality, they're the second aspect of consciousness engineering that allows you to advance your human potential and step into the extraordinary.

But here's the problem. Most of us are using systems that have long become obsolete. As Bill Jensen said in his book *Future Strong:* "Even as we enter one of the most disruptive eras in human history, one of the biggest challenges we face is that today's systems and structures still live on, past their expiration dates. We are locked into twentieth-century approaches that are holding back the next big fundamental shifts in human capacity."

UPGRADED SYSTEMS FOR AN UPGRADED LIFE

Good software is constantly being updated. It would be ridiculous to still be running Windows 95 when you could be running the latest version. Yet when it comes to our systems for living—our internal software—we run systems that are highly suboptimal.

But what if you start viewing your systems for living in much the same way you view the apps you download on your smartphone? When you swap outdated models of reality for empowering ones and pair them with new systems for applying your new models day to day, your life will improve exponentially—and fast.

In this chapter, you'll learn how to think about your systems for living in a very structured way so that you get to do more and create more, in less time, while having more fun.

Let me give you an example related to that night on Necker Island with Richard Branson.

I had been thinking about writing a book for a long time but had no idea how to start. I simply was not ready.

I wanted to write in a style that contained practical lessons scattered among fascinating stories that could keep the reader entertained. One of my favorite books of this type was actually Branson's 1998 autobiography *Losing My Virginity*. I loved it because of the personal stories peppered with really powerful personal growth lessons. That book became one of the role model books for the kind of book I wanted to write.

However, I was nowhere close to Branson in terms of life accomplishments or life adventures. So I stayed stuck—thinking I'd "someday" write such a book when I could prove myself by getting my business to a gigantic level.

That same night on Necker as we were talking about parenting and I shared with Branson some of my philosophies, he interrupted me and said, "You should write a book."

I was silent, stunned. That little push from Branson (and he probably doesn't even remember it) was just the boost of confidence I needed to start seriously thinking about this book.

Still it took me three years to figure out what I wanted to write about.

Then it took me one whole year to get a framework done.

And then it took me three months to write the first chapter.

It was slow and painful.

But each day, I kept optimizing my systems.

I developed a method for coming up with titles, a method for creating a framework, and a style for writing personal stories. I even tested different types of whiskey to see which helped me create the most interesting writing. (Scotch versus Kentucky versus Japanese. If you must know, Jim Beam Kentucky bourbon won.)

As I fine-tuned these systems, I experienced exponential productivity in my writing abilities. Now, I can write a chapter in a single day. Three months ago, this would have been next to impossible. Here's my efficiency plotted on the graph below that shows how far I came as I optimized the system. Note how hard it was to start but how much I could speed up as I formalized my system.

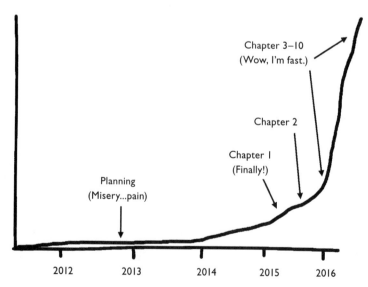

When you optimize your systems for living, you can experience exponential growth in areas that truly matter to you.

EXTRAORDINARY PEOPLE DISCOVER EXTRAORDINARILY EFFECTIVE SYSTEMS

Extraordinary people don't just have extraordinary models of reality. They strive to ensure that their systems for living—that is, DOING what they do in the world—are well defined, structured, and continuously optimized.

I try to upgrade at least one of my systems for living every week, not because I feel like things are always broken but because I know how energizing it is to try something new. It's exciting to think that we can just swap in a new system like downloading a new app.

There's a three-step method for effectively upgrading your systems for living:

1. THE DISCOVERY PROCESS. Many people discover new systems from books, conferences, or online courses. Maybe you read about the benefits of a particular approach to weight training. You do some research and decide to incorporate it into your workouts. In a month or two, you assess the results. Or you hear about a new management strategy at a conference and decide to try it with your team and track how it's working. I make it a habit to read nonfiction books on a wide variety of topics that matter to me, such as parenting, work, and exercise, and to continually discover new systems. Think of it like browsing the App Store. It can be fun and enlightening when you find something that seems to work for others and might also work for you.

2. YOUR REFRESH RATE. Your refresh rate is how often you upgrade your systems for living. For example, I try to experiment with a new exercise system every year. In 2013, for example, I spent thirty days straight on Les Mills's BODYPUMP. The next year I experimented with Minimum Effective Dose exercises such as Christine Bullock's Total Transformation program. This year I'm trying kettlebells. None of these was randomly chosen. I discovered them after reading books, having conversations with friends who were passionate about fitness, and knowing what my needs were (love handles begone!). I made these changes not necessarily because my previous exercise system was broken but because I simply realized I'm

more likely to work out if I switch things up regularly so I don't get bored. It also ensures that I'm working different muscle groups and keeping my whole body fit and healthy.

3. SET POINTS AND MEASUREMENT. How effective are your systems for living? Is your new system for living really better than a previous one? We'll look at ways to measure and maintain the effectiveness of your systems for living as you discover and refresh them. This is the important bit that people often forget—are you measuring the effectiveness of your system? A set point is a level of performance that you do not allow yourself to slip below. For example, I have a waist measurement set point that has kept me at the same waist size for ten years. I measure it by seeing which hole is used when buckling my favorite belt. If I ever go even slightly beyond that set point, I make it a discipline to diet or exercise to get back to my set point. I'm not allowed to buy a new belt.

Here's how all three stages come together to allow you to create effective systems for governing your life.

The Discovery Process

Patrick Grove is one of the most successful entrepreneurs in Australia and the Asia Pacific region. His entrepreneurial success has made him a member of the Business Review Australia's Rich 200 list, and he's known as the Asia Pacific's IPO whiz kid because he holds the seemingly incredible record of starting four companies and taking each of them public. He's also a close friend. I once bumped into Patrick in a local Starbucks in the neighborhood where we live, where I found him scribbling furiously on a piece of paper. When I asked what he was up to, he said, "I'm trying to solve this massive problem."

"What is it?" I asked.

"I'm trying to figure out how I can make $100 million in one year," he answered.

I smiled. But I knew Patrick was serious. He's one of the biggest thinkers I know. Making $100 million in one year sounds impossible to most people, but to an extraordinary mind like Patrick's, it's a reasonable question. It was not a function of "is it possible?" but rather "when is it possible?"

That encounter happened in 2008. In 2013 Patrick pulled it off. He acquired three small used car websites across Southeast Asia, renamed the group iCar Asia, took it public in Australia, and drove this investment to over $100 million in valuation. All in ONE year.

Patrick likes to get out of the office and ask himself big, tough questions, and then he says that the inspiration for his business ideas often comes to him. He makes sure that he gives himself the space and time to do this. Too many of us are so busy *doing* that we never step back and think about *how* we're doing. Or *why* we're doing it. I call this the do-do trap. You're so busy doing what needs to be done, you don't really know whether your systems for living might be obsolete, or even (pun intended) absolute crap.

This is why people like Patrick get out of the office and find the time and space to question their systems and set new, bolder goals.

Awareness is the essence of discovery. Every now and then, *stop doing and gather some research.* I know many people who have a disciplined system for going to the gym a few times weekly. But are your gym workouts fully optimized? For example, once a month I might actually skip going to the gym one day and instead read about new workout routines, buy a new fitness app, or study a new fitness method to *optimize* my gym time. This is what I mean by the discovery process. You step back from what you're doing and seek to discover new ways to do it better.

At Mindvalley we bypass the do-do trap through a technique called Learn Day. On the first Friday of every month, nobody works (unless it's something crucial). Instead, everyone focuses on learning about how to work better. Customer support agents may research the art of writing personalized replies or review customer feedback for ideas on improving our products. A programmer may experiment with a new coding language. People are allowed to sit and read all day, provided it's a book related to their career. Through this process, new ideas form, new systems emerge, and new ways of working are born.

Whether related to work, health, fitness, personal growth, culture, or anything else, discovery is a life-affirming tool. It's not just about making life a little more interesting. It allows you to be better at what you want to do. Patrick Grove is the chairman of four public companies, and he still has time to step back and rethink his systems. Some might say that this is *why* he's chairman of four public companies. Surely all of us can find the time to think in a different way about how to solve our own problems—massive or otherwise.

Your Refresh Rate

When was the last time you read a book about a topic you were interested in but knew nothing about? Signed up for a class? Sought honest feedback from a friend? Sat in a Starbucks and scribbled notes about crazy dreams you wanted to pursue? Or otherwise revitalized the systems in your life? Keeping your systems fresh is a system in itself. Your frequency of doing this is your refresh rate.

Exercise: What's Your Refresh Rate?

Let's go back to the Twelve Areas of Balance we looked at in Chapter 3. Have you updated the systems in any of these parts of your life recently? If not, it's time to hit the refresh button.

Write down the areas where you know you need to make some changes. It could be how you interact with your partner, the way you raise your kids, how you deal with people and projects at work, how you're pursuing a job hunt, whether your home and other creature comforts make you feel good, or whether you're making time for big dreams, amazing new experiences, spiritual insights, or creative growth. Maybe you want tune-ups in all of these areas. You'll get there.

The important thing is to remember to study and invest in learning about how to improve your systems for living. Below are the twelve categories; for each, I've added my personal favorite book as a suggestion for something that might give you a bold new perspective on the subject:

1. **YOUR LOVE RELATIONSHIP.** *Men Are from Mars, Women Are from Venus* by John Gray. This book is a beautiful and somewhat humorous look at how to live with and love the opposite sex.

2. **YOUR FRIENDSHIPS.** *How to Win Friends and Influence People* by Dale Carnegie. I read this book seven times before I turned twenty; an amazing book for anyone.

3. **YOUR ADVENTURES.** *Losing My Virginity* by Richard Branson. This book inspires you to live a life of adventure and to have fun while pursuing big goals.

4. **YOUR ENVIRONMENT.** *The Magic of Thinking Big* by David J. Schwartz, PhD. This book inspires you to upgrade your quality of life and to dream bigger about your home, your office space, the car you drive, and more.

5. **YOUR HEALTH AND FITNESS.** Here I have different recommendations for men or women. For men, it's *The Bulletproof Diet* by Dave Asprey. Dave is a friend and the most famous biohacker in the world. This is science meets eating. For women, it's *The Virgin Diet* by JJ Virgin, which will challenge your rules about calories and exercise and show you that it's not about how much you eat, but how you combine the right foods in the right order for your body's "chemistry lab."

6. **YOUR INTELLECTUAL LIFE.** What better way to optimize your intellectual life than by upgrading your learning systems, learning to speed-learn and improve your memory? I recommend courses by Jim Kwik.

7. **YOUR SKILLS.** *The 4-Hour Workweek* by Timothy Ferriss is a great book on finding fast hacks to developing unique skills.

8. **YOUR SPIRITUAL LIFE.** *Conversations with God* by Neale Donald Walsch is the best book I've read on spiritual growth. But a close tie is *Autobiography of a Yogi* by Paramahansa Yogananda, which was Steve Jobs's favorite book.

9. **YOUR CAREER.** *Originals* by Adam Grant is one of the best books I've read on how to be more creative at work and how to think outside the box, sell your ideas, and make a difference.

10. **YOUR CREATIVE LIFE.** *The War of Art* by Steven Pressfield inspires you to shed your artist inertia and get moving with your creative work. It is also one of the most beautifully written books I've come across.

11. **YOUR FAMILY LIFE.** I believe the root cause of most family issues is the lack of self-love, so I suggest *The Mastery of Love* by Don Miguel Ruiz.

12. **YOUR COMMUNITY LIFE.** *Delivering Happiness* by Zappos CEO Tony Hsieh is an inspirational read on starting epic businesses and giving back to the world in a big way.

Want to jump-start your progress? Aim to read one book a week. If you find this hard, start by first learning to speed-read. (You're upgrading your reading system.) With a few simple tricks, you can rapidly boost your reading speed.

Reading is an easy and excellent way to boost your refresh rate. But you should also consider online courses, masterminds, networking groups, and seminars. Patrick Grove is a learning junkie. We became friends because of our mutual interest in personal growth and the seminars and courses we attend.

My visit to Necker Island was part of a learning experience, too. I was there to bond, connect, and share ideas with other entrepreneurs looking to build big businesses while having daily sessions with Branson, who served as a mentor to us. The reason I founded MindvalleyAcademy.com, which at the time of this writing has more than a million members, was to provide people with the opportunity to learn new models and systems from the world's greatest teachers. These teachers teach and run webinars in the academy, many of which are completely free to attend.

The more you seek opportunities to learn and then apply your learnings, the faster your refresh rate.

Set Points and Measurement

It's great to refresh your systems for living. But once you've got a good thing going, how do you maintain it?

You know what it feels like to set out to make a big life improvement, only to see your results slip away a little bit at a time. You work hard to take off the pounds; then they start to creep back. You fall back into your procrastination habit. You spend more and save less. Or you stop keeping up with friends, or with your meditation practice, or connecting with your kids, or snuggling so much with your sweetheart.

I struggle with this as much as anyone. But I've figured out a way to reset myself when my systems start to slip. I devised a tool called non-negotiable set points.

Here's an example of how I apply this in my life.

I love my wine, whiskey, chocolate, and cheese. But I like to stay in shape because I feel and perform at my best when I'm at peak physical energy.

As I get older, I've been setting up simple mental and physical hacks to slow down my aging and maintain my sense of well-being. My non-negotiable set point for my body is that at any time, I should be able to drop and do fifty push-ups. No excuses. I can come off a twenty-hour flight from L.A. to Kuala Lumpur and plop into bed at home. But after a good sleep if I get out of bed and can't do fifty—something's off. Fifty push-ups is my health pulse check. I can always tell when my travel schedule or a few good meals with family and friends has nudged me off my peak, because I have a hard time doing my usual fifty push-ups during my workout. If that happens, I know that I need to really pay attention to how I'm treating my body and make some changes.

We can establish these system checks for our finances, the time we spend with our kids, our endurance, the number of books we read per week, and so on.

Things slip when we don't have a detection method for knowing when it's happening. Set points are that detection method.

Exercise: Your Non-Negotiable Set Points

A set point is simply a bare-minimum threshold you establish for yourself that you promise you will not go below. A set point differs from a goal. Goals pull you forward, while set points help you maintain what you have. You need both.

You can establish set points for anything important to you. And here's a secret: You can use set points not only to prevent or reverse slipping but also to *improve* over time. Imagine getting fitter as you get older . . . more intimate with your partner . . . more secure financially . . . or closer to your kids. There's a super-simple set point mind trick you can deploy that ups your game in amazing ways. So, let's get you started on setting up your own set points.

Step 1: Identify the areas of your life where you want to create set points.

Look back at the Twelve Areas of Balance list from Chapter 3. In which categories did you score the lowest? Where are you slipping? Pick two or three to focus on, for which you'd like to set specific, achievable set points. Eventually, you can expand your list, but start with a few that are really important to you.

Step 2: Determine your set points.

Next, create set point targets for each area you've selected. Now, this is very important: *Make sure that your set points are absolutely achievable.* You'll see why in a minute.

For things you can measure (your weight or your bank account, for example), you can establish specific amounts: My weight set point is X. My bank account set point is Y. You can establish set points for your intellectual life (I will read X books per month) or even your work (I will spend two hours a week researching or studying something that will make me better at my job). The more specific you are, the easier it will be to keep track of the set point and actually stick with it.

Here is an example of potential set points you can choose for each of the Twelve Areas of Balance:

1. YOUR LOVE RELATIONSHIP. Set up set points for how much time you spend together, whether it's the frequency of date nights, working out together, or even regularly scheduled lovemaking.

2. YOUR FRIENDSHIPS. Create set points for keeping in touch; for example, calling a close friend at least once a week, inviting friends for brunch or dinner once a month, writing a short weekly note to someone going through a tough time.

3. YOUR ADVENTURES. Consider setting set points for the frequency of holidays or adventure trips. I go on at least two long trips with my entire family every year. We don't have to be going somewhere exotic or expensive, but by committing to extended time with my family, I have a chance to show them how much I love them while we create lasting memories together. You could commit to going to one new place every month, even if that place is somewhere in your neighborhood. It doesn't have to cost any money at all, but your world will feel bigger and brighter when you regularly expose yourself to new corners of it.

4. YOUR ENVIRONMENT. Set a few simple set points for keeping your home tidy; for example, making the bed every morning, making sure the sink is clear of dirty dishes at night, sorting the mail as soon as you get it and recycling what you don't need to keep, and so on. You can also create set points for the level of quality of your life; for example, a weekly full-body massage or spa treatment.

5. YOUR HEALTH AND FITNESS. Set some specific set points as fitness benchmarks. For me, it's my push-up routine. It could also be maintaining a specific waist measurement or getting in the

routine of going to one yoga or Pilates class per week, or even tracking your eyesight or blood pressure.

6. **YOUR INTELLECTUAL LIFE.** Start to incorporate some systems for bringing intellectual richness into your life. It might be reading a few pages each night before bed, visiting a gallery or exploring one room of a museum each week, or attending one play per month. A great set point here is to read at least two books per month.

7. **YOUR SKILLS.** Commit to spending a certain number of hours per week reading or studying material to improve skills in your field. I have a set point of taking off one day per month from work to focus on studying and learning how to work better.

8. **YOUR SPIRITUAL LIFE.** You might make fifteen minutes of meditation per day part of your spiritual practice, read several pages of spiritual literature each day, or pray or send your thoughts to someone dealing with a problem. My set point in this category is fifteen minutes minimum of daily meditation.

9. **YOUR CAREER.** Join a professional group and make sure you go to a certain number of meetings per year. Read one book per month on career issues. If you're looking to change careers, commit to reading a certain number of articles online per week about this new field and how to break in.

10. **YOUR CREATIVE LIFE.** Choose and pursue a creative outlet, and set a reachable set point for making it part of your life. It could be spending twenty minutes journaling each day, joining a weekly improv class, or setting goals to move forward on a creative project that's been stalled or you've been meaning to start. I have set points for the amount of writing I do every week.

11. **YOUR FAMILY LIFE.** Set a goal of spending a certain amount of time doing family-oriented activities per week, whether with your kids, the entire family, your parents, or other relatives. It could be calling your mom or dad every couple of days just to say hi, going out for Sunday breakfast as a family, having playtime with your children each evening.

12. YOUR COMMUNITY LIFE. Decide on an amount to donate annually to good causes, or identify a place where you'll volunteer on a regular basis. I have an annual set point for money donated to charity. Each year I ensure I can give away a healthy sum to good causes I believe in.

Step 3: Test your set points and correct if you miss.

I test my fifty push-ups set point once a week. If I can't do fifty—whether because I've been slacking off on exercise, my energy levels are low, or I've put on weight—I immediately initiate a set-point correction procedure.

My set-point correction procedure is a specific method to get me back on track. When it comes to fitness, it's what I do when I need to get back into shape to do fifty. What works for me is to immediately go on a low-carb diet for a week to get my weight back to normal and commit to working out at the gym three times a week. Typically in *one* week I'm back to fifty.

I turn forty the year this book is published. I intend to live to one hundred. And even at that age I expect to be able to do fifty. I don't believe in letting this slip.

The set-point correction procedure is a crucial part of this process. When you slip and can't maintain a set point, you must be disciplined enough to correct it. This brings us to Step 4.

Step 4: Turn up the heat—in a good way.

When you slip off your set point, set a goal to get back to the set point *plus a little bit more*. Suppose fifty push-ups is your fitness set point. If you slip, aim to get back to fifty and a little more—say, to fifty-one. If you've stopped your weekly date nights with your partner, go back to the weekly date night but now add next-day mooky (my term for morning nooky). That's turning up the heat—but so gradually that you don't notice it. Once you reach that new level, make that your new set point.

Now you've not just prevented stagnation, you're actually *growing*. Here's what the set point system looks like when you map it out:

Most people slip with age. But when you apply non-negotiable set points,

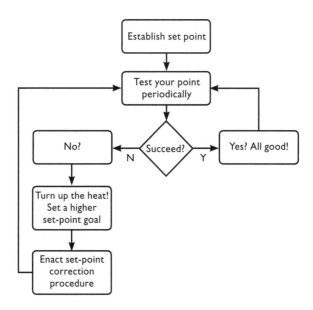

you grow with age. I believe we all can be better than ever as we gain mileage in life—just make sure you make your set points non-negotiable. You can learn more about set points on www.mindvalley.com/extraordinary.

THE POSITIVE PSYCHOLOGY OF SET POINTS

There's a powerful reason why set points work. It's a natural human tendency to feel that we've failed when we slip from our goals. But with set points, a failure is turned into a challenge. If you can't attain your fifty push-ups, you enact a new goal. Get to fifty-one. You replace the feeling of failure with the positive feeling of striving for a goal.

The key is to make the new goal easily achievable. Notice that my set-point correction procedure for push-ups was to turn up the heat from fifty to fifty-one, not to fifty-five or sixty. Setting the bar too high is just punishing; it's unrealistic that you'll make all of that progress in one giant leap. Turning up the heat just a little bit allows you to regain some momentum without setting yourself up to fail.

When you correct your set points by aiming slightly higher than before, you can put yourself on a path to constant improvement in every aspect of life.

This brings us to Law 5.

Law 5: Upgrade your systems for living.

Extraordinary minds consistently spend time discovering, upgrading, and measuring new systems for living applied to life, work, heart, and soul. They are in a perpetual state of growth and self-innovation.

THE SYSTEMS OF THE FUTURE

I'm going to ask you to do an exercise with me.

If you're reading this book on a plane or subway or anywhere else with people around you, I want you to try to smell your neighbor. Go ahead. Lean just a little toward them and take a whiff.

If you're reading this alone, try smelling yourself.

What do you smell? In most cases it's going to be perfume, aftershave, a certain soap, or deodorant. Or not much of anything.

And that's exactly the way it should be.

But if you were doing this exercise 150 years ago, everyone around you would have *stunk*. Back then, we didn't have the practice of a daily shower. We weren't trained to brush our teeth. Cologne and perfume were mostly used by the very wealthy. Deodorant didn't exist. In the 1900s, humanity simply got used to its own stinking smell.

Today we do all kinds of things in the morning to clean and prepare our bodies for the day. We brush, shower, spray on cologne, and dress well, all to keep our physical bodies fresh and clean. Yet billions of us wake up each morning feeling worry, stress, anxiety, and fear and don't do anything about it. We assume this is normal, but it's not. Just as we can wash our bodies, so we can have systems to completely "wash" our minds of these debilitating feelings.

As the "smell your neighbor" exercise shows in a fun way, we pay far more attention to systems for taking care of our bodies than to systems that take care of our mind and spirit.

We've created a society where it's considered normal to wake up with feelings of stress, anxiety, fear, and worry. But it isn't. These feelings aren't meant to be constant states. They're alarm systems, evolved to alert us to things we need to deal with, not just live with. You're not supposed to hate your work or dread your day. "Happy hour" shouldn't be the drinks you have on Friday to celebrate getting through another week.

Instead of taking pills or engaging in unhealthy habits to suppress our feelings, we can install systems to be free of them. What's inspiring is how popular these new systems are proving to be—and how fast and powerful the transformations are. I call these systems transcendent practices. They include exercises on gratitude, meditation, compassion, bliss, and other practices that take you beyond or above the range of normal or merely physical human experiences.

Now that you understand how to discover, refresh, and create set points around your systems for living, we're going to focus the rest of this book on systems for consciousness—in short transcendent practices. These systems can have an amazing payoff when applied to life and work, as you'll see in the next chapter. But first I wanted to share some insights into how one of the world's most powerful women is applying transcendent practices to run her business and life.

HOW ARIANNA HUFFINGTON RULES HER MIND

I got the beautiful opportunity to interview Arianna Huffington in 2014, just when her book *Thrive* was coming out. I adore Arianna; she radiates calmness and kindness while also running a massive media empire centered around the *Huffington Post*. Arianna shared with me some of the transformations that had been occurring in her life since she started adding transcendent practices to her busy day.

Arianna's shift happened on April 6, 2007. She was two years into building the *Huffington Post*, having incredible success but working herself to the bone. And that's when it hit her that money and power were not the only two metrics for success—there was a third that was not getting nearly enough airtime. She explained to me:

When building a start-up, it's easy to buy into the delusion that we have to work around the clock trying to make everything happen. And then, of course, we have lives outside of work as well. As we were building the *Huffington Post,* I was taking my older daughter around to check out colleges to see where she wanted to apply.

I came back from the college tour and collapsed from burnout, exhaustion, and sleep deprivation. I hit my head on my desk, broke my cheekbone, and needed four stitches on my right eye. As I was going from doctor to doctor to see if there was anything medically wrong with me, I was asking myself all of these questions that we often stop asking when we leave college: "What is a good life? What is success?" And I came to the conclusion that the way we define success, centered only on the two metrics of money and power, is just a very inadequate way to define life. It's like trying to sit on a two-legged stool—sooner or later, we topple over. And that's when I came up with this idea of the third metric of success, which consists of four pillars: well-being, wisdom, wonder, and giving.

Arianna went on to describe her daily systems for living. She spoke about meditation:

I don't want just to be effective or productive. I want to be joyful. After eight hours of sleep, I also meditate every morning for at least twenty minutes. On the weekend, I try to do an hour or an hour-and-a-half. I love it.

Then we discussed gratitude:

I used to wake up and the first thing I would do was check my smartphone. Now I don't do that. And just taking this time—sometimes it can be literally a minute to just look ahead at my day and fill myself with gratitude for the blessings in my life, and set my intention for the day—it immediately takes away this false urgency that we bring into our lives that creates such unnecessary stress.

I love Arianna's message. Her systems for living involve meditation, movement, gratitude, and setting an intention for the day. And that's how one of the most powerful women in the world starts her day.

I once polled one of my audiences to learn their biggest challenges with meditation. Turns out one of the biggest challenges people have with meditation is that they simply can't find the time. I call this the busyness paradox. It's a paradox because meditation actually adds time to your day by optimizing your thinking and creative process to make you more functional.

Arianna is busy. She's been named to *Time* magazine's list of the world's one hundred most influential people and the *Forbes* ranking of the one hundred most powerful women in the world.

Yet she told me:

> It doesn't take a lot of time. But then I can bring that quality into my day. Things happen in the course of my day, your day, I'm sure everybody's day that are challenging, that require us to deal with problems. So when that happens, as it inevitably does, I am in a place where I can address them without being overreactive, prioritizing what I need to handle right away, and without stressing about bad things happening.

She suggested that you can start with as little as five minutes a day:

> Eventually you can build it up to twenty minutes, thirty minutes, or more. But even just a few minutes opens the door to creating a new habit and all the many proven benefits it brings, and I have fifty-five pages of scientific endnotes in the book about it.

I could probably have written an entire book from the wisdom I learned from Arianna. She is truly an amazing woman who shared many more of the systems she formed as daily habits that make her truly extraordinary.

You can watch a video of my full conversation with Arianna at www.mindvalley.com/extraordinary and learn about more systems that she uses in her daily life to set herself up for success and peaceful, happy living.

TRANSCENDENT PRACTICES
AND WHERE WE'RE GOING NEXT

We can tie Arianna's wisdom to philosopher Ken Wilber's eloquent words in Chapter 3 about the need to apply transcendent practices to our models and systems in the modern world.

I believe we're about to enter a new age of alignment between our physical bodies, our intellect, and our spirit. That is what we're going to explore in the next part of this book as we go into your inner world.

PART III

RECODING YOURSELF

TRANSFORMING YOUR INNER WORLD

As you practice consciousness engineering, something beautiful starts to happen. As you gain a new sense of power and freedom from Brules that no longer hold you back, your growth starts to accelerate.

At this point a great yearning often starts building in you.

You want to do more, be more, contribute more.

This part of the book will give you the means to do so.

In previous chapters, you focused on the world around you and learned to shed models from the past. Now we'll look at your present and your future, and we'll focus on a new world—your inner world with all its conflicting habits, beliefs, emotions, desires, and ambitions. We'll be bringing a beautiful order and balance to this world.

You'll be asking yourself two questions:

- What exactly is happiness, and how can I be happy in the present?

- What are my goals and visions for the future?

You'll learn new systems for living that allow you to dramatically raise your levels of happiness, including three powerful approaches that you can apply to be more blissful on a daily basis—I call it Blissipline: the discipline of daily bliss.

You'll also discover how to create exciting goals for your future without succumbing to the Brules of the culturescape. You'll learn the difference between end goals (a brilliant idea) and means goals (a bad idea). Best of all—you can do all of this by asking yourself three simple but profound questions.

When you're happy in the present moment and pulled forward by a vision for the future, your inner and outer worlds mesh seamlessly. It almost feels as if luck is on your side, and the universe has your back. When you're in this state, life seems to unfold for you in the best possible way—as if you've been blessed. I have a term for this. I call it bending reality.

CHAPTER 6

BEND REALITY

Where We Identify the Ultimate State of Human Existence

I have realized that the past and future are real illusions, that they exist in the present, which is what there is and all there is.

—ALAN WATTS, ZEN PHILOSOPHER

LOVE AND ITS CAREER REPERCUSSIONS

I was hardly a poster boy for "Person Most Likely to Succeed" after college. My scorecard the first three years after graduation looked like this:

- I tried and failed trying to launch two start-ups.

- When I did try to get a decent job, I was fired. Twice.

Finally in 2002, after being a couch-crasher for a while, I got my dialing-for-dollars job selling legal software and got good enough at that (thanks to the practices I talked about in Chapter 3) to be promoted to director of sales and relocated to New York City to open the company's East Coast office.

Then I hit another snag.

Love.

My girlfriend, Kristina, was amazing—the kind of woman who turned heads everywhere she went. But there was one big problem. She lived in Tallinn, Estonia, 4,167 miles away. Yes, I counted.

We tried to compensate by seeing each other every four months. We'd meet in Paris or Greece, and like star-crossed lovers on a budget, we'd have the most romantic holidays we could in the cheap hotels that were all we could afford. It's not every day that you meet a woman who's so incredible you'll tolerate a three-year long-distance relationship. So eventually I proposed for two reasons: romantically—because we couldn't wait to be living in the same city together and financially—because all those transatlantic flights and holidays were causing me to run out of cash.

So I asked my boss for four weeks off. The idea was to get married in Europe and then go on a honeymoon and spend some time visiting our folks. It all went well. But the day I arrived back in New York with Kristina, I received a call from my boss. "You know I think you're great, and I really like you," he said, "But I couldn't keep the position open. I had to replace you. Business is business."

I was dumbstruck. I had no US green card and no way to find another job. Neither did Kristina. "Tell you what," he said, "I can find another position for you. But it'll be half your previous pay."

I remember standing there holding the phone, feeling as if my soul had collapsed onto the floor. Calmly, I replied, "Umm . . . okay. I'll do it."

Inside I wanted to scream expletives that would make a Marine blush.

Kristina, not having a green card, couldn't work in the United States. Money was going to be tight, but we would not give up on our American dream.

Sometimes from the crappiest situations, opportunity arises. Since I had two mouths to feed and a salary that had been cut in half, I had to find other ways to make money. I'd read a couple of books about online marketing and figured that with my knowledge of coding and marketing, I could easily build a simple website to promote and sell a product I could buy wholesale. Since meditation was something I was interested in, I thought selling a meditation product would be a great way to start. I registered the first cheap domain I could find—mindvalley.com—and launched my little e-commerce store. I worked on it a few hours every evening after I got home from the office.

In my first month, I lost $800. In my second month, I lost $300. In my third month, I made a profit—a grand total of $4.50 for every day I worked. Still, it felt good. It bought breakfast at least. I loved my morning cup of Starbucks coffee. Now, I had a tiny website that earned me enough to buy a Starbucks coffee every single day. At first it was a Grande Café Mocha, but the growth of my microbusiness did not stop. Soon I was making $5.50 a day. I could upgrade to a Venti. That was a pretty exciting moment.

By month six, I was earning $6.50 every day—enough for a Venti with (drumroll please) hazelnut flavoring. A few months later, my little site was buying me my daily Starbucks *and* a Subway sandwich for lunch. Exciting times, indeed. I remember having beers with some friends at a bar, proudly telling them of my little side business that paid for breakfast and lunch each day—and how in a few months, it would pay for dinner, too.

That was basically how Mindvalley started. It wasn't about building a business. No big goals. No deadlines. Just this little game to see how much food I could get with my profits. Without realizing it, I'd stumbled upon a secret that video-game designers and psychologists had long been aware of. I was "gamifying" my life.

The money continued to grow. I soon had a new goal. I knew my minimum livable income was $4,000. That was what Kristina and I needed to eat, pay rent, live in Manhattan on a modest budget, and reinvest in the business. I was earning $7,500 from my job, but I really needed just $4,000 to survive in New York with Kristina at that time. Right before Thanksgiving 2003, I hit that number for Mindvalley's monthly earnings. I called my boss and resigned.

FROM GAME TO GRIND

Quitting my job as a law firm software salesman meant that I no longer had a US visa. Kristina and I faced a choice. We could return to Estonia, her home, or to Malaysia, where I was born. Estonia is a beautiful nation, but its winters are dreadful, so we settled on Malaysia for its warmer weather.

I'd like to be able to say that this is the whole story for why we left. But there's more. In the years following September 11, the United States was on high alert. For some reason, I was put on a watch list called Special Registration, which was designed to monitor foreign visitors from specific countries. Malaysia unfortunately made the list, and someone in the State Department decided that I was "suspicious" enough that I should be monitored.

I could travel only via certain airports, and it included an exhaustive two- to three-hour extra wait at immigration for special screening. But worst of all, every thirty days while in the United States, I had to register myself at the local immigration office. I would be required to wait in a line—sometimes standing outside in the cold for four hours in a line that stretched more than a block long, until an officer could see me, fingerprint me, take a photograph, and check my credit card purchases to see if I had made any dangerous purchases. It was horrible and demeaning.

After tolerating this for four months, Kristina and I decided we had to give up our American dream and move to a new country. I never stopped being in love with the United States. Although I grew up in Malaysia, I still feel more American than anything else, but I couldn't stay in the country I loved while being forced to live according to parolelike rules.

So I ended up home in Kuala Lumpur, Malaysia. I was precisely halfway across the world from my close friends in New York, my favorite city in the world, and my customers and business vendors.

At first the Malaysia office of Mindvalley included just me and my faithful Labradoodle, Ozzy (whom I listed as my PR manager: "the first dog in the country to hold a paid position in e-commerce"). Soon, though, we started growing. I hired my first employees and expanded into a small office space at the back of a warehouse in a run-down part of the city. We then started ramping up with more staff and projects. Suddenly, I had to run a "real" business. Rent. Hiring. Payroll. Filing taxes. Dealing with banks. I loved the work itself but was dragged down by all the worries of running the day-to-day. Being so far removed from the United States posed its challenges.

I struggled, working crazy-long hours. And to make matters worse, I was hitting a glass ceiling. The next four years would be relatively unremarkable. There were ups and downs, and we grew to eighteen people, but our business was still finding its way. At least it paid the bills. By May 2008, I found myself in a dilemma. The company was making a quarter-million dollars of revenue per month, but losing $15,000 per month. If the bleeding didn't stop, I'd have to start laying off some of our eighteen employees.

The game had become a grind. It was definitely one of those dips we talked about in Chapter 1. But something really beautiful was about to happen. I just didn't know it yet. It would cause a major shift in my models of reality. It would spark me to adopt new systems of living for my life and work. And the result would be so powerful that in just eight months, I would grow the company beyond my wildest imaginings and forever change my own life.

What Happened Next

What exactly shifted in me? I'll get to that in a minute. First, here's what happened in just eight months after the shift.

- THE BUSINESS EXPLODED. From being on the verge of laying people off, we grew 400 percent in revenue in just eight months. We'd never experienced growth like this. In May 2008, we did $250,000 in sales. Eight months later, by December of the same year. we'd had our first million-dollar month.

- WORK BECAME FUN. I no longer felt suffocated by the pressure or the grind.

- WE STARTED GETTING DREAM CLIENTS. No more working the phones and haggling. Often clients came to us. Part of my role became learning to say no.

- WE GOT AN AMAZING TEAM. In a year, we grew from eighteen employees to fifty.

But the best was yet to come. By May 2009, just one year after almost going bust, my life had completely transformed. That was a month I'll never forget. I spent just six days in the office and twenty-one days on beaches around the world. I attended a friend's wedding in Cabo, Mexico. I spent nine days with Tony Robbins in his resort in Fiji. I got to spend several days with Richard Branson and others on his private island, Necker—a dream come true for me. While all of this was happening, our company had its best-ever month and a new single-day sales record. I was at Tony Robbins's private villa in Fiji with Tony and his wife when I got the news on my phone. I had an incredible business. A wife and a family. An amazing life. And for the first time, I loved it all.

Magic seemed to be happening all around. My wildest dreams were coming true. It was as if I had been blessed with sudden luck. So, what was the insight that caused my life to shift so rapidly in such a short time?

BENDING REALITY FOR FUN AND PROFIT

If you've been reading the previous chapters and doing the exercises, you probably have a pretty good idea of the way we humans tend to live in our heads according to "truths" that we absorbed from the culturescape. You've identified important Brules that have been limiting your life, and you've started applying the principles of consciousness engineering to detect the models of reality and systems for living that may be holding you back. Thus, you've adopted a new and robust framework for personal growth.

But there's more to come. As you start playing with consciousness engineering and experimenting with new ways of thinking and living, life starts to feel more spacious and exciting. You become ready to do more, be more, and really thrive as a human being. Having mastered the art of liberating yourself from the culturescape, you're ready for a new level of mastery: mastery of your own inner self. You're now ready to recode yourself into a new type of human being and to make your own dent in the universe.

But you're not going to do it in any conventional way (culture hackers just don't work like that). Instead, you're going to question and redefine two of the biggest pillars of how we define success—namely, happiness and the attainment of goals.

You're going to get both in massive quantities, but not through struggle and striving. Rather, they'll come through attaining a balance—a delicate balance in your state of being between your levels of happiness and your vision for your future. I call living in this state "bending reality" for a reason—I've found that when I put myself in this state, it almost seems as if the universe has my back and luck seems to be on my side. It's as if I can bend reality to make my days perfect and my visions unfold at spectacular speed. This was the state I entered in the summer of 2008 when my life and business started expanding at a massive rate. Like a good engineer, I decided to try to decode this state so I could replicate it in myself and others.

IT'S ALL HAPPENING IN YOUR MIND

In the spring of 2008, as my business was struggling, I decided to stop what I was doing and take a break from the countless start-up and marketing strategies I was studying about and working long hours to implement. Instead, I decided to pour myself into personal growth.

I knew something was off. I just did not know what. But I knew it was something internal. I studied countless books and attended a number of seminars. Books by Bob Proctor and Neale Donald Walsch and seminars by T. Harv Eker and Esther Hicks gave me deep insights—the biggest of which was the idea that our beliefs shape our world.

I knew this intellectually, but I could not seem to make it work in a powerful way. And so I kept beating my head against a wall trying to make my business survive and thrive. I watched as our bank savings dwindled, and the threat of layoffs loomed ever larger. I came to work trying to act confident in front of my staff, but deep inside I felt like a failure.

I can't remember when the key insight came to me, but when it did, it was profound. And it went like this: *Stop postponing your happiness. Be happy now. Your thoughts and beliefs do create your reality, but only when your present state is joyful.* I realized I was running on empty and the fuel I desperately needed was happiness. I did have much to be happy about, but I was so obsessed and stressed out about meeting our revenue goals that my dominant thoughts were fear and anxiety.

I thought back to the early years when I would celebrate making $4.50 a day by buying myself a Starbucks coffee. It seemed so simple back then—I was grateful for every small win—and I realized there was no reason I couldn't adopt that same model of reality now. *Keep the big goals—just don't tie your happiness to your goals. Be happy now.*

I decided to change my game and my mind-set. I set new goals to get us out of the revenue slump, but I also decided to make fun and happiness a key part of my day. I was not going to postpone my happiness until I attained some future goal.

As I started hacking my life and work in this way, the needle started to move. I wrote down my target for June: to hit $300K in revenue. We hit it. I took my entire team to a beach holiday to celebrate and have fun. There we set a new target: $500K for the month. I still have on my wall today a picture of my team from 2008 holding up a sign on the beach with that goal on it. We pushed hard—but we did it *while* having a blast. We hit $500K by October. Then we set a new goal: $1 million.

I don't know how it happened. But we crossed the million-dollar mark that December. From May 2008 to December 2008 we had grown our monthly revenue from $250K to $1 million in a mere eight months. And I was having fun and the ride of my life all along.

It all started with that shift in my mental model:

Have big goals—but don't tie your happiness to your goals. You must be happy before you attain them.

I've since formulated this model into the philosophy I call bending reality. Bending reality is so named because when you're operating in this state, you tend to have a feeling that everything in life is bending in your direction, that you are effortlessly making things happen—and that anything is possible.

And so it's a subtle balance:

1. You have a bold vision for the future pulling you forward.

2. Yet . . . you're happy in the NOW.

But here's the key: BOTH of these stem from the present. As Paulo Coelho said in *The Alchemist*:

> Because I don't live in either my past or my future. I'm interested only in the present. If you can concentrate always on the present, you'll be a happy man.

There's no point dwelling in the past and letting it define you, nor in getting lost in anxiety about the future. In the present moment, you're in the field of possibility. How you engage with the present moment will direct your life.

When you're bending reality, your vision is continuously pulling you forward—but it doesn't feel like work. It feels like a game, a game you love to play. But at the same time, your happiness does not seem to be tied to that future vision. You're feeling elated and happy right now, in this moment. You're happy as you pursue your vision, not only when you attain it. You're thus grounded in the present.

Are you ready to try out this new model? Here's what I now understand about how it works.

THE FOUR STATES OF HUMAN LIVING

Think of happiness in the now and vision for the future as two ingredients that can be combined, but that have to be in balance. Too much of one or the other creates imbalance and limitation. Depending on how they're combined, at any moment in life, we can be in one of four different states of mind. This napkin drawing will help you see it.

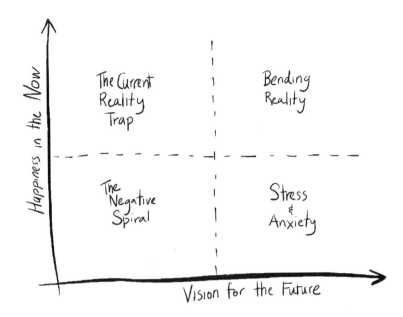

1. **THE NEGATIVE SPIRAL.** In this state, you're not happy in the now, nor do you have a vision of your future. With little to enjoy or look forward to, this is a painful place to be, and certainly not one where you want to spend any significant amount of time. Often when in this state you're feeling depressed.

2. **THE CURRENT REALITY TRAP.** This state feels great because you're happy in the now. There's nothing wrong with being in this state now and then—for example, when you're having an amazing experience or are on vacation. But remember, happiness alone can be fleeting. You can get happy from smoking a joint. But long-term happiness and fulfillment come from something more—the need to contribute, grow, and do meaningful things. While this state may bring you temporary happiness, it won't bring you long-term *fulfillment.*

3. **STRESS AND ANXIETY.** This is the state I was in during the years I struggled to build my business. A lot of entrepreneurs are in this state, as are a lot of career-driven people. In this state, you may have big goals, but you've tied your happiness to those goals. You're waiting to sign the next big deal, move into that new office, hit that next revenue milestone—before you celebrate. It's great to think big

and to want to accomplish amazing things, but it's not an optimal state if you're postponing your happiness along the way. If you're working hard but aren't making progress or if you feel you have a lot to offer but aren't getting where you want to go, you may be stuck in this state.

4. **BENDING REALITY.** This is the ideal state where you're happy in the now, and you have a vision for the future that drives you. Your vision pulls you forward, but you're happy now—despite not having yet attained that vision. When you're in this state, there's a feeling of growth and enjoyment. It's about the journey as well as the destination. An interesting observation about this state is that it often seems as if the universe "has your back." Call it what you want—but it starts to feel as if you're lucky. The right opportunities, ideas, and people seem to gravitate to you. It's as if your happiness is rocket fuel moving you toward your vision.

THE TWO ELEMENTS OF BENDING REALITY

Now that you have a sense of where bending reality falls on the spectrum of life, let's take a closer look at the two key elements that must be in play in order to get there.

I. Be happy in the now.

A key ingredient of this state is that your happiness is not tied to attaining your vision. It comes from the pursuit of your vision, combined with a sense of gratitude for what you *already* have.

That way, you don't have to wait for happiness. It's just the natural by-product of pursuing your vision. You feel a deep sense of fulfillment. And you feel insanely motivated to keep moving forward. Your work becomes like a craving. You can work twelve hours straight, and you might feel tired, but you won't burn out. All the truly great people I know have this beautiful happiness associated with pursuing their goals. Indeed, I think it's the only way to truly attain your goals—to be happy as you make the long, sometimes difficult climb toward great visions.

On Necker Island, as we were masterminding with Branson and getting life lessons from him, someone from my group asked him, "You're always happy. What do you do when you're sad?"

Branson replied, "I can't remember the bad times. I only remember the good things that happened in my life."

That was certainly one thing I noticed about hanging out with him: He's always about having fun. He has huge goals. He's one of the biggest thinkers I've ever met, yet he's perpetually in play.

And it's not just Branson. Go back a hundred years and there's another influential titan of his time who penned this little poem:

I was early taught to work as well as play,

My life has been one long, happy holiday;

Full of work and full of play—

I dropped the worry on the way—

And God was good to me every day.

That titan was John D. Rockefeller, who wrote the poem at age eighty-six. During his time he was one of the richest men in the world. Rockefeller speaks so simply and clearly here about dropping worry and about merging work and play into a life that is "one long, happy holiday." And where he says God was good to him, others might replace that with "luck" or "fortune" or "the universe."

So, no matter where you are in your life today, you must remember this lesson: Your happiness cannot be tied to your goals. You must be happy even before you attain them. Doing so will make life joyous and full of play and bring your goals to you faster than ever.

Getting There: Insights for Hacking Happiness

We make it hard for ourselves to achieve happiness because we've been trained to think about it in the wrong way. Many of us have fallen into the trap of the "if/then" model of happiness: *If X happens (if I get the right job, find the perfect mate, buy that dream house, have a baby, write a bestselling book, etc., then I'll be happy.*

To me, that's a flawed model in two ways:

1. **IT PUTS HAPPINESS OUTSIDE OF OUR OWN POWER.** It gives it to a job, another person, a house, a baby, or a book, among other things—and how crazy is that?

2. **WHEN WE'RE HAPPY, WE PERFORM BETTER, ATTRACT OTHERS, AND IN GENERAL KICK ASS IN LIFE.** I got stuck in stress and anxiety because I had hitched my happiness bandwagon to the future success of my business. So when the business went into crisis, I went into crisis, which put me in the totally wrong mind-set to get the business out of crisis, which threw me into a deeper crisis, which became a swirling spiral of unhappy crises. I have seen this happen to many successful people.

We shouldn't do things so we can be happy. We should be happy so we can do things.

Your happiness will accelerate your movement toward your goals, but it should not be tied to them. The best thing you can do to meet your goals is to find a life balance that allows you to *be happy now*. Integrate practices into your daily routines that allow you to feel content and focus on the journey, not the destination. That's how you'll break free of stress and anxiety and be in the best position to fulfill your vision. We'll explore such practices in the next chapter.

2. Develop an exciting vision for your future.

I've observed that almost all of the extraordinary people I've met or read about have one thing in common: They have a vision for their future. It may be a new piece of art to create, a service or product to bring to the world, a mountain to climb, or a family to raise.

These people live in the future in some way. Conventional spiritual growth advocates talk about the need to be "present." I believe that being present is only part of the story. Happiness in the now grounds you in the present. But you need bold dreams pulling you forward, too. Extraordinary people intend to leave a mark on the world.

Now, a word of warning. You need to make sure that your goals aren't Brule-based, or you might end up chasing something that feels meaningless once you acquire it—as happened to me when I got my first big gig at Microsoft—or as happens to countless entrepreneurs when they build a business with the goal of earning a living, only to feel trapped in the usual nine-to-five when they achieve their goal.

Instead, you want a vision for the future that speaks to your soul. This vision is typically what we call an end goal—which you'll learn how to set for yourself in Chapter 8 using a process called the Three Most Important Questions.

Getting There: Insights for Hacking Vision

I've lost count of the number of books I've read that give instructions on goal setting, from growing a business to simply getting organized. But just as we've been trained to think about happiness in a limiting way, so modern goal setting leads us astray. It happens in three ways:

1. WE CONFUSE BRULES WITH GOALS. When we set a goal that we must have a certain kind of job, a certain kind of lifestyle, or a certain kind of appearance, often these are Brules installed by society. Extraordinary minds pay little attention to the infectious "wants" of the culturescape. Instead, they create their own goals.

2. WE CAN ONLY VISUALIZE WHAT WE KNOW. While there's nothing wrong with visualizing and pursuing what we think will make us happy, we can really only visualize what we already know. What if there are even more wonderful visions and goals you could attain—gifts that only you can give the world—if only those unseen, unknown visions could be brought to the surface? We'll explore this in Part IV of the book.

3. WE'RE NOTORIOUSLY BAD AT PREDICTING JUST WHAT WE CAN DO IN A GIVEN TIME FRAME. We tend to a) bite off way more than we can chew in the short term, and b) not expect nearly enough of ourselves in the long term. Both tendencies work against successful visioneering. We tend to overestimate what we can do in one year and underestimate what we can do in three years.

In the next two chapters, we'll dive deeper into the practice of creating happiness in the now and the art of establishing beautiful visions for your future. But for now, this brings us to Law 6.

Law 6: Bend reality.

Extraordinary minds are able to bend reality. They have bold and exciting visions for the future, yet their happiness is not tied to these visions. They are happy in the now. This balance allows them to move toward their visions at a much faster rate while having a ton of fun along the way. To outsiders, they seem "lucky."

Exercise: The Eight Statements

The simple set of eight statements below will help you gauge where you are on the path to bending reality. Indicate how true each statement is for you by selecting one of the choices offered. There are no right or wrong answers. If you're still in the starting gate, no worries. We'll be talking more about how to get there.

1. I love my current job to the point where it does not feel like work.

    NOT AT ALL TRUE   SOMETIMES TRUE   VERY TRUE

2. My work is meaningful to me.

    NOT AT ALL TRUE   SOMETIMES TRUE   VERY TRUE

3. There are often moments at work that make me so happy the time just flies by.

    NOT AT ALL TRUE   SOMETIMES TRUE   VERY TRUE

4. When things go wrong, I don't worry at all. I just know something good is on the horizon.

    NOT AT ALL TRUE   SOMETIMES TRUE   VERY TRUE

5. I feel excited about my future, knowing even better things are always on their way.

    NOT AT ALL TRUE   SOMETIMES TRUE   VERY TRUE

6. Stress and anxiety don't seem to faze me much. I trust in my ability to attain my goals.

NOT AT ALL TRUE   SOMETIMES TRUE   VERY TRUE

7. I look forward to the future because I have unique and bold goals on the horizon.

NOT AT ALL TRUE   SOMETIMES TRUE   VERY TRUE

8. I spend a good amount of time thinking excitedly about my visions for the future.

NOT AT ALL TRUE   SOMETIMES TRUE   VERY TRUE

If you answered "Very true" to statements 1 through 4, you are likely happy in the now.

If you answered "Very true" to statements 5 through 8, you likely have a good vision for your future.

If you can answer "Very true" for all eight statements, you're likely in the state of bending reality.

Most people, however, find that they tend to be able to answer "Very true" to either the happiness-related statements or to the vision-related questions, but not to both.

HOW BENDING REALITY FEELS

Bending reality feels almost magical. Everything seems to "click." You're working, but it doesn't feel like work because you love what you're doing. When I'm in this state, I almost feel as if work doesn't exist. Plus, intuition and insights seem to come easily, out of the blue. Maybe this is because your mind is focused so intensely on your vision that you're alert to everything that will help achieve it and you're in a happy, joyous state that opens you up to creativity. Sometimes it seems as if the right people, coincidences, and opportunities come to you, nudging and pushing you toward your goals. Is this the mystical law of attraction? Or is it what's known as the brain's reticular activating system? To me it doesn't matter. It's a model of reality that serves me well.

If you can choose any model of reality you want and accept it as true—why not choose a model that suggests that you can literally bend reality to your wishes?

For all of these reasons, I call this the ultimate state of human existence. From a purely practical standpoint, I also believe it's the ultimate productivity hack. When you're in this state, it feels as if you're bending reality to accelerate yourself toward the visions you have in your mind, visions that come to you easily and without anxiety.

Almost everyone has experienced this sensation at one time or another, but the trick is staying in this ultimate state for longer and longer periods. The most extraordinary people know how to do this.

It's actually a discipline you can learn and practice. I call it Blissipline. And it's coming up next.

I first presented these ideas on bending reality at a speech in Calgary, Alberta, in 2009, when I shared the stage with His Holiness the Dalai Lama. My speech included the story in this chapter and expanded it to applications within businesses and teams. Back then, I described it as "being in flow." I have since changed the terminology as I have become better at the practice through the years. As you yourself master it, you will begin to see that it is not only your own "flow" you can mold but rather the full spectrum of the world around you. You can watch that full speech on www.mindvalley.com/extraordinary.

CHAPTER 7

LIVE IN BLISSIPLINE

Where We Learn about the Important Discipline
of Maintaining Daily Bliss

> It turns out that our brains are literally hardwired to perform
> at their best not when they are negative or even neutral, but
> when they are positive. Yet in today's world, we ironically
> sacrifice happiness for success only to lower our brain's suc-
> cess rates.

—SHAWN ACHOR, *THE HAPPINESS ADVANTAGE*

THE BILLIONAIRE WHO DANCES ON TABLES

It was another beautiful night on Necker Island, Richard Branson's gorgeous getaway in the British Virgin Islands. Kristina and I were sitting at a huge long wooden table with Richard and his other guests, dining on delectable food and free-flowing drinks. We'd just returned from the beach, and everyone was in a playful mood—perhaps because our host, Branson, radiated that vibe.

But as the meal went on, I noticed that several entrepreneurs there seemed to try to steer the conversation toward more serious matters. They started hitting Richard with business questions. Someone asked about an investment opportunity. Another asked for advice about running a large company. I can't blame them. When you're in the presence of such a legendary entrepreneur, you can't help but want to glean a few nuggets of his wisdom. Still, I felt that their timing was off. This was meant to be a fun, casual dinner.

Then Richard did something surprising. He politely halted the conversation. In his flip-flops, he climbed onto the table amid our plates and glasses. He then extended his hand to Kristina, who was sitting next to me, and helped her up onto the table.

"Let's dance," he said.

And they did. A beautiful slow dance right there in the middle of the feast while everyone else watched—surprised and amused—cutlery and wine glasses be damned.

It was the perfect reminder that life is not all business. We're here in this brief span of time to be happy together. And it was so perfectly Richard Branson, who is an inspiration to me as an extraordinary person who's mastered the art of working toward big visions while being persistently happy in the present.

INTRODUCING BLISSIPLINE: THE DISCIPLINE OF DAILY BLISS

When Richard Branson restored fun to a special dinner, he was demonstrating that happiness is under our control. When things get out of balance, you can bring yourself back to bliss.

Science is showing us that one of the key things that lets us function optimally in the world is our ability to control our happiness level. It's a requirement for learning to bend reality. While it's a trainable skill, many of us still find it elusive.

In this chapter, I'll introduce a simple system for mastering happiness in the now. It goes beyond feeling peaceful to feeling truly joyous. It combines spiritual mastery with the real-world desire to meet your goals and make your intentions come true. I call it Blissipline: the discipline of daily bliss.

Why Happiness Matters

Studies abound on the link between happiness and effectiveness. Here are just a few of the compelling findings.

HAPPINESS CAN IMPROVE PERFORMANCE AT YOUR JOB. In the brilliant book *The Happiness Advantage*, Shawn Achor describes a common med school exercise in which doctors in training make a diagnosis based on a rundown of a patient's symptoms and history. It's a test of the doc's knowledge and ability to think outside the box, not getting wedded to one diagnosis (known as anchoring). In one study three groups of doctors were asked to do this kind of analysis. One group was "primed to feel happy" before the exercise, another group was asked to read "neutral" medical material beforehand, and the "control" group wasn't given anything prior to the exercise. The happiness-primed docs were almost twice as speedy at making the right diagnosis compared to those in the control group—and beat them soundly at avoiding anchoring, too. What was this mysterious priming? The doctors in the happiness group were given a little candy. And they weren't even allowed to eat it to avoid possibly skewing the study results by performing with elevated blood sugar! Which leads to the amusing question that Achor asks in his book: "Perhaps patients should start offering their doctors lollipops, instead of the other way around."

GOOD ATTITUDES YIELD BETTER RESULTS. Martin Seligman, PhD, a pioneer in the field of positive psychology and author of *Learned Optimism*, screened 15,000 newly hired salespeople at MetLife using a test he developed to measure optimism levels, and then followed their performance for three years. The salespeople who scored in the top 10 percent for optimism performed a whopping 88 percent better in sales than the reps in the top 10 percent for pessimism. Dr. Seligman found that the power of optimism held in other professions, too. He concluded that in general, optimistic salespeople performed an impressive 20 to 40 percent better than pessimistic salespeople.

HAPPINESS MAY HELP KIDS LEARN. In his book *The Happiness Advantage,* Shawn Achor describes a study with four-year-olds who were given some "learning tasks" to do. One group was asked to think of something that made them happy; the other wasn't. The happy-thought group did a speedier job on the task and didn't make as many mistakes—which makes you wonder what might happen if we designed schools to take into account a student's happiness.

With so much evidence on how happiness boosts performance, it seems evident that learning to control and maintain our happiness is an important part of extraordinary living. But first we have to answer the question—what exactly is happiness?

How Happiness Happens

Before we dive into the practice of Blissipline, it's important to first define the idea of happiness. I believe that there are three distinct types of happiness.

1. Happiness from Special and Unique Experiences

This is the happiness that comes from unique human experiences. There's the heart-pounding bliss of incredible sex. The fist-pumping elation of winning a sports game. The chest-thumping excitement of closing a major deal. The mind-bending bliss of ecstatic experiences, chemically induced or otherwise. This bliss is powerful—present moment and short-lived. Sometimes there's a crash or letdown afterward as your brain chemistry descends from this high. In small doses, it's fantastic, but it can be distracting, addictive, and potentially destructive. If we were hooked up to instant bliss machines that pumped this chemistry through us 24/7, civilization would cease to progress (and we'd be too blissed-out to care). Happiness from unique experiences is a kind of short-term happiness—but it can't be the only kind.

2. Happiness from Growth and Awakening

While bliss from experiences is wonderful, there's a second type of happiness. It's more rare but seems to be more enduring. It's the happiness advocated by spiritual practitioners and transcendent practices. I call it happiness from growth and awakening. This type of happiness comes from reaching higher states of consciousness. People seek awakening in many different ways—from mindfulness practices to spiritual paths and practices of all kinds. The millions who pursue some type of spiritual path show how important this level of happiness is to human beings.

3. Happiness from Meaning

I adore my kids, but let's be honest: There are times when parenting is no fun. I've had nights of no sleep, dealt with icky diapers, and walked the floor for hours at a time with a wailing baby. So, I wouldn't say I'm always happy as a parent. And studies bear this out: Having kids tends to lessen happiness. But even on the difficult days, I wouldn't trade it for anything. The overwhelming majority of parents say the same thing.

Social psychologist Roy Baumeister, PhD, has found that this "parent-hood paradox" is explained when the search for meaning is added into the equation. Parenting is highly meaningful, even though it's also highly demanding and requires personal sacrifices that go against short-term happiness. What's interesting about the parenthood paradox is that it seems to indicate that we humans find meaning so important that we'll sacrifice a certain amount of happiness for it.

Meaning is what we get from having a healthy vision for the future, as we discussed in Chapter 6. It's a critical component of happiness. In the chapters that follow, we'll take a deeper dive into how to find the meaning and mission that will put you on your personal path to extraordinary living.

These three types of happiness tiptoe with us through life. Opportunities to find unique experiences, growth and awakening, and meaning are always around us. Most of us just don't look as hard as we could. And the reason for this is that we get tuned to function at a particular preset happiness level.

Your Happiness Gauge

Think back to a time of supreme happiness in your life. Maybe it was the day you fell in love, got married, had a baby, achieved a dream goal, had a spiritual epiphany, or just felt glad to be alive. Spend a few moments feeling those feelings. Incredible, right?

Now, sense how you're feeling right now.

Chances are, you're neither at your highest high nor your lowest low right now. You're likely somewhere in between. We don't generally spend too long at the very top or the very bottom of our emotional spectrum.

Studies show that each of us has a particular level of happiness that we tend to return to after things happen, good or bad. Researchers call this phenomenon hedonic adaptation. While hedonic adaptation can help insulate us from being forever flattened by tragedy, it can mean that even the joy of hugely positive events doesn't stick with us for long. We humans are so good at adapting that we adapt to whatever has happened and then continue along in life.

But research has found that our happiness is hackable. You've already learned how to raise your set points for the Twelve Areas of Balance in your life. Happiness is no different. It's all part of optimizing your systems for living. It turns out that you can actually raise your happiness level to experience higher levels of happiness every day of your life, too, no matter what is going on around you. There are three specific systems for living that can be especially helpful for this.

THE PATH TO BLISSIPLINE: THREE SYSTEMS FOR ADVANCING YOUR HAPPINESS LEVELS

The three Blissipline systems below will help you upgrade your quality of life every day. They're called transcendent practices: conscious practices that you internalize or embody. You'll know if they're working because you'll experience higher levels of satisfaction in daily life—and the boost in happiness usually comes instantly.

Does this mean that bad things won't happen or that you'll never be unhappy? Of course not. But it does mean that you'll have the Blissipline to deal with adversity from a positive place and the capacity to recover to a higher happiness set point than before.

The three systems below are all scientifically proven to create a boost in happiness; in some cases, a long-lasting boost that can span months. These are the three systems I used to pull myself out of stress and anxiety in 2008 and revive my career and business. These systems will also help you weather the inevitable dips you might face as you pursue a thrilling, "unsafe" life outside the Brules.

Blissipline System 1: The Power of Gratitude

Perhaps no single exercise leads to as big a happiness boost as the practice of gratitude—so much so that gratitude is getting significant notice in research and scientific circles. The list of scientifically proven benefits for the practice of gratitude now includes:

- More energy
- More forgiving attitudes
- Less depression

- Less anxiousness

- More feelings of being socially connected

- Better sleep

- Fewer headaches

A study by Robert A. Emmons, PhD, and Michael McCullough, PhD, showed that people who simply wrote down five things they were thankful for from the previous week showed a 25 percent difference in happiness levels compared to people who wrote down five negative things from the week. They also exercised more and said they felt healthier.

Dr. Emmons did another study in which people wrote down positive things each day. Not only did they report an even greater gratitude boost, but they also said they helped other people more. Apparently gratitude leads to giving, which in turn boosts the happiness and gratitude of others. That's the kind of social contagion I can get behind.

Appreciating the Reverse Gap

So, how can you make the experience of gratitude a daily occurrence in your life? Switch your "gap." This idea comes from entrepreneurial coach Dan Sullivan. As shown in the diagram below, most of us are trained to watch the forward gap—the gap between where you are now and where you want to be. The problem is that we tell ourselves we'll be happy *when* we reach that new revenue target at work . . . finally get married . . . have a baby . . . have X amount of money in the bank, and so on:

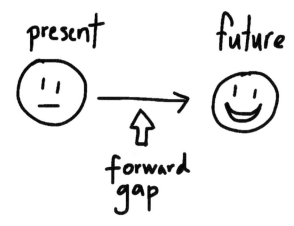

But there's a problem here. If you're chasing the forward gap, the chase will never end. No matter how good life gets, you'll always be chasing the next idea on the horizon. And just like the actual horizon, you can't catch it. It will always remain ahead of you. Tying happiness to the attainment of some future goal is like trying to catch up to the horizon. It's always going to be one step beyond your reach.

Instead, Dan suggests we look backward—to the past—and appreciate how far we've come. Dan calls this the reverse gap:

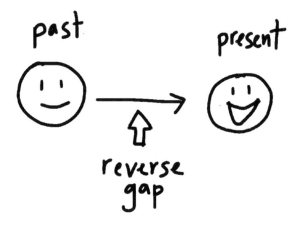

Dan explains it this way:

> The moment I start feeling disappointed or discouraged or I start feeling really tense, I immediately say, "Okay, what are you measuring against?" and sure enough, I'm measuring against the ideal. And the moment I say, "Okay, turn around, where did you come from?" And the moment I turn around and I measure backwards [from] my starting point for this particular activity—bang, I feel great.... I've learned a lot. We've made tremendous progress.... In a matter of a few seconds, I go from the negative zone of being in the gap to the positive zone of measuring my actual progress.

Even in tough times, you can look back and see how far you've come, how much you've learned, and the support you've received along the way. Paying attention to the "reverse gap" is a perfect exercise in gratitude and is far more likely to give you a boost of happiness than striving for happiness in the future. That's why gratitude is such a powerful system for Blissipline.

I believe every day should begin and end with gratitude. I practice it every day in my morning meditation. Each morning, focusing on the reverse gap, I think of five things I'm grateful for in my personal life. Then I think of five things I'm grateful for in my work and career. A typical list might look like this:

PERSONAL LIFE

1. My daughter, Eve, and her beautiful smiles

2. The happiness I felt last night relaxing with a glass of red wine and watching *Sherlock* on BBC

3. My wife and life partner

4. The time I spent with my son building his newest Lego Star Wars creation

5. The wonderful cup of gourmet coffee my publicist, Tania, left on my desk

WORK LIFE

1. My leadership team and the amazing talent they bring to our company

2. A particularly great letter we received for my online course Consciousness Engineering

3. The incredibly fun Culture Day we had in the office yesterday

4. The fact that plans are coming together to hold our upcoming A-Fest at another amazing location

5. Having coworkers who are friends and who greet me with hugs when I come to the office

This entire practice takes me no more than ninety seconds. But it's perhaps one of the most important and powerful ninety seconds I can spend each day.

Exercise: Daily Gratitude

In Chapter 4, you learned two gratitude exercises that take just a minute or two each and help prevent negative models of reality from taking root. Here, we'll take the process a little deeper. Each day, take a few minutes to focus on the reverse gap—what has happened in your life that you're grateful for? Think about:

Three to five things you're grateful for in your personal life

Three to five things you're grateful for in your work life

For some people, expressing gratitude for things in their immediate environment might feel awkward. That's okay; too many of us have fallen into a gratitude-free way of living, which means that it's all the more important to push through the discomfort. Here are a few hints for enhancing the process as you get the hang of it:

FOCUS ON THE FEELINGS. A lot of people turn this into a mechanical list-making exercise or list things they "should" feel grateful for (usually a sign that a Brule is running the show). To avoid these pitfalls, focus on your *feelings*: happy, optimistic, comforted, confident, tender, proud, sexy, filled with laughter, filled with love. For each item, spend five to ten seconds letting the feelings well up. When you land on something for which you truly do feel gratitude—whether it's for your great child or your great skin—it will feel like a straight shot to bliss.

DO THESE EXERCISES TWICE A DAY, MORNING AND NIGHT. Just as Arianna Huffington describes her meditation system as a way to kick-start her morning in the right direction, taking just a moment to express gratitude in the morning can have an amazing impact on the rest of your day. Similarly, ending the day with gratitude allows you to establish a more positive model of reality.

SHARE THE GOODNESS OF GRATITUDE. Think about ways to use or adapt these exercises with others in your life. Try them with your kids, as I do, or with your partner over a glass of wine at the end of the week (that's happy hour for real). The benefits will be even greater if you share them, and hearing what others feel grateful for may inspire you to find more gratitude in your own life.

Blissipline System 2: Forgiveness

In Silicon Valley, the Quantified Self movement is growing in popularity. People known as biohackers are measuring every aspect of their being. If you've ever used a sleep app on your smartphone to gauge the quality of your sleep or if you've used wearable tech to record how many steps you've taken in a day, you're part of the Quantified Self movement. In short, you're using measurements and metrics to improve your well-being.

Quantified Self is now coming to meditation in a big way through traditional brain wave measurement machines—but with a fascinating twist.

I recently got to experience this firsthand at the invitation of my friend Dave Asprey. Dave is the formidable entrepreneur behind the Bulletproof coffee brand and is one of the fittest, sharpest, and most intelligent people I've ever met. But less than ten years ago, he told me he weighed over 300 pounds, and his life was a mess. Dave said everything shifted when he experienced this new form of meditation.

I flew all the way to Victoria, British Columbia, to meet Dave and try out this program called 40 Years of Zen. Why the odd name? Well, the scientists who developed this technology studied the brain waves of many remarkable people—billionaires, intuitives, creatives, monks, and mystics. What they found was that when you meditate using these methods, your brain takes on the same patterns as someone who has spent twenty-one to forty YEARS in Zen meditation.

And so I started my journey into this program with some of the most remarkable people I had ever met. Our group of seven consisted of a famous Hollywood actor, a guy who'd just sold his company for a billion dollars, a top medical doctor, nutrition and fitness expert JJ Virgin, legendary marketing mind Joe Polish, and Dave.

In some respects, the experience was similar to the way we use sleep apps to measure the quality of our sleep, but in a super-high-tech way: We were hooked up to some of the most cutting-edge, specialized biofeedback equipment to measure our brain waves. The equipment beeped different sounds depending on the brain waves we were producing (alpha waves, associated with high creativity, compassion, insight, forgiveness, and love; theta waves, correlated with flashes of creativity and intuition; and delta waves, associated, we were told, with "altering reality"). We'd also see numbers on our screens indicating our brain wave amplitudes (higher amplitudes are better) and the coherence between both hemispheres of our brain (better coherence signifies better states of mind).

The difference between 40 Years of Zen and, say, classic meditation or mindfulness is simple. It's based on actual biofeedback. When you're meditating with your brain hooked up to a machine that's recording every peak and trough of your brain waves, it's easy to pinpoint exactly what works and what doesn't. You can see the results of what's going on in your mind.

Instantly.

The main focus of our sessions was to teach us how to increase our alpha waves, which would allow us access to higher states of creativity, a more relaxed mind, better problem-solving abilities, and in general many of the same benefits one would get from years of meditation.

All of us were making major breakthroughs. By the end of my time there, I was feeling a noticeable difference. In fact, my practice has never evolved so fast in such a short time.

As it turned out, the big secret to increasing alpha waves was just *one* thing. And we spent seven full days focusing on it.

Forgiveness.

The people behind the program discovered holding onto grudges and anger is the single biggest factor suppressing alpha waves. So it was critical for us to be able to release every last bit of that out of our systems.

Nobody mentioned forgiveness in the brochure when we signed up for the program. We signed up to improve our thinking and creativity skills, to experience deep states of meditation, to tame stress and anxiety. Yet forgiveness gave us all of the above. We could see the results in our neurofeedback data.

We had to forgive every single person in our lives who had wronged us, even if it was in the slightest way imaginable.

I had to forgive high-school teachers, business partners, family members—everyone I could think of who I believed had wronged me, big or small.

And every time I did a round of forgiveness, my alpha waves spiked. The method they taught us was unbelievably effective.

For me it was timely. I had some major forgiveness to do.

Recovering from a Nightmare

Sometimes, life puts you in funny, almost ironic situations.

Just three months before attending this training, I had had one of the most horrible experiences in my life. I employ some 150 people in one of our offices. And I had discovered that someone whom I had trusted to run the operations and offices of the company had been skimming money from us. He had created fake vendors—from air-conditioning repairmen to cleaners and janitorial services—and then paid his own companies exorbitant sums to service our office. So the person I had hired to run our employee housing and office maintenance was in fact paying his own companies to provide services for our company. This was illegal and highly corrupt.

By the time he was caught, he had pocketed more than $100,000. It was a massive blow to me. I couldn't believe that someone I had trusted so deeply could take advantage of me in this way. I had trusted this man for four years. I felt sick to my stomach, but I could not tell if it was from hurt or disgust.

Unfortunately, as painful as the discovery was, the worst was yet to come. When we finally fired him and filed a case against him with the police, he proceeded to go on a rampage to make my life difficult. From threats that gangsters would beat me up, to threats of my car being followed by gang members, to disrupting our business activities by sending the fire department to investigate fake charges that our office was a firetrap— he did everything he could for months to distract us from our work. It was a nerve-wracking time for me and my family and probably one of the most stressful things I've ever had to endure.

When we were doing the forgiveness exercises at 40 Years of Zen, I decided to leave him for last.

Finally, there I was in the dark chamber, meditating. Forgiving a man who had stolen from the company. Betrayed my trust. Threatened to hurt me. As I finished the exercise, I heard the machine let out a sudden beep.

I had scored my highest brain wave record.

Forgiving this man liberated me. I'd always known that forgiveness was extremely powerful, but never to this extent. I was also genuinely surprised that I was able to so thoroughly forgive him. But more than that, I felt a deep sense of compassion for him.

Even though I'd been plagued by the actions of this person, I believe if I were to see him today, I could comfortably sit down with him, have a coffee, and take the time to understand him and not be unnerved or upset.

This is what is meant by the phrase, "Forgive into love."

So, for anyone who's looking to master Blissipline, forgiveness is key.

Exercise: Liberate Yourself and Truly Forgive

Here's how to do a simplified variation of the forgiveness exercise I learned.

Preparation

In a notebook or on your computer, make a list of people you feel have wronged you or situations where you've been hurt. They could be recent or from the distant past. This may not be easy to do, especially if you're dealing with a very hurtful or long-standing situation. Be patient with yourself and remember that forgiveness, like happiness, is a trainable skill. In my own life, I have found it well worth the time and effort needed to release anger and hurt from my heart. When you're ready, pick one of the people on the list and start the exercise.

Step 1: Set the Scene

First, with your eyes closed, for about two minutes or so, feel yourself in that very moment when it happened. Picture the environment. (In one of my sessions, for example, I imagined my bullying school headmaster in the basketball court where he had made me stand for hours in the hot sun as punishment.)

Step 2: Feel the Anger and Pain

As you see the person who wronged you in front of you, get emotional. Relive the anger and pain. Feel it burn. But don't do this for more than a few minutes.

Once you bring up these emotions, move on to the next step.

Step 3: Forgive into Love

See that same person in front of you, but instead, feel compassion for him or her. Ask yourself: *What did I learn from this? How did this situation make my life better?*

As I was doing this process, I remembered a quote from one of my favorite authors, Neale Donald Walsch: "[The universe] sent you nothing but angels." It implies adopting a model of reality that everyone who has ever entered our lives, even those who have hurt us, are nothing more than messengers to teach us an important lesson.

Think about what lessons you could derive from this situation, as painful as it might have been. How did these lessons help you grow?

Next, focus on the person who wronged you. What pain or anguish could they have gone through in their life that made them do what they did?

Remember that hurt people, hurt people. Those who hurt others are doing it because at some level, at some time, they were hurt, too. Think about how they may have been hurt in their childhood or in recent years.

When I did this exercise, I saw the man who had stolen from me and tried to imagine him as a little boy. Perhaps he came from poverty. Perhaps he had an abusive parent. Perhaps his life was a constant struggle, and the only means of survival as a child was to steal. I don't know the reality of his history, and I don't need to know it, but it was helpful for me to imagine him in a situation where I could feel compassion for him rather than just anger.

This process could take a few minutes. Afterward, you should feel a slightly lesser negative charge toward this person. Repeat the process until you feel comfortable forgiving into love. For a serious offense, this could take hours or days. For a small offense like a minor issue with a coworker, five minutes may be all you need. I learned from this experience that you don't have to ask the other person to forgive you. You just have to forgive them. And that's completely within your control.

Now, there's something important to distinguish here. "Forgiveness into love" does not mean to simply let go (in my case, to drop the charges against the man with the police). You still need to protect yourself and take action if need be. Criminal acts, especially, need to be reported to authorities.

But the pain of what happened should not eat at you.

My friend Joe Polish, who took the training with me, sent a quote he found on the web to me in a text message the next day:

> UNFUCKWITHABLE: When you're truly at peace and in touch with yourself. Nothing anyone says or does bothers you and no negativity can touch you.

When you learn to truly forgive, you become unfuckwithable. Someone could be mean to you, and, yes, you'll take defensive action and protect yourself if necessary. But you're able to go on with your life without having to waste your energy on them.

The thing that truly made 40 Years of Zen the most powerful personal growth experience I've ever had was the sense of liberation I felt at the end of it. I had cleaned myself of so many grudges I'd held onto for years. I let go of painful memories I'd forgotten I had that were weighing me down. And I finally released the negative charges I felt against people who I believed had wronged me.

Today, I have never felt more at peace with myself. You can do this, too.

Blissipline System 3: The Practice of Giving

The Dalai Lama once said: To be happy, make others happy.

Giving is the path for doing this.

Giving is a natural segue from gratitude. Gratitude fills us with positive feelings and energy for life. When our cup is full, we have the capacity to give to others. Dr. Emmons's study found that people who practiced gratitude were more caring. Dr. Baumeister's research found that being a self-described "giver" was linked with a greater sense of meaning in life. He also found that meaning in life was connected with doing good things for other people.

Giving happiness to others is hugely powerful, lifts up both giver and receiver, and it's easy, because happiness is contagious. It can be anything from smiling and saying good morning with gusto to leaving little notes in briefcases or lunchboxes; from going the extra mile on a project to doing an extra house chore without being asked; from leaving a thoughtful note of appreciation on a coworker's desk to meeting your sweetheart at work with surprise tickets to an evening concert "just because."

Giving is the path for doing this. I believe that the only currency that truly matters in an uncertain world is the kindness and generosity passed from one human being to another.

In 2012 I decided to try an experiment with giving at Mindvalley. I frequently apply a method I call culture hacking to help create healthier, more collaborative culture in my workspaces. In culture hacking, you apply consciousness engineering within a group to allow the members to grow and collaborate. This time I wanted to see what would happen if I created more appreciation and connections between coworkers. The method I decided to use revolved around the art of giving. Valentine's Day was coming up, and I had been hearing too many singles grumbling about it. So, here's the experiment that came out of that: For the week before Valentine's Day, each person in the company drew a fellow employee's name out of a hat. They became the secret angel of that particular "human" for the week. We gave each secret angel a simple instruction: Do one nice thing a day for "your" human for five days. Morning coffee and croissant, candy, flowers, cards, or just a simple note of appreciation left on someone's desk—these are just a few examples of what people might give. At the end of the week, there'd be a big reveal, and lots of laughter and hugs all around. We called it Love Week.

People ended up going out of their way to organize the most spectacular surprises for their humans. These included elaborate lunches being cooked and delivered, hand-picked handicrafts, covering someone's entire desk in flowers or balloons—and even once, a plane ticket to a holiday destination.

There was a second surprise, too. The vast majority of employees polled said they actually enjoyed the act of giving more than the act of receiving their gifts. They loved planning a daily surprise of something they knew their human would enjoy. If they didn't know their human well, much of the fun came from finding secret ways to learn about him or her from coworkers and coming up with creative ideas for what to give.

The experiment was so successful that we now do it every year. By the end of Love Week, the entire office is buzzing with happiness. And while you might think that no work gets done with all this fun going on, Love Week is actually one of the most effective productivity hacks we do each year. A Gallup study of more than ten million workers found that those who answered yes to the statement: "My supervisor, or someone at work, seems to care about me as a person" were found to be more productive, contributed more to profits, and were significantly more likely to stay with their company long term.

Giving is a powerful system for bringing bliss into your life. A compliment to a coworker, a handwritten note of appreciation, inviting someone to get ahead of you in line—all of these seemingly little things will help elevate your happiness while creating tiny ripples that you may not see but when multiplied, help us make this world a far kinder and more beautiful place.

Be merciless with your kindness.

Exercise: Ways of Giving

Step 1. List all the things you could give to others.

Ideas include: time, love, understanding, compassion, skills, ideas, wisdom, energy, physical help, and what else?

Step 2. Drill down and get specific.

What skills (accounting, tech support, tutoring, legal assistance, writing, office skills, art skills)? What kinds of wisdom (career counseling; working with kids; helping others deal with an experience you've had, such as going through an illness or being the victim of a crime)? What types of physical help (fixing things, assisting the elderly, cooking, reading to the blind)?

Step 3. Think about where you could give help.

within your family or extended family? At work? In your neighborhood? Your city? Local businesses? Spiritual community? Local library? Youth organizations? Hospitals or nursing homes? Political or nonprofit organizations? What about starting a group or raising awareness about an underserved cause?

Step 4. Follow your intuition.

Review your lists and mark the items where you feel a surge of excitement.

Step 5. Take action.

Put out feelers, watch for coincidences that bring opportunity your way, and explore the possibilities.

You can also bring systems like Love Week to your office or workplace. Mindvalley has produced a guide for companies on how to implement this in their workspace. You can watch a quick video and learn the steps on www. mindvalley.com/extraordinary. Then join us each Valentine's Day week as we initiate Love Week together with thousands of other companies.

ON YOUR WAY TO BLISSIPLINE

I'd like to tell a story from my wife, Kristina, about an encounter she had with one of the wisest beings living on this Earth.

Kristina worked for an NGO at the time and was a volunteer at the UNHCR, the United Nations High Commission for Refugees. Life for refugees in Asia can be abysmal, and while Kristina's work was rewarding, it was also extremely stressful to see such misery on a daily basis. In her words, it sometimes made her "feel almost guilty about being so happy and fortunate in my own life."

These issues were very much on her mind when the opportunity came up to ask the Dalai Lama a question while we were at that incredible conference together in Calgary. Kristina asked, "How is it possible to be happy when seeing so much misery and tragedy every day?"

The Dalai Lama's answer was actually a question, and it was simply this: "But who can you help if you're unhappy?"

And this is perhaps one of the most important things to understand about Blissipline. You can be surrounded by pain. You can be empathetic and feel for others, but ultimately the discipline of bliss allows you to help spread more bliss in the world. That is the highest expression of the extraordinary life.

This brings us to Law 7.

Law 7: Live in Blissipline.

Extraordinary minds understand that happiness comes from within. They begin with happiness in the now and use it as a fuel to drive all their other visions and intentions for themselves and the world.

I hope that this chapter has shown you how easy it is to bring Blissipline into your life and how incredibly powerful the results can be. Live Blissipline and share it, and it will take root and grow.

CHAPTER 8

CREATE A VISION
FOR YOUR FUTURE

Where We Learn How to Make Sure That
the Goals We're Chasing Will Really Lead to
Long-Term Happiness

Man. Because he sacrifices his health in order to make money.
Then he sacrifices money to recuperate his health. And then
he is so anxious about the future that he does not enjoy the
present; the result being that he does not live in the present
or the future; he lives as if he is never going to die, and then
dies having never really lived.

**—JAMES J. LACHARD,
ON WHAT IS MOST SURPRISING ABOUT HUMANITY**

FORWARD MOMENTUM

Dreams, visions, aspirations, goals—call them what you will—these are
essential to an extraordinary life. I call them forward momentum. When
life doesn't hold meaning for us, it's like living in the desert, parched for
water.

In this chapter, you'll learn how to embark on your own path toward the
extraordinary by getting bolder and better with your goals. Every extraordinary mind I've ever met—including those mentioned in this book—
dreams boldly and unapologetically. I'll share a simple, enjoyable, yet
focused system for setting goals and pursuing dreams in all areas of your

life. I want you to wake up ten years from now and not say "What have I done?" but "This has been incredible—now, what's next?"

THE DANGERS OF GOAL SETTING

Goal setting is an absurd practice that I gave up long ago. It simply is too dangerous when done without the right training.

See, modern goal setting, as it's explained in countless college courses or to high-school kids, is really not about teaching you how to pursue what will really help you lead an extraordinary life. Rather, it's about teaching you to pursue common Brules of the culturescape—Brules that often lead to your chasing things that you'll ultimately find do not really matter. It's about safety rather than about truly living.

The biggest of these Brules is the idea that you need to map out your life to move you toward some ridiculous idea called a career. As a result, when most people think about setting goals and their visions for the future, their dominant model focuses on career and money. Bullshit.

As Zen philosopher Alan Watts famously said:

> Forget the money, because if you say that getting the money is the most important thing, you will spend your life completely wasting your time. You'll be doing things you don't like doing in order to go on living—that is, to go on doing things you don't like doing. Which is stupid. Better to have a short life that is full of what you like doing than a long life spent in a miserable way.

Too many of us pursue goals we *think* will make us happy—only to wake up one day in our forties, wondering what on earth happened to us as we find ourselves stuck in uninspiring, boring, stagnant lives. How does this happen?

First, the big problem with life in many industrialized countries is that far too often, we're expected to choose a career before we can legally buy a beer. As a nineteen-year-old college student, I was supposed to choose and pursue a career in computer engineering before I even knew what I truly loved. It took years of increasing misery and the drama of getting fired from Microsoft before I figured out what a rut I'd dug myself into. There is a fundamental flaw in our modern system of goal setting: With our minds clouded by Brules, we confuse the *means* and the *end*.

CHOOSE END GOALS; SKIP MEANS GOALS

You've probably heard the expression "it was a means to an end." It applies to goals, too. Often people confuse means goals with end goals. We choose college majors, career paths, life paths as if they were ends in themselves, when in reality they're a *means to an end*. We may invest years of toil and money for means goals masquerading as end goals. This can get us into trouble. The difference between a means goal and an end goal is one of the lessons that I wish more people could learn earlier in life. End goals are the beautiful, exciting rewards of being human on planet Earth. End goals are about experiencing love, traveling around the world being truly happy, contributing to the planet because doing so gives you meaning, and learning a new skill for the pure joy of it.

End goals speak to your soul. They bring you joy in and of themselves, not because they confer any outward label, standard, or value attached by society. Nor are end goals undertaken for the purpose of pay or for material reward. They are the experiences that create the best memories in our lives.

My most amazing end goals were:

- Reaching the top of Mount Kinabalu and gazing down at the clouds below me as the sun rose over the island of Borneo.

- My honeymoon with Kristina in Svalbard, Norway, hiking through blizzards in Arctic weather.

- Inviting my employees to witness a gorgeous, state-of-the-art new steampunk office I'd been dreaming up for years, and witnessing the look of awe on their faces when we opened the doors for the first time.

- Seeing my baby daughter dance for the first time (to Billy Ray Cyrus's "Achy Breaky Heart").

But for most of my life, I pursued means goals. Means goals are the things that society tells us we need to have in place to get to happiness. Almost everything I wrote down as a goal was actually a means to an end, not an end in itself, including:

- Graduating from high school with a good GPA.
- Qualifing for the right college.
- Securing a summer internship.
- Getting a job at Trilogy Software in Austin, Texas.

Other common means goals include hitting certain income levels, getting good reviews and promotions to a certain level at work, and being with one particular someone.

But when means goals become your focus, you miss the point.

I love this advice from author Joe Vitale: "A good goal should scare you a little and excite you a lot." Scary and exciting are two beautiful feelings that good end goals often bring out. Scary is a good thing because it means you're pushing your boundaries—that's how you take steps toward the extraordinary. Excitement signifies that your goal is genuinely close to your heart—not something you're doing to please someone else or to conform to society's Brules.

THE DAY I QUIT

My wake-up call happened in 2010. I had made a promise to myself that if I ever woke up two weeks in a row dreading going to work, I should quit and think of another job. In 2010 for the first time, I felt that dread.

Mindvalley was a different company back then, and I ran it with Mike, my cofounder and college friend from the University of Michigan. Mindvalley was a venture builder, a small start-up spinning off different small web businesses with the goal of generating revenue. We had launched several e-commerce stores, a software algorithm for calculating the quality of a blog post, and even a social bookmarking engine that we had sold.

Mike and I were both good at what we did, but our friendship had long ended and working together no longer had that certain spark. While Mindvalley ran on its own, I was pursuing other business ventures, and so was Mike. One of my goals was to start and exit a start-up, so I could notch another entrepreneurial win on my belt. And I was close. My second start-up, a daily deals site for Southeast Asia, was picking up steam and had just received a healthy round of venture capital funding. I was running two businesses at once, and according to my goal list, I should have been happy:

- Fast-growing business. Check.

- Funding. Check.

- Press and media attention. Check.

- Money. Check.

- Titles and rewards. Check.

Yet I wasn't happy. I was bored at work. I hated what I did and dreaded going to the office. I felt lonely. When most of your friends are your business partners or employees and you dislike your work, friendships suffer, too. Mindvalley existed to generate cash flow but not to fulfill any grand meaning for me or contribute to humanity.

How had things gotten this way?

I was bending reality: I had been happy, and I had visions pulling me forward. And I had become wildly successful and wealthy. But while I had hit all my goals as an entrepreneur, something was missing.

I had inadvertently fallen into the trap of confusing means goals with end goals. I had ended up as an entrepreneur with a business and cash in the bank. I was my own boss. But I had not bothered to set true end goals that went beyond this.

So, what did my heart truly crave?

- I wanted to be able to travel to exotic countries and beautiful locations around the world.

- I wanted to be able to stay at five-star hotels with my family and experience luxury.

- I wanted to be able to travel with my kids and expose them to unique learning opportunities.

- I wanted to have friends from all around the world who were amazing men and women driven by humanity-focused values and doing big things in the world.

- I wanted to meet many of the business and personal growth legends who had inspired me.

- I wanted to be able to teach and put down on paper my personal growth models for the world.

- And I wanted my job to be spectacular fun.

In 2010 I wrote down these goals. It was no longer just about start-ups, making money, and growing a business. I wanted a life that was enjoyable and meaningful.

Something interesting happens when you give your mind a clear vision. Whether the goal is a means goal or an end goal—your mind will find a way to bring it to you. This is why I say that to the untrained mind, goal setting can be dangerous. You could end up somewhere you don't want to be. But when you learn about end goals and their significance and do the exercise I'll share in this chapter, you're more likely to end up with what your heart and soul really crave.

When I made that list, I had no idea how those goals were going to come about. But the human mind, driven by an exciting vision, can be an amazing force for change. Sometimes the path to your end goal can be unexpected. It certainly was in my case.

Bored, lonely, and thirsting for meaning and adventure, I was definitely experiencing one of those life dips we've talked about in earlier chapters. And in the depths of those doldrums, I got the crazy inspiration to start a festival.

While attending a lot of seminars to invest in my growth, I had been turned off by how many hosted dodgy speakers pitching shady, get-rich-quick models under the guise of personal growth. But I was inspired by events that brought together tribes of like-minded souls for networking and learning. I had been invited to speak at events like Summit Series and loved the tribal dynamics I saw as people connected with each other outside the seminar room. *How could I make these better?*, I thought.

I was speaking on stage in Washington, DC, sharing some of the ideas in this book. At the end of my speech, I asked the audience if anyone wanted to come and spend a weekend with me exploring these ideas further. I had no date and no event plan—yet sixty people expressed interest. I invited them to a room and asked them what they would like to experience. What I learned was that people wanted to understand more about my unique models for personal growth, and they wanted to do it with a curated tribe, in a fun, paradise location. "This is going to be awesome," one of them said.

"I like the word," I replied. "Let's call this *Awesomeness Fest* for now." Then and there, with no date or location, I sold $60,000 worth of tickets. I now had seed funding.

Over the next several months, I put together the "fest." I invited several amazing speakers, including hotelier Chip Conley, MBA professor Srikumar Rao, Summit Series founder Elliott Bisnow, plus a host of fitness experts, and other speakers. Working with just my assistant, Miriam, we planned an entire event for 250 people in Costa Rica. It was a wild success.

We later renamed it A-Fest—and that's how it started. Now every year thousands of people from forty-plus countries apply for limited tickets to two A-Fests happening somewhere on the planet. I, along with a roster of world-class speakers and trainers on different aspects of human performance, share our latest learnings on personal growth onstage, with themes like Biohacking, Brain and Body, and Belief Hacking. In the evenings the guests experience spectacular adventures and parties that bring people together to connect and create profound memories.

We rent space at some of the most spectacular spots in the world, from paradise islands in the Caribbean to castles in Europe to world-class cultural spots in Bali. We bring in music, art, and other elements to create environments where people connect so deeply that best friendships, marriages, and business partnerships are formed. And in the midst of all this, I have some of the most incredible fun and adventure I can imagine—and get to share it with hundreds of extraordinary people who become new friends.

A-Fest grew and grew. It has become one of the most exciting things I do. Yet it fits in no category or box. But here's the beautiful thing—it fulfills all the goals I set that were missing in my life at that time:

- Friendship. *Check.*
- Being able to stay in amazing hotels. *Check.*
- Traveling to wonderful locations around the world. *Check.*
- Exposing my children to amazing minds and learning opportunities. *Check.*
- Meeting experts and business legends whom I admire. *Check.*
- Spectacular fun. *Double check.*

A-Fest was never a goal in itself. Rather, it *emerged as an evolution of* all the items on my bucket list coalescing, merging, dancing with each other, and pointing me toward the creation of a model of reality that was completely new in the world.

And that's the most important aspect of end goals. They help take you off the beaten path and move you away from the restrictive models of reality, systems of living, and Brules that school and society prod you into following. End goals help you step off the treadmill of the ordinary and get on a trajectory toward the extraordinary.

Today, 80 percent of my closest friends in the world are people I met at A-Fest. And it was just one thing in my life that emerged from focusing on end goals. But other things happened, too.

I sold my second business. It was making me miserable. I off-loaded shares to a friend and got out. The money was not worth it.

I decided I would either leave Mindvalley or remake it into something I felt proud of. And if my business partner and I did not get along, one of us would need to leave. Since I had started the company and felt it close to my heart, I decided to buy him out. I went into debt to pay him millions of dollars to buy back every share. By 2011, I owned my company again. I was broke—but I was happy. Fueled by this happiness, I grew the company 69 percent in one year, and I've not looked back since.

Correcting the way I set goals helped me shift my life from a mundane and tiresome slog to a life of adventure and meaning. I only wish I had learned about the idea of end goals sooner—I wouldn't have wasted so many years pursuing goals that seemed great on the outside but that contributed little to what my heart felt was important.

So, don't choose a career, lest you end up in a mind-numbing occupation. Nor should you just declare that you want to be an entrepreneur—lest you turn into a stressed out, bored one. Instead, think of your end goals and let your career or creation *find you*.

Now, how do you know if you're on the right path? Here's how you can check whether your goals are means goals or end goals.

THE IMPORTANT DISTINCTION: MEANS GOALS VERSUS END GOALS

It's a simple distinction, really, with four hallmarks to watch for.

HOW TO IDENTIFY MEANS GOALS

1. MEANS GOALS USUALLY HAVE A "SO" IN THEM. Means goals don't stand alone but are stepping-stones to something else. They're part of a sequence. For example: Get a good GPA *so* you can get into a good college. This often means that goals get strung together into (life) long sequences, like this one: Get a good GPA *so* you can get into a good college, *so* you can get a good job, *so* you can make lots of money, *so* you can afford a nice house, car, etc., *so* you'll have money saved to do all the stuff you really want to do after you retire. Does your goal have a "so" attached?

2. MEANS GOALS ARE OFTEN ABOUT MEETING OR CONFORMING TO BRULES. Is your goal one you think you "should" meet as part of achieving your ultimate goal—for example, thinking that you should get a college degree in order to have a fulfilling job or that you should get married in order to have love in your life? Many means goals are cleverly concealed Brules. You do not *have* to get married. Or get a college degree. Or be an entrepreneur. Or join the family business. What you really want is to be in beautiful loving relationships, to have consistent opportunities to learn and grow, and to have freedom. These can come in many different forms. See the difference?

HOW TO IDENTIFY END GOALS

1. END GOALS ARE ABOUT FOLLOWING YOUR HEART. Time flies when you're pursuing them. You may work hard toward these goals, but you feel it's worth it. They remind you of how fantastic it is to be human. When you're working on an end goal, it doesn't feel like "work." You could be doing it for hours on end, but it genuinely makes you happy or gives you meaning. You don't need to step away to get "recharged." Working on the end goal itself recharges you—it doesn't drain you. For example, for me, writing this book is an end goal. It's so much fun that I'd do it even if I never got paid.

2. END GOALS ARE OFTEN FEELINGS. To be happy, to be in love, to consistently feel loving, to consistently feel joyous are all very good end goals. A diploma, an award, a big business deal, or other

achievements can certainly bring good feelings, but they are not end goals UNLESS you're happy AS you're pursuing them—in other words, unless the act of studying for your diploma or closing the business deal itself brings you happiness. End goals have happiness baked into the pursuit.

THE THREE MOST IMPORTANT QUESTIONS

How do we avoid the means goals trap? I developed this improved goal-setting technique to get you there. I call it the Three Most Important Questions. When these questions are asked in the correct order, this exercise can help you jump straight to the end goals that really matter in your life.

I've found that all end goals fall into three different buckets.

The first is experiences. No matter what you believe about humanity's origins, one thing is clear. We're here to experience all the world has to offer—not objects, not money, but experiences. Money and objects only generate experiences. Experiences also give us happiness in the now, a key component of the extraordinary life. We need to feel that daily life holds wonder and excitement to sustain our happiness—which fuels our movement toward our goals.

The second is growth. Growth deepens our wisdom and awareness. It may be growth we choose or growth that chooses us. Growth makes life an endless journey of discovery.

The third is contribution. It is what we give back from the wealth of our experiences and growth. What we give is the special mark we can make on the world. Giving moves us toward awakening, the highest level of happiness, by providing meaning in our lives, and it is a key component of the extraordinary life.

Think about these three essentials framed as questions.

THE THREE MOST IMPORTANT QUESTIONS

1. What experiences do you want to have in this lifetime?

2. How do you want to grow?

3. How do you want to contribute?

As you do the Three Most Important Questions exercise later in this chapter, you'll see how the Twelve Areas of Balance that you've been exploring and developing in chapters throughout this book match perfectly with the Three Most Important Questions. In fact, I derived the Twelve Areas of Balance from these questions. The graphic below shows how and where they fit.

Your Love Relationship
Your Friendships
Your Adventures
Your Environment
} **Experiences**

Your Health and Fitness
Your Intellectual Life
Your Skills
Your Spiritual Life
} **Growth**

Your Career
Your Creative Life
Your Family Life
Your Community Life
} **Contribution**

Let's play out these questions in more detail. I suggest you read through the process and finish this chapter (which ends with tips for doing the exercise). Then do the exercise when you feel ready.

Question 1: What Experiences Do You Want to Have?

In this section, you are asking yourself this question:

If time and money were no object and I did not have to seek anyone's permission, what kinds of experiences would my soul crave?

Let's apply this to the first four items in the Twelve Areas of Balance. Each of these four items relates to experiences:

1. **YOUR LOVE RELATIONSHIP.** What does your ideal love relationship look like? Imagine it in all its facets: how you communicate, what you have in common, the activities you do together, what a day in your life together looks like, what holidays are like, what moral and ethical beliefs you share, what type of wild passionate sex you are having.

2. **YOUR FRIENDSHIPS.** What experiences would you like to share with friends? Who are the friends you'd share these experiences with? What are your ideal friends like? Picture your social life in a perfect world—the people, the places, the conversation, the activities. What does the perfect weekend with your friends look like?

3. **YOUR ADVENTURES.** Spend a few minutes thinking about people who've had what you consider to be amazing adventures. What did they do? Where did they go? How do you define adventure? What places have you always wanted to see? What adventurous things have you always wanted to do? What kinds of adventures would make your soul sing?

4. **YOUR ENVIRONMENT.** In this amazing life of yours, what would your home look like? What would it feel like to come back to this place? Describe your favorite room—what would be in this wonderful space? What would be the most heavenly bed you can imagine sleeping in? What kind of car would you drive if you could have any car you wanted? Now imagine the perfect workspace: Describe where you could do your best work. When you go out, what kinds of restaurants and hotels would you love to visit?

Question 2: How Do You Want to Grow?

When you watch how young children soak up information, you realize how deeply wired we are to learn and grow. Personal growth can and should happen throughout life, not just when we're children. In this section, you're essentially asking yourself:

In order to have the experiences above, how do I have to grow? What sort of man or woman do I need to evolve into?

Notice how this question ties to the previous one? Now, consider these four categories from the Twelve Areas of Balance:

5. **YOUR HEALTH AND FITNESS.** Describe how you want to feel and look every day. What about five, ten, or twenty years from now? What eating and fitness systems would you like to have? What health or fitness systems would you like to explore, not because you think you ought to but because you're curious and want to? Are there fitness goals you'd like to achieve purely for the thrill of knowing you accomplished them (whether it's hiking a mountain, learning to tap dance, or getting in a routine of going to the gym)?

6. **YOUR INTELLECTUAL LIFE.** What do you need to learn in order to have the experiences you listed above? What would you love to learn? What books and movies would stretch your mind and tastes? What kinds of art, music, or theater would you like to know more about? Are there languages you want to master? Remember to focus on end goals—choosing learning opportunities where the joy is in the learning itself, and the learning is not merely a means to an end, such as a diploma.

7. **YOUR SKILLS.** What skills would help you thrive at your job and would you enjoy mastering? If you'd love to switch gears professionally, what skills would it take to do that? What are some skills you want to learn just for fun? What would make you happy and proud to know how to do? If you could go back to school to learn anything you wanted just for the joy of it, what would that be?

8. **YOUR SPIRITUAL LIFE.** Where are you now spiritually, and where would you like to be? Would you like to move deeper into the spiritual practice you already have or try out others? What is your highest aspiration for your spiritual practice? Would you like to learn things like lucid dreaming, deep states of meditation, or ways to overcome fear, worry, or stress?

Question 3: How Do You Want to Contribute?

In keeping with His Holiness the Dalai Lama's message, as I mentioned earlier, if you want to be happy, make other people happy. This question explores how all of your unique experiences and growth can help you contribute to the world. It doesn't have to be a big dramatic gesture—perhaps it's inviting the new neighbors over for a cookout or taking the new hire out for lunch, playing the piano at a nursing home, helping rescued animals get adopted, or spearheading a clothing drive at work.

In this section, you're essentially asking yourself:

If I have the experiences above and have grown in these remarkable ways, then how can I give back to the world?

Again, notice how this question connects to the previous two. Imagine what you can give in these areas of the Twelve Areas of Balance:

9. **YOUR CAREER.** What are your visions for your career? What level of competence do you want to achieve and why? How would you like to improve your workplace or company? What contribution to your field would you like to make? If your career does not currently seem to contribute anything meaningful to the world, take a closer look—is that because the work is truly meaningless or does it just not have meaning to you? What career would you like to get into?

10. **YOUR CREATIVE LIFE.** What creative activities do you love to do or what would you like to learn? It could be anything from cooking to singing to photography (my own passion) to painting to writing poetry to developing software. What are some ways you can share your creative self with the world?

11. **YOUR FAMILY LIFE.** Picture yourself being with your family not as you think you "should" be but in ways that fill you with happiness. What are you doing and saying? What wonderful experiences are you having together? What values do you want to embody and pass along? What can you contribute to your family that is unique to

you? Keep in mind that your family doesn't have to be a traditional family—ideas along those lines are often Brules. "Family" may be cohabiting partners, a same-sex partner, a marriage where you decided not to have children, or a single life where you consider a few close friends as family. Don't fall into society's definition of family. Instead, create a new model of reality and think of family as those whom you truly love and want to spend time with.

12. YOUR COMMUNITY LIFE. This could be your friends, your neighborhood, your city, state, nation, religious community, or the world community. How would you like to contribute to your community? Looking at all of your abilities, all of your ideas, all of the unique experiences you've had that make you the person you are, what is the mark you want to leave on the world that excites and deeply satisfies you? For me, it's reforming global education for our children. What is it for you?

This brings us to Law 8.

Law 8: Create a vision for your future.

Extraordinary minds create a vision for their future that is decidedly their own and free from expectations of the culturescape. Their vision is focused on end goals that strike a direct chord with their happiness.

Applying the Three Most Important Questions to Work, Life, and Communities

You can do the Three Most Important Questions exercise alone or with others. Schools in the United States and in villages in Africa have used it to inspire students. Companies use it to create more bonding and employee engagement. Many people do this exercise with a partner—sharing your answers creates instant connection. Try the exercise with your partner on your respective birthdays or on your anniversary. It's fascinating to see how your own and others' goals evolve and change over time.

Blueprints for the Soul

The Three Most Important Questions exercise is so important that we do it with every person who joins the Mindvalley family. New hires go through a training in consciousness engineering, following a curriculum similar to this book. They end their induction by doing the Three Most Important Questions exercise. On a piece of letter-size paper, they draw three columns marked Experiences, Growth, and Contribution. Within the columns, they write down their visions and aspirations for each of the three areas. In the end, the sheet looks like this:

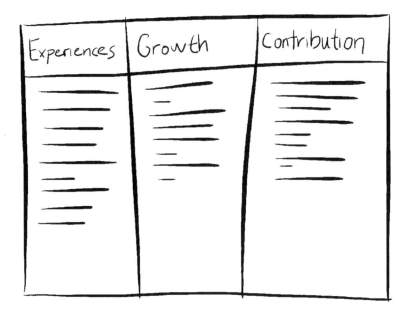

These are more than just sheets of paper to me. Each represents the dreams, ambitions, and motivations of someone who has joined our company. And so we lovingly call these sheets "blueprints for the soul."

We post everyone's blueprint, along with their photo, on a giant corkboard so we can see and share our dreams. Each floor in our office has a corkboard with the blueprints of the people who work there. Seeing all of those shining aspirations collected in one place gives off indescribable power. It's one of the most beautiful things to behold at Mindvalley—the collective dreams of hundreds of employees on one giant wall.

It's also the ultimate in transparency: Coworkers know what drives other coworkers. Managers know what drives their team members. I know what drives everyone, and they know what drives me.

Many success stories started as blueprints on this wall. Amir joined Mindvalley from Sudan. He did the exercise when he was twenty-two, and he had big dreams. He wrote about how he wanted to be a professional speaker and write a book. Those were incredibly bold dreams considering his circumstances, but by age twenty-six, Amir had scratched off most of them. He'd written that book: *My Islam: How Fundamentalism Stole My Mind— And Doubt Freed My Soul*, which *Foreign Policy* magazine recommended as one of the twenty-five must-read books of 2013. Today he writes, consults, and speaks at top-tier venues, from Google to Columbia University.

Luminita Saviuc joined our team from Romania. On her list she wrote goals such as "be a world-renowned author and speaker" and "be a world leader in the field of spirituality." The goals came to her in the most interesting way. She had written a blog post called "15 Things to Give Up to Be Happy" on her personal blog PurposeFairy.com. Somehow a year later the post resurfaced and went viral on Facebook. It touched a nerve and 1.2 million people shared it. Within months she got a book deal. Two big goals checked off.

These stories are not unusual. Time and time again I would see the big goals being checked off in the most unusual ways.

Best of all, this model is an opportunity for growing and giving: We can look at the board, see what others are doing, and say, "I love that!" and add it to our own blueprint. After all, there is no monopoly on dreams.

The wall also allows collaboration on shared visions. Mariana, a product manager from Ukraine who worked for us, dreamed of going to Nepal to hike the Himalayas. She scoured the wall for others who had Nepal on their blueprints and found three others. All four took a week off to hike in Nepal, bonding as they supported each other in striking an item off their list.

Talking openly about your dreams and end goals helps to make them a reality. It's rare that people confide their dreams—or even admit them to themselves. The Three Most Important Questions exercise brings dreams to light for the universe—that's you, me, and the mysterious beyond. That's what makes the Three Most Important Questions exercise one of the most powerful ideas in this book.

As a bonus tip, remember that once you know the blueprint for your team members or a family member, you can always practice giving by offering them simple little gifts or reminders to help them grow. Over time, I developed a simple management technique that I consider one of the most important tools I use as a leader. I take a picture on my smartphone of every employee's Three Most Important Questions sheet and carry it with me. I then read their blueprints and surprise them with a book to help them achieve their dream. For example, one recent new hire had written that she dreamed of learning public speaking and someday giving a TEDx talk. I bought her a copy of *Talk Like TED* and wrote a little note of appreciation inside the book. Something magical happens when you do this at work. You aren't just showing that you care—you are making someone totally light up as they recognize that their dreams are supported by others. It's a great way to build trust. Meaningful gestures need not be expensive; they simply need to be genuine.

Exercise: Ask Yourself the Three Most Important Questions

BEGIN BY KEEPING IT SIMPLE. All you need is a place to write down your responses—it could be your journal, your computer, a smartphone, or anything else. For each category, set a timer or your watch for three minutes or so. Setting a timer helps shut down your logical mind so your intuitive and creative mind can come out to play before hairy old Brules or outdated models of reality can rear up and rain on your parade. With the timer, you can complete the entire exercise in ten minutes.

DON'T OVERTHINK IT. Trust your intuition to know the answers to these questions. Don't spend too long, and don't worry about being grammatical. Just let your words flow. Draw pictures if that helps. This is why the three-minute timer works. It forces your logical mind to shut up so your intuitive mind can be allowed a free-flowing expression of what you truly want. You can always go back after the three minutes are up and spend time analyzing and sorting out your list. But start with the three-minute rule.

REMEMBER THE DIFFERENCE BETWEEN A MEANS GOAL AND AN END GOAL. The quickest way is to focus on feelings. What feelings will a goal bring? For example, a feeling-focused end goal about your environment might be: "I want a house I'm blissfully happy to wake up in every morning" or "At least twice a month, I get to go out for a delicious meal with friends or family I love to be with."

FOLLOW THESE FIVE STEPS TO STAY ON TRACK. Use this quick guide to double-check your goals to see if they're in full alignment with what you really want. Mia Koning, our chief facilitator at A-Fest, designed these five steps, which added further clarity to the process:

1. Identify a goal.

2. Answer this question exhaustively until you have no more answers: When I achieve this goal, I will be able to __, __, __, [etc.].

3. Answer this question exhaustively, until you have no more answers: When I achieve all this, I will feel __, __, __ [etc.].

4. Identify the true underlying objectives of your goal, based on your answers to questions 2 and 3.

5. Compare these objectives with the original goal and ask:

   - Is this original goal the only way/best way to achieve these objectives?
   - Is this original goal enough to achieve them?
   - Can I achieve them in a more effective way?

When you do this, you will often find that what you think is an end goal is really a means goal. You will also get clarity on what the actual end goal might be. This will free you to ensure that you're really pursuing the right end goal.

WHAT TO DO WITH YOUR LIST. Stick it up on a wall where you can see it and keep consciously and subconsciously working toward your goals. Share it with others for all the reasons I mentioned. You'll be empowering others to grow and giving yourself new opportunities to grow as well. I cannot express how powerful this is as an exercise for companies. It's one of the most important exercises for cultivating great culture at Mindvalley, and thousands of companies are doing the same. Why not introduce it to your workplace?

THE GOOD NEWS

The good news is that you're already on your way. Something amazing happens when you set big, beautiful end goals. Your brain latches on to what you're seeing and feeling. It goes to work, hacking its way toward your goals. Steve Jobs said it wisely:

You can't connect the dots looking forward; you can only connect them looking backward. So you have to trust that the dots will somehow connect in your future. You have to trust in something—your gut, destiny, life, karma, whatever. Because believing that the dots will connect down the road will give you the confidence to follow your heart even when it leads you off the well-worn path; and that will make all the difference.

When you ask the Three Most Important Questions right, you're "believing that the dots will connect down the road." You will start noticing and discovering the paths that bring you closer and closer to where you want to be. Scientists may call this one thing (such as the brain's reticular activating system); mystics may call it another (the universe, God, fate, synchronicity, the law of attraction, or thoughts create reality). Steve Jobs calls it "your gut, destiny, life, karma, whatever."

I call it the extraordinary mind.

Use this weapon wisely.

To provide you with additional resources for the Three Most Important Questions, Mindvalley has produced several short videos that you can access on www.mindvalley.com/extraordinary:

- A guided summary of the brainstorming process

- How to bring the Three Most Important Questions to your own organization: Watch how Mindvalley applies the process within its own organization. (I strongly feel every company should be doing this and every manager should take an interest in the blueprints for the soul of the people they lead.)

PART IV

BECOMING EXTRAORDINARY

CHANGING THE WORLD

In Part I you learned to observe the culturescape, the world around you, and see it for what it is.

In Part II you learned that you get to choose the world you wish to experience. Through consciousness engineering, you can choose your own models of reality and systems for living and speed up your growth and awakening.

In Part III you learned about the world within and how to strike a balance between happiness in the now and having a vision for the future. Taken together, these abilities allow you to seemingly "bend reality."

In Part IV I build on all of these to take you to the next level. Here you learn to change the world.

Extraordinary minds are not content to merely be in the world. They have a calling, a pull, to shift things. At this point in your journey toward the extraordinary, you may begin feeling an urge to shake up the culturescape by creating new models, new ideas, and new ways of life and living that move others to new places, too. You go from escaping the culturescape to returning to it and helping it evolve. All extraordinary minds go through this passage. They return to shake things up and change things.

But this is no small feat. To do it, you need to learn the final two laws.

In Chapter 9 we start with the first lesson: Be unfuckwithable. Trying to change the world requires a certain level of boldness and toughness.

In Chapter 10 we'll look at finding your quest—how to know WHAT to change. You'll learn that you are not alone and that there is an inner guidance system that is going to come to your aid.

Finally, in the appendix, Tools for Your Journey, you'll learn how to take all the systems for living I've shared with you and put them together in a daily fifteen-minute practice that allows you to bring together everything you've learned from this book.

CHAPTER 9

BE UNFUCKWITHABLE

Where We Learn How to Be Fear-Proof

Train yourself to let go of everything you fear to lose.

—YODA, *STAR WARS*, EPISODE III: REVENGE OF THE SITH

HOW TO BE A SPIRITUAL BADASS

There is a great myth in spirituality today: that in order to be spiritual, we must resign ourselves from the world. In other words, to be spiritual, one must avoid big goals, ambitions, and wealth.

Rubbish. I believe the most spiritual people in the world today are those who are doing things to push the human race forward. To be extraordinary is to be connected to this spiritual aspect of yourself and to feel it move you to create, change, invent, and rattle the world.

Ken Wilber, perhaps the greatest living philosopher in the world today, wrote a beautiful essay on this subject called "Egolessness."

In it, he says:

> The typical person wants the spiritual sage to be less than a person, somehow devoid of all the messy, juicy, complex, pulsating, desiring, urging forces that drive most human beings. . . . We want our sages to be untouched by them altogether. And that absence, that vacancy, that "less than personal" is what we often mean by "egoless."
>
> But egoless does not mean "less than personal"; it means "more than personal." Not personal minus, but personal PLUS—all the normal personal qualities plus some transpersonal ones. Think of the great

yogis, saints, and sages, from Moses to Christ to Padmasambhava. They were not feeble-mannered milquetoasts but fierce movers and shakers—from bullwhips in the temple to subduing entire countries. They rattled the world on its own terms, not in some pie-in-the-sky piety; many of them instigated massive social revolutions that have continued for thousands of years.

And they did so, not because they avoided the physical, emotional, and mental dimensions of humanness, and the ego that is their vehicle, but because they engaged them with a drive and intensity that shook the world to its very foundations.

Ken Wilber's profound words helped me resolve some of my own inner conflicts on being spiritual. I think there are many ways to be spiritual, and one of them is to be spirited—filled with forward-looking energy and the courage to challenge the status quo, like the scientists, entrepreneurs, and titans who are working on projects to push humanity forward. What could be more uplifting than that? We don't have to choose between Buddha or badass. The idea is to be both. Indeed, sometimes the only way to be effective at one is to master the other.

BUDDHA OR BADASS?

There is a scene in *Star Wars* where Yoda sits an angry teenage Anakin Skywalker down and tells him, "The fear of loss is a path to the Dark Side. . . . Train yourself to let go of everything you fear to lose." But to Anakin this advice seems difficult. Not only does he remain attached to his fear of losing his wife, but his fear grows to be the driving force in his life—eventually turning him into Darth Vader. That scene has been much debated on the Internet: How could Yoda expect Anakin to not fear the loss of loved ones? It's human after all.

Here is what I believe Yoda was saying.

To truly be a great warrior in the world, you must step past your fears. It's inevitable that we get attached to people, to our goals, and fear losing them—but a true Jedi knows that attachments to people and goals can hinder us. It is possible to move toward a goal or to be madly in love with someone—without attachment. Often what we really fear is not losing the other but losing that part of ourselves that this someone or something makes us feel. This happens when we attach our sense of self-worth and happiness to someone or something outside of ourselves.

Go ahead and love well. Work hard toward a goal, but know that when you make your feelings of love and fulfillment come from an internal reservoir and not from the other person or the goal, you become much stronger. In fact, you may discover that you can love better and pursue your goals with much more ease. But it starts with a feeling within.

Before we come to finding your own particular quest—that aspect of the world that you can "rattle"—you first need to find your "badassery."

This idea comes from my experiences at 40 Years of Zen, the biofeedback course where I discovered deep inner peace and clarity after working intensively on forgiveness. That feeling was one of being unfuckwithable. I don't know the origin of that word. It started to appear in 2015 on the Internet in the form of an image accompanied by this text:

Unfuckwithable: A Definition

When you're truly at peace and in touch with yourself. Nothing anyone says or does bothers you and no negativity can touch you.

Sounds good, right?

The question is: How do we get there?

There are two models of reality that can help you get to this stage. Not only do they make you feel more grounded in terms of who you are but they also give you immense control over your state of mind and feelings.

Law 9: Be unfuckwithable.

Extraordinary minds do not need to seek validation from outside opinion or through the attainment of goals. Instead, they are truly at peace with themselves and the world around them. They live fearlessly—immune to criticism or praise and fueled by their own inner happiness and self-love.

THE FIRST COMPONENT OF BEING UNFUCKWITHABLE: SELF-FUELED GOALS

What happens when you go as far as you can with end goals, when you keep asking the "so" question, as we discussed in Chapter 8, until you get to a genuine feeling you crave to consistently feel? My epiphany about this came in the middle of the desert in August 2014.

I was at Burning Man, the famous annual art festival in Black Rock City, Nevada, where people from all over the world come together in the desert and create a city from scratch. Thousands of structures and art installations are erected—a carnival of creativity, ingenuity, and culture to astonish the mind and senses—all burned or dismantled at the end as the hordes depart. More than 75,000 burners, as festivalgoers call themselves, attended the 2014 event. Many see it as a deeply spiritual experience.

Each Burning Man has a unique installation called the temple near the center of the festival. That year, it was a beautiful domed structure of wood panels cut in floral and nature patterns. Thousands meditated and prayed there daily. As night fell and the heat ebbed, a breeze sifted across the desert. I pedaled along the dusty, hard-packed earth as I'd done every night since arriving, headed for the temple where I'd sit on the soft playa sand and meditate among hundreds of burners.

The temple is filled with incredible, indescribable energy. Since the temple is a temporary structure, every available surface is covered with handwritten notes expressing wishes, dreams, and odes to friends and family, dead or alive. The place vibrates with the concentrated power of human thought and emotion.

I went to the temple to reflect on my goals and my life. One night, as I sat in meditation, an insight hit me that would fundamentally change the way I selected end goals:

A good end goal is something you have absolute control over. No object or person can take it away from you.

I now call goals like this self-fueled end goals. For example, let's look at end goals for a fictional character named Vanessa, newly married to Dan. Vanessa might write down this goal:

"To be madly in love with Dan."

Is this an end goal? It might seem so—but it's not. Why? Because the attainment of this goal is largely dependent on someone else. What if she and Dan fall out of love?

A better end goal for Vanessa might be this:

"To be consistently surrounded by love."

The beauty of this end goal is that Vanessa controls it. It is thus "self-fueled." If she and Dan have a long, healthy marriage, this goal manifests. But even if the marriage doesn't work out, Vanessa can still be surrounded by love—from friends, family, a new partner—or best of all, from her own love for herself.

Setting expansive and truly powerful end goals like these is simple. And goals like these are largely within our control.

At Burning Man, I realized that when it came to love, the best end goal I could write for myself was not "To be in a loving relationship with Kristina" or "To be close to my children," but rather: "To be consistently surrounded by love."

This goal freed me from having to depend on others for love or to require it from them. I love my kids and my wife, but I cannot demand that they love me back, and setting goals for myself that are largely dependent on someone else leaves me powerless. This is true for everyone. We should not be attached to receiving love from someone else.

A similar idea can be applied to our relationship with our children. "Having a close, loving relationship with my kids" sounds like a proper end goal, but what if our kids decide at a certain age to move far away or they don't need our closeness anymore? So I changed my family life goal from "To be close to my children" to: "To be the best father I can be." Because that IS in my control, and it encourages me to pay attention to what my kids need from me on an ongoing and ever-changing basis.

When I shifted these goals, my mind's guidance system kicked in, pulling me into opportunities and situations to attain them. My relationships improved significantly. Neediness on my end stopped. I began to love and appreciate my own self at a level I never had before. Doing so freed me to be more loving and appreciative of others because, empowered by my own self-love, I stopped unfairly demanding love from others.

After much contemplation, I adjusted my goal about travel and adventure (did I really want to experience bungee jumping or was I just conforming to a trend?) and replaced it with: "I will always have the most amazing and beautiful human experiences."

See, I can control what I define as an amazing human experience. I can be in my nineties and unable to use my body with the same ease as now, but I can still have amazing human experiences, which might be holding my great-grandchild in my arms or enjoying a glass of fine whiskey with my wife.

With that new goal, I made a decision to take my family on a special holiday each year to experience an amazing part of the world. We've since traveled to Edinburgh, Scotland, and to New Zealand and had incredible experiences. But even if I can't travel or decide I don't want to anymore, with this expanded goal I can still have the most beautiful human experiences simply being at home, playing with my daughter or building the latest Lego Star Wars toy with my son. Recently I found myself incredibly happy just sitting on my sofa drinking a wonderful red wine I had discovered and eating the most delicious chocolate (Royce Rum Raisin, if you must know) while watching *The Daily Show* on Comedy Central. It *is* that simple.

The third self-fueled end goal I now have is: "I am always learning and growing." For a long time I'd had specific learning goals such as "Read a book a week." And there's nothing wrong with goals like that. But for me it had become stressful: Between managing a company with hundreds of employees and having two kids, I was finding less time to read. Sitting in the temple, I had an intuitive hit that it was time to reboot my learning goals.

It turned out that for me, reading a book a week had become a means goal. What I really wanted was to gain knowledge.

Once I expanded my goal, I got into experimenting with alternative ways of learning, such as mastermind groups, online courses, and "brain exchanges," where I'd get on a sixty-minute call with a friend who was an expert on a topic and we'd share notes on our best practices.

When your goals change, your means of attainment change. A good goal can open up new and innovative ways of reaching it.

THE ULTIMATE BEAUTY OF SELF-FUELED END GOALS

Below are the three expanded end goals that I currently live by. Can you see what they all have in common?

1. I will always be surrounded by love.

2. I will always have the most amazing and beautiful human experiences.

3. I will always be learning and growing.

They are all directly within my own power. *No one* can take these away from me. This means no failure can stunt me. I could be homeless and alone, sleeping on the streets of New York City—but I can still be surrounded by love because my love comes from within. I can learn and grow as long as I can find an old newspaper or a thrown-away book to read. I can even have beautiful human experiences because I can see the joy in everyday life, even just walking through Central Park.

When you identify self-fueled end goals that put them within your power—you will have nothing to lose. Not love. Not learning. Not beautiful human experiences. You will be free to live life on your own terms and to explore opportunities that might once have seemed out of reach or inconceivable. Too many people stay stunted in their growth because of fear of loss—but when you go deep enough with this exercise, you realize that there is no loss. Happiness is completely within your control, and when you have nothing to lose, you're free to think and dream boldly.

Replacing fear with courage is one of the key components of being unfuckwithable. Most people live their lives consistently bothered and worried about not being loved enough, about not succeeding fast enough, not being significant, not being impressive, losing the things that make us happy. But when you let go of the Brules that lead you to the wrong priorities, look beyond your means goals and create self-fueled end goals, you've effectively bother-proofed yourself. You stop worrying about what others will think of you or might take from you, and you free yourself to dream big and be creative in other areas of your life.

When you become unfuckwithable, it doesn't mean you're settling for small goals. Instead, it means you've stopped setting goals for things you *think* you need to get from other people. These days, I have massive visions based on my Three Most Important Questions. My goals for Mindvalley are to create a school for humanity—to get a billion people onto a single education platform where adults and children can access the education they truly need to get to a point where they can truly be extraordinary—not just the industrial-age education that we currently get. It's a big goal, and I work long days to make it happen—but I feel peaceful where I am now simply because my happiness is not just tied to building a billion-dollar education company. That certainly fuels me and excites me—but my happiness itself comes from those three simple end goals that I have daily control over and that no one and no circumstance can take away from me.

My happiness in the now fuels my vision for the future, and that vision fuels my happiness, because a key part of it (love, learning, and human experiences) is already happening. It all connects.

I believe this is what the ancient Zen masters (and Yoda) meant by nonattachment to goals. They didn't mean "do not have goals." Have goals. But your happiness should not be attached to the completion of your goals. The feeling you get from completing those goals you can learn to generate *now*. When you realize this, the fear of loss disappears. You can explore every facet of your dreams. Be bold. Act fearlessly. And be happy—now.

THE SECOND COMPONENT OF BEING UNFUCKWITHABLE: REALIZING YOU ARE ENOUGH

In Chapter 4 I introduced you to Marisa Peer, the famous British hypnotherapist and the work she did with me to help me see how my childhood insecurities were affecting my achievement and goal setting in my adult life.

It's nearly impossible to go through childhood without some situation or person infecting you with the belief that you are not enough. Marisa Peer, in her much-watched A-Fest speech, calls the mental models we carry around that say we are not enough the "Biggest Disease Affecting Humanity."

Because the model of reality that we are not enough is terribly painful, we live our lives trying to prove that we're enough. Sometimes this can be an asset; for example, my drive to prove I was enough led me to a certain degree of entrepreneurial success.

But it's not the optimal path, because working to disprove the model of not being enough has a hidden cost. That cost is that you will depend on others for validation.

You may come home from work and expect to be greeted or treated in a certain way by your spouse. If this does not happen, you feel out of sorts or rejected.

You may expect to be praised, noticed, or have your ideas heard by your boss or a superior at work. If that doesn't happen, you decide you are not appreciated, not respected, or that your boss is an asshole.

Or maybe your son or daughter doesn't call you enough, or a brother or sister doesn't remember your birthday in the way you expect. Boom—the feeling creeps back in.

In all of these situations, chances are you won't literally think, "I'm not enough." No, the sneaky thing about this model is that if you have it, it's hard to admit you have it—or even to realize that it's there. So instead, you bury it and create a model of reality about the person you're seeking validation from. Your brain's meaning-making machine goes into overdrive and you decide:

- My husband's such an inconsiderate asshole sometimes.

- That son of mine really doesn't appreciate me.

- My sister doesn't care about her family—how awful of her.

- My boss is an unappreciative jerk.

This is the most disempowering kind of model to have, because you're blaming outside circumstances for what happens in your life. This model robs you of your own ability to control your life. While you can't control what others do, you can control how you react to others. In order to be truly unfuckwithable, you need to lose your need to seek validation or love from others and to judge them when you perceive that they are not giving you what you need.

FROM HOLE TO WHOLE

When you create meaning around others' actions or judge others who don't provide what you need, chances are you're really just compensating for a hole within yourself that they reminded you of. In every case, the root cause of this is a feeling of not being enough. So we look to others for validation, love, or praise and get hurt when we observe what we believe is criticism, judgment, or rudeness.

But remember, you're in control of filling the hole within.

And here's the paradox. When you plug this hole within yourself and stop demanding that others fill it for you, you actually improve the chances of having the kind of great relationships you long for.

There is nothing more attractive than a person who loves himself or herself so deeply that their positive energy and love spill over to others and to the world.

BECOMING IMMUNE TO OTHERS' BEHAVIORS, CRITICISM, OR JUDGMENT

You know you have a hole to plug when you find yourself feeling hurt or creating meaning around someone else's action or words.

You can't control someone else's behavior toward you, but you can control your own reaction and how your meaning-making machine construes that behavior. The key is to override our inner desire to prove ourselves or our tendency to feel as if we're not enough without the love or validation of others.

I had such a moment as a teenager that's funny in retrospect, but it was so painful at the time that I still remember it vividly today. The year was 1990. I was fourteen, and Vanilla Ice's hit song "Ice Ice Baby" was at the top of the charts. I loved that song, and like every other cool kid in school, I had tried my best to memorize the lyrics.

One day at recess, I spotted the group of cool kids that everyone in class wanted to hang out with. They were sitting around a desk rapping "Ice Ice Baby." Their baseball caps were on backward, and they were snapping their fingers, looking as cool as teenagers in the nineties could look.

When they got to a particular verse, I knew this was my chance to prove I was hip. I jumped in and sang the verse. Loudly. With my rap face on.

But I sang the wrong line. The other kids stopped and stared at me. Jaws dropped. How dare I fudge the brilliant verses of Vanilla Ice? It was sacrilege. And then the cool girl in the group we were all trying to seek validation from, said: "Jeez, what a nerd."

I walked away with my head down. Devastated. A failure. Their lack of validation tortured me.

Twenty-five years later I still remember that moment. It is incredible to think that I derived so much meaning about fitting in from knowing those lyrics. It makes no sense to me today (especially given Vanilla Ice's musical track record), but it did then. If you think back, you've probably experienced this sort of thing, too. (The funny side-effect is that today I know the entire lyrics of "Ice Ice Baby" by heart. I'm never ever messing that one up again.)

When you look back at the formative experiences of your life—whether they are the most painful or the most positive—you're likely to find your meaning-making machine running on high. Someone's words or actions influenced you in some way, and you created a meaning around them.

In order to be unfuckwithable, we need to be immune to such words and actions—to praise as well as to criticism. Every time you give someone the power to build you up with praise, you're also unknowingly giving that person the power to destroy you with criticism. Therefore, accept praise and criticism as nothing more than someone else's expressions of their models of reality. They have nothing to do with who you really are.

You were born enough. And we should be able to feel secure and complete in our own skin without others having to support us. Fortunately, there are some powerful tools and practices to help.

EXERCISES FOR BECOMING UNFUCKWITHABLE

I learned the following exercises from several remarkable men and women. These three exercises are systems for living that you can apply to truly create deep love for yourself, deep appreciation for who you are, and to center yourself and remove fear or worry. Combined, these help make you unfuckwithable.

Exercise 1: The Person in the Mirror (for Creating Self-Love)

I learned this exercise from Kamal Ravikant, a Silicon Valley entrepreneur and investor. He also shared this with me in a training session on my Consciousness Engineering Program.

Kamal came out of a major illness and depression when he realized that the root of his discontent was a lack of self-love. He tells the story in his remarkable little book *Love Yourself Like Your Life Depends on It*.

One of Kamal's techniques is for you to look at yourself in the mirror and say the words, "I love you." Talking to yourself in the mirror is like speaking directly to your own soul—especially when you're gazing at yourself in the eye. Have you noticed how uncomfortable it can be to really look someone in the eye for an extended period of time? Turns out it's uncomfortable because it brings out feelings of connectedness and love.

Start by focusing on one eye. Once your gaze is fixed on that eye, repeat to yourself (aloud or silently) "I love you." Do this for as long or as short a time that you feel is right.

Kamal suggests you do this every day. It should be a regular practice like going to the gym. Tie it to your habit of brushing your teeth in the morning. After you put down your toothbrush, get close and comfy and look at yourself in the mirror.

I can vouch for the power of this technique. After Kamal shared it with me and I started practicing it, I experienced remarkably elevated feelings of self-love and security. In less than a week I could feel myself operating in a wholly new way with the people around me.

To learn more about this technique, you can watch Kamal talk about this model at his 2013 A-Fest speech. The video is available on www.mindvalley .com/extraordinary.

Exercise 2: Self-Gratitude (for Appreciating Yourself)

Make it a point to do the "What I Love about Myself" exercise we talked about in Chapter 4. This exercise is a powerful way to shut down the meaning-making machine. It also helps combat negative childhood indoctrination that might have caused you to feel unworthy.

Simply think about what it is about you as a human being that you love. Is it your sense of humor? Or maybe your taste in books? (Why, thank you.) Did you leave a big tip for your last waiter? Maybe it's your commitment to daily personal growth. Or the fact that you have a good amount of cash sitting in a bank account. Or maybe it's that you're broke—but still happy. You can identify qualities that are big or small, but particularly if your meaning-making machine is working overtime, make sure you pinpoint three to five things every day that make you proud to be who you are.

I do this exercise daily in the morning as I wake up. Go ahead and express gratitude for the events of your day or the beauty of life—but make sure you include yourself in your inventory of life's beauty by expressing gratitude for all those things that make you so gosh-darned beautiful as a human being. See what a difference it will make in the rest of your day.

Exercise 3: Becoming Present (to Remove Sudden Fear and Anxiety)

Every now and then you might need a quick fix to get back to your unfuck-withable state when sudden anxiety creeps in. It happens to me, too.

It was a regular family Sunday in November 2015. Halloween had just ended, and I had recently returned from a two-week trip with my wife and kids that included a visit to Universal Studios in Orlando, Florida, attending A-Fest in Costa Rica, and visiting friends in Los Angeles and Phoenix. It was good to be home, but as I sat in a local restaurant with my family, I sensed something was off.

Inside my chest I felt my heart beating unnaturally fast. I felt an unusual gnawing pain within. It was part fear, part anxiety. Being away for two weeks had its costs. I was returning to work as the CEO of a growing company, but I was feeling overwhelmed. Four hundred–plus e-mails were waiting to be answered. The manuscript for my new book—this book— was due in two weeks. And then there were family errands, a sleeping baby in a stroller next to me, and an eight-year-old who needed help eating. I felt unpleasant and overstressed. I felt the weight on my shoulders of all the things I ought to be doing *next*.

Suddenly I remembered advice from my friend, the author Sonia Choquette: *Be present.*

I took my attention away from the fears and worries. Instead, I focused on the leaves of the plant on the restaurant table before me. I noticed the subtle veins running through the leaves, observed the sunlight falling on the green surfaces, and used my fingers to feel the texture and pliability of the stem. In one minute, I felt as if I had just popped a relaxation pill. Everything went almost back to normal. This is the power of becoming focused on the present. It takes your mind off whatever stress, fear, judgment, anger, or frustration you're having with the world or the people in it—and it forces you to remember who you are and to be present in the now.

The next time you feel an apparent urge to lose your cool, or you feel judged, insulted, or hurt by a loved one, remember to be present. This quick mental hack to autocorrect your mental state can instantly pull you out of stress and anxiety and return you to happiness in the now.

When I interviewed Arianna Huffington, she shared a profound tip for how she gets present-centered. Focus on the rising and falling of your breath for ten seconds whenever you feel tense, rushed, or distracted. Arianna said:

> This allows you to become fully present in your life. You know about the thread that Ariadne gave to Theseus so that he could find his way out of the labyrinth after he killed the Minotaur? The thread for me is my breath. Returning to it during the day, hundreds of times when I get stressed, when I get worried, when judgments come up, has been an incredible gift—and it's available to all of us. There's nobody alive who is not breathing.

THE PARADOX OF BEING UNFUCKWITHABLE

Shortly after filming Marisa Peer speaking at an event, Al Ibrahim, our cameraman, realized he had a question about this matter of being "enough," so he asked Marisa about it.

In a nutshell, his question was this: If it is true that "I am enough" and if we don't need to get validation or praise from others, what is the driving force that pushes us to do big things in the world? What would prevent us from just being happy couch potatoes, doing nothing but enjoying the present?

Marisa replied:

> If you sit on the couch all day and do nothing, it is precisely because you don't think you're enough. You're afraid. You're afraid of failure. You're afraid of rejection. You're afraid that those things will be proof positive that you indeed are not enough. So you do nothing.

Marisa continued:

> But if you believe that you're enough, that's when you take action. That's when you go out and try something new. That's when you

apply for that job you really want. That's when you ask for that raise. Because you're enough. And even if you fail, you won't take rejection personally because it's not you—you ARE enough—so it must be your methods or your approach or skill or whatever—and because you know you're enough, you know you can then improve those methods and skills and your approaches and then try again.

I found that to be a beautiful paradox: Knowing we are ENOUGH gives us the courage to do MORE, do BETTER, do our BEST. When we learn to be unfuckwithable, the biggest fears that hold so many back no longer bother us. We boldly pursue big dreams and goals.

But we'd be happy even if we lost all our goals and possessions because our end goals are self-fueled goals—feelings that we desire to have, such as being surrounded by love, enjoying beautiful human experiences, or learning and growing.

When you learn how to fill the holes within, and you no longer need outside validation to know you are enough and when you set end goals that come from your deepest feelings about living a meaningful life, you have graduated to the next level in recoding yourself and moving forward on your path toward the extraordinary. You're now armed with the fortitude you need to take on truly massive goals—goals that change the culture-scape itself and create a dent in the universe.

When you become unfuckwithable, it makes all the smaller problems meaningless. You're no longer bothered about that date who didn't text you back, the rising price of gas, or that naysaying coworker. You have more urgent things to worry about.

The problem with most people is that their problems aren't big enough.

You don't get bogged down by petty problems and by other people's misbehaviors, grudges, and rivalries. You have no time for politicking, finger-pointing, pot-stirring, backstabbing, bullying, tattling, throwing under the bus, and other time sucks that fill the days of bored and unhappy people.

When you're unfuckwithable, you rise above all of that. Instead, you're thinking of far bigger things—of problems to solve that could change the world and help others move forward. Your goal becomes to tackle these problems.

We call these goals "your quest." We'll explore them in the next chapter.

You can watch Marisa Peer's excellent speech from A-Fest 2014 on "The Biggest Disease Afflicting Humanity: I Am Not Enough." The video is available on www.mindvalley.com/extraordinary.

CHAPTER 10

EMBRACE YOUR QUEST

Where We Learn How to Put It All Together
and Live a Life of Meaning

> Even the smallest person can change the course of the future.
>
> —J. R. R. TOLKIEN, *THE LORD OF THE RINGS*

WHERE WE'VE COME FROM

Each part of this book represents an evolution of sorts. With each evolution, you ascend to a new level in terms of your awareness of the world and your ability to influence it.

In a simple diagram, this gradually expanding progression would look like this:

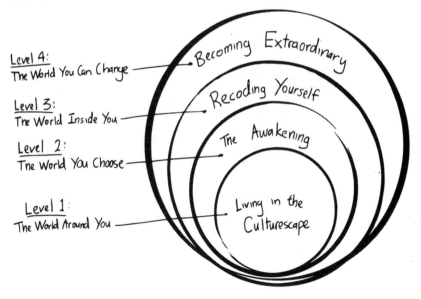

Level 4:
The World You Can Change — Becoming Extraordinary

Level 3:
The World Inside You — Recoding Yourself

Level 2:
The World You Choose — The Awakening

Level 1:
The World Around You — Living in the Culturescape

Level 1: Living in the Culturescape

In Part I of this book, you became aware of how the culturescape dominates many of us. You learned about how the rules of cultures—some of which go back thousands of years—influence who you are today. You learned about Brules and how to recognize and avoid them.

At Level 1, you are being controlled and shaped by the world around you. Life happens TO you. But as you start to expand in awareness and influence, you move to Level 2.

Level 2: The Awakening

At this level, in Part II, you learned that you can choose the world you want to live in. You take a stand and decide that you will *choose* to create the world you want to experience. Life happens as you CHOOSE. Here you start practicing the skill of consciousness engineering. You learn that your models of reality and your systems for living are the two components that determine who you become. You learn to swap out bad models and take on empowering ones. You discover that you can create a filter so only the most empowering models of the culturescape come through to you. In the process, you start to realize that you have the ability to do more, think bigger, and be in control of your own happiness. These realizations open you up to Level 3.

Level 3: Recoding Yourself

At this level, you connect with the world inside you and learn that happiness in the now, combined with a vision for the future, put you in a balanced state for moving powerfully toward your goals. You start to find that your dreams and ambitions come to you with ease. You realize that you can influence the world outside by changing the world inside you. You turn on your internal engine of power. We call this state of being "bending reality." There's a feeling of limitless opportunity. You're shifting up to Level 4.

Level 4: Becoming Extraordinary

At this level, you feel secure and confident in your own abilities and strengths. You are unfuckwithable. At the same time, you start to actually change the world around you so that you contribute to the growth and expansion of other human beings. You decide that you have a greater purpose and role to play, and you decide to influence the world in a positive way. You feel a calling, a push to make the world a better place. Life happens THROUGH you.

Thus as you ascend the levels, your relationship with life changes:

First Life happens TO you.

Then Life happens as you CHOOSE.

Then Life happens FROM you.

Then Life happens THROUGH you.

At Level 4, life is working through you to cause you to give back to life. You become a servant to a higher calling. This calling is what we call your quest.

FINDING YOUR QUEST

Like a character in a computer game or a hero in an ancient tale, you've been on a path of intense learning, gathering and honing your skills and insights in crucial areas.

But there's one thing left to accomplish. In every great tale that has captivated generations and stood the test of time, the hero is not a hero without a quest. This chapter is about finding your quest.

Make no mistake: You could remain in Level 3 and be a highly effective human being. But as you bend life more and more skillfully and start seeing the power unleashed by this new way of living and as you get used to the feeling of living in this heightened way, you may start to wonder if there are even greater uses of this power that you haven't yet thought of.

Level 4—the level of the quest—awaits those curious and venturesome souls.

WHAT EXTRAORDINARY PEOPLE HAVE IN COMMON

What keeps the men and women whose stories I have shared in this book going and going and going, willing to take big gambles and risks?

They're driven by a vision so big that they're operating at a level beyond the conventional rules and limitations of work and life. When I think about the extraordinary people I know, there's something about them that is inherently positive. They pour that positive energy into a mission they're passionate about. Arianna Huffington is running a media empire, but she still pursues her calling of helping people live meaningful lives and stay healthy. X Prize founder Peter Diamandis is looking to incentivize dramatic advances to help solve the world's problems. Dean Kamen is working to bring science and technology to the forefront in the United States so kids will grow up to be scientists who can change the world. Elon Musk is set on making humanity an interplanetary species.

What I've learned from years of studying personal growth and speaking with many unusual thinkers and doers is this:

The most extraordinary people in the world do not have careers. What they have is a calling.

How do we define a calling? It's pretty simple: A calling is your contribution to the human race. It's something that helps us leave the planet better for our children. It doesn't have to be a massive new business or a game-changing piece of technology. It can be a book you're working on. It could be dedicating your life to raising remarkable children. It could be working for a company with a mission to change the world in a way that resonates with you.

The key is that when you have this calling, work dissolves. What you're doing excites you. It's a passion; it's meaningful. You'd probably do it for no money, since it's anything but work. I once witnessed someone ask Richard Branson how he maintains work-life balance, and his reply was, "Work? Life? It's all the same thing. I call it LIVING." When your work becomes a calling, the old model of work disappears.

Amy Wrzesniewski, associate professor of organizational behavior at Yale University, has been studying a classification system that can help you recognize your orientation toward your work and attain greater job satisfaction.

She defines work in three ways:

1. **A JOB** is a way to pay the bills. It's a means to an end, and you have little attachment to it.

2. **A CAREER** is a path toward growth and achievement. Careers have clear ladders for upward mobility.

3. **A CALLING** is work that is an important part of your life and provides meaning. People with a calling are generally more satisfied with the work they do.

That's what I'm talking about when I talk about having a calling.

Mindvalley is my calling. The mission is to touch one billion lives, put enlightened ideas into the world, and shake up how people live, work, and take care of their minds and bodies. Through Mindvalley, I'm inviting others to become extraordinary through personal growth and learning—a personal value for myself. Education—the transmission of knowledge, enrichment, and power from one person to another—is a particular expression of love that I find compelling and beautiful. This mission makes my work deeply meaningful and makes me happy. Even in the lean start-up years, when I was banging away on my computer in a tiny apartment in New York City, I was happy because I was fulfilling my vision of spreading meditation to the masses. Obviously my life today is very different. But while there's a limit to the rewards of money, there's no limit to the rewards of having and pursuing a mission.

THE BEAUTIFUL DESTRUCTION

If you've been pondering and practicing what I've talked about in the later chapters of this book, you're already on your way toward this stage.

Finding your calling starts with identifying your end goals. As you do the Three Most Important Questions exercise in Chapter 8 and create your list of experiences, growth opportunities, and contributions, you're setting the stage for something magical to happen. You may not know exactly how to get to your end destination or even what that destination is. But there's something mysterious about the human mind: Once you choose a destination, often the right synchronicities, opportunities, and people emerge in your life to get you there. Some people call this luck. I beg to differ. I believe luck is under our control. When you pursue the right end goals while making sure you're happy in the now, happiness unlocks the door for luck to come calling.

In fact, it often seems as if you don't find your quest. Rather, your quest *finds you.*

The path may not be a straight line. You might have old Brules, models of reality, and systems for living (your own and maybe others') to challenge or dismantle first. You may experience dips, stops, starts, and speed bumps. But it's all part of the process. Those bumps are often signposts designed to turn you in the right direction and get you moving toward your calling. This recoding of your life won't always be neat and tidy. Remember:

Sometimes you have to destroy a part of your life to let the next big thing enter.

I call this the *beautiful destruction.* Trust is the key that unlocks it. I once asked Arianna Huffington the same questions I asked Elon Musk: "What makes you Arianna? If we could distill you and try to extract your essence, what is it that makes you you?"

Arianna replied:

> I would say trust. I have an incredible trust in life. One of my favorite quotes is a little misquote: "Live life as though everything is rigged in your favor." I really profoundly believe that whatever has happened in my life, including the biggest heartbreaks, the biggest disappointments, was exactly what was needed to help me get to the next stage of my own personal evolution and growth. I always had a sense of that, but now I believe that so profoundly. I can literally see the hidden blessing in every bad thing that happened.

There are names for these little nudges that move you toward your calling.

ENTER *KENSHO* AND *SATORI*

My friend Dr. Michael Bernard Beckwith, the inspiring founder of the Agape International Spiritual Center in Los Angeles, talks about two different paths to life growth: *kensho* and *satori*. *Kensho* is growth by pain. *Satori* is growth by awakening.

Kensho is a gradual process that often happens through the tribulations of life. A relationship breaks up, but you learn from it and your heart becomes more resilient. You lose a business, but you use the hard-earned wisdom to start your next one. You lose your job, but you learn who you are beyond your career. You suffer a health problem, but you discover personal reserves you didn't know you had. *Kensho* is the universe giving you tough love.

Bottom line: You go through some kind of pain or difficulty through which you learn different ways to feel, think, and be. You might not even notice these changes while they're happening. Imagine the tectonic shifts of the continents. We can't see them happening, but mapped over time, it's clear the world has changed.

In retrospect, you might even view these painful events as positive forces that pushed you to challenge beliefs and systems that were holding you back in ways you hadn't realized (what we often call the blessing in disguise or the cloud's silver lining). Dr. Beckwith suggests that *kensho* is our soul's way of calling on us to grow.

Kensho was having my salary cut in half at work after I got back from my honeymoon. It forced me to start a side business that ended up becoming Mindvalley.

Kensho was losing my US visa. It moved me to Malaysia, where I had no inkling of the impact I would have on entrepreneurship in that country.

Kensho was Mindvalley about to go bust in May 2008, leading me to discover new models for using my mind that led to a 400 percent increase in the company's revenue.

In contrast, Dr. Beckwith defines *satori* moments as big insights that happen suddenly and change you forever. They can happen anytime, anywhere—while you're out in nature, listening to music or seeing inspiring art, holding hands with a loved one, quietly contemplating, or being in a personal growth situation, such as with a therapist, teacher, or healer. Once you've had a *satori* moment, the stuff that used to scare you or hold you back is left in the dust. You've leveled up and can operate on a whole new plane. If you were to plot your growth as quality of life over time, *satori* moments would look like sudden bursts upward, while *kensho* moments would start with a dip and then shoot upward as you recover and then assimilate your new learnings.

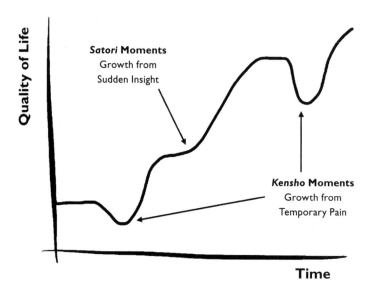

So, you see, here's a new model for understanding the problems that happen to us in life. It could be that our problems are nothing more than a friendly universe whispering in our ear as we hike through life: "Hey, you're on the wrong path. Check out the view from *this* angle."

Dr. Beckwith once shared with me this little wisdom-bomb during an interview:

> Behind every problem, there's a question trying to ask itself.
> Behind every question, there's an answer trying to reveal itself.
> Behind every answer, there's an action trying to take place.
> And behind every action, there's a way of life trying to be born.

That new way of life trying to be born is your calling. And who knows how this calling might influence the world and those around you?

YOU ARE THE CHOSEN ONE

Do you choose your calling, or does your calling choose you? There is a model of reality emerging that suggests that the universe comes calling— and your job is to listen.

My friend Emily Fletcher, a wonderful and vivacious meditation instructor who has spoken at Harvard Business School and at Google, told me in an interview this story about pop music legend Michael Jackson and the universe, which she refers to as "nature":

> If you watch the documentary, *Michael Jackson's This Is It,* they interview his manager. He said that Michael used to call him all the time at like three, four, five in the morning. And the manager was saying Mike would be like, "Fireflies. We need fireflies." And his manager would be like, "Michael, it's four in the morning. We'll talk about this tomorrow." And Michael would say, "No, I need you to write it down. I need you to get up and write it down. Fireflies." And his manager would say, "Why? We'll talk about it tomorrow." And he's like, "If we don't do it, Prince will."
>
> I like this story because to me it's illustrating that Michael . . . knew that if he didn't take action, if he didn't lead with creation, that nature would look for someone else. It's like nature is just trying to create all the time, and it's looking for people who are awake. It's looking for people who are willing to raise their hands and bring something from the unmanifest into the manifest. And I don't think that it's choosy about who it is. It's like, "Well, if you don't do it, then fine. I'll choose this other person." And so this is why the more we create, the more of nature's support we get. It's like imagine that nature is the CEO of the company and then we're all the employees. And if you're the CEO of a company, which of your employees are you going to give the raise to? Which of your employees are you going to give more important jobs to? The one who is not executing on anything or the one who is creating and executing and coming in with new ideas every day?

Emily is saying that when a mission needs to manifest, the universe (or, as she calls it, nature) may knock on your door and bless you with that intuition. But it's up to you to jump on it. If you don't, the universe will move on to the next person. The universe doesn't care who's going to change the world. It just wants someone who'll seize the idea and run with it.

In the book *Big Magic: Creative Living beyond Fear,* Elizabeth Gilbert talks about a similar phenomenon. Gilbert talks about how she would come up with a very specific book idea, and then something would happen in her life to distract her from working on the book. She'd later find the exact same book emerging from another writer's mind—a writer who chose to act on it.

Gilbert writes, "I believe inspiration will always try its best to work with you—but if you're not ready or available, it may indeed choose to leave you and to search for a different human collaborator."

There's even a name for this sort of occurrence. It's called multiple discovery. Gilbert describes it as:

> . . . inspiration hedging its bets, fiddling with the dials, working two channels at the same time. Inspiration is allowed to do that if it wants to. Inspiration is allowed to do whatever it wants to, in fact, and it is never obliged to justify its motives to any of us. (As far as I'm concerned, we're lucky that inspiration talks to us at all; it's too much to ask that it also explain itself.)

So, let's say this model is true—that the universe does indeed come calling. Well, then, you damn well better take those marching orders!

But here's the insight that makes me smile. If it's true that the universe does come calling and has chosen you for its grand new design, whatever that is, then it means that just like every great hero in legend, film, or the best computer games, you are literally the Chosen One for your particular quest.

Ain't that something?

You can access the full session with me and Emily Fletcher discussing this idea in further detail on www.mindvalley.com/extraordinary.

THE GODICLE THEORY

As you ascend the levels and get to Level 4, several unique and beautiful new models of reality will open up to you. I found the models below to be consistent in every person I interviewed for this book. Each is a unique approach to living, and each leads to the other:

1. Extraordinary people feel a unique connectedness and kinship to all life.

2. Extraordinary people are open to intuitive insights they attain through this connection.

3. Extraordinary people allow their intuition to lead them to a vision that pulls them forward.

4. As extraordinary people serve this calling, the universe blesses them with luck.

This feeling of being lucky reinforces their sense of connectedness and kinship to all life. It's a virtuous circle because each leads to the other. The feeling of being lucky or blessed leads to a feeling of even greater connectedness with the world as you seek to share these blessings. Illustrated, it looks like this:

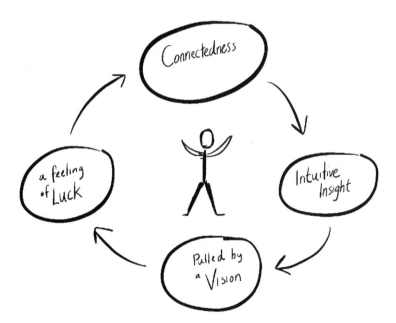

Combined, I call this model of reality the Godicle Theory. Here's the idea: If there is a God, or Universe, or Life Force, or whatever we choose to call it, I believe that it is deeply connected with all of life and all of humanity.

If this is so, then we are particles of this "God." I call these particles Godicles. The idea is that you, me, and every other human being on this planet are Godicles experiencing creation.

Whether you choose to interpret this as meaning that we are the metaphysical essence of God or we that are made from stardust is your choice. Either way, it's an empowering model of reality. (Remember, models of reality do not have to be scientifically true. You can take on a model as a philosophy if it empowers you.)

The Godicle Theory is interesting to me because of what it implies:

First, that all of us are connected, all life is connected, and we're all in this together.

Second, if we're all connected, then we're capable of intuitive insights gained from this connection.

Third, there is a higher collective mind that seeks new visions for the betterment of itself and that picks individual Godicles to work on them. These Godicles experience this calling as their "quest."

And finally, if we are particles of God, then it's beautiful to think that we are endowed with certain God-like powers.

Perhaps this is why we sometimes seem to bend reality when we're pursuing our quest.

All of this is, of course, just theory. It's a personal spiritual model of reality that I play with. But it also comes from observation of the extraordinary people I have met. They embody these ideas. You do, too. You just have to step outside the culturescape and go within.

Let's look at how the elements of the Godicle Theory might play out in your life at Level 4.

I: You Feel a Connectedness with All Life

At this level, you start to feel a deep connectedness with the world. All of humanity—all cultures, all nations, and all people seem to resonate with you as part of one family. Ken Wilber describes this phenomenon as moving into world-centric consciousness. Simply put, people in Level 4 start to see past the Brules that divide them and understand that different cultures, different religions, and different countries are not so different after all. We're one species, on one planet. The only difference is what's in our heads. At Level 4, you can have an ardent patriotism for your own country, an appreciation for your religion, but you're equally in awe and respectful of other cultures, nations, and religions. Interestingly, the overwhelming majority of people I meet who are at Level 4 are humanists, not subscribing to any one world religion but instead having an appreciation of and reverence for humanity as a whole.

It's important to make a qualifying statement at this point in our journey. Many men and women throughout history have had a sense of extreme mission—but rather than push humanity forward, they ended up starting wars, engaging in massive failed social experiments (think Joseph Stalin), or becoming prone to dangerous ideas such as religious fundamentalism. All of these have one thing in common—they viewed a particular idea or group of people as being superior to another group. This is the opposite of true connectedness, for true connectedness does not recognize borders, color, or other such models of differentiation. The truly extraordinary have reverence for humanity as a whole.

2: You Are Tapped into Intuition

Your intuition at this level becomes incredibly strong. You feel drawn to people or opportunities as if you had a homing beacon. You often wake up with amazing ideas floating around in your mind. These intuitive impulses seem to guide you toward the right opportunities and ideas.

I agree with Dr. Beckwith's beautiful idea that when we're in this state, the calling isn't coming from us. It's coming *through* us. I believe intuition is a conduit for that. This is why Blissipline is so crucial. Happiness is the fuel for intuition. When you're stressed or fearful, you shut intuition down.

Thanks to intuition, when you set end goals, you don't necessarily need to know HOW to attain them. Too many people trap themselves in the chains of realistic goals because they refuse to see beyond the HOW. Don't worry about the HOW. Start with the WHAT and the WHY. When you know what you want to bring forth in the world and WHY you want it, choose it. Then take whatever action intuition guides you toward taking.

3: You Are Pulled by a Vision

At this level, your goals are plugged into your larger mission. A mission provides the fuel that keeps us going. Without a mission, work is a four-letter word. With a mission, work dissolves. As many mission-oriented workers say, their job stops being work and becomes something that adds to the quality of their life, rather than detracting from it.

And so traditional goals don't motivate you; instead, you're pulled by bigger visions to serve the world. Dr. Beckwith shared this insight with me about living with purpose:

> It's a much higher way of being. So you don't give up goals, you don't give up tasks . . . you still have them but they don't run you. . . . When you are living under a goal-oriented model, you are pushed; you need motivation. [But] when you are living your purpose, you are now pulled by a vision.

At this level, you wake up every day excited about what you're working on. It may be your day job, or it may be a volunteer project or a venture you're working to get off the ground. Whatever it is, the calling to serve is strong. It drives you. It lights a fire under your ass to move. In the old paradigm of goals, you needed motivation to go after your goals. A whole industry of motivational tools has been born to support such efforts. But motivation is only needed when you're chasing a Brule—a means goal. When you chase end goals, especially end goals related to your calling, you no longer need to be "motivated." Instead, you are PULLED by your vision.

4: You Feel As If Luck Is on Your Side

At this level, all sorts of coincidences, synchronicities, and lucky breaks seem to happen to push you forward. You thus tend to be positive, enthusiastic, and optimistic about the world and life.

When you're working on a goal that is out of alignment with your calling, very often you will face roadblocks. This is why we sometimes fail to reach our goals. But think of these roadblocks as *kensho* moments—as gentle taps to get your blinders off so you can see what you're really meant to be doing with your life.

Here's a new model worth considering. Failure is often nothing more than good luck in disguise: the destruction of an old way of life so you can create the next grand vision of yourself. When you finally get on the right track, pointed toward that mission that life chose you for, just like the chosen one of countless films, you start to find huge reservoirs of untapped power and support coming your way. Some people call it luck. You know better. You're just another Godicle being pulled toward your quest.

This brings us to Law 10.

Law 10: Embrace your quest.

Extraordinary minds are motivated by a quest or calling—a drive to create some positive change in the world. This drive propels them forward in life and helps them to gain meaning and make a meaningful contribution.

GETTING STARTED

When it comes to finding your mission, it helps to remember these two ideas from the culturescape as potential Brules that might hold you back.

Brule 1: You Have to Be an Entrepreneur

When I give talks, especially to college students, I'm struck by how many people think that in order to make a meaningful contribution in life, they have to become an entrepreneur. When I tell them, "No—you do not have to be an entrepreneur in order to move toward your mission," I can almost hear the sighs of relief. There's been a Brule going around in recent years that the greatest achievers become entrepreneurs, and employees are just working stiffs. Not true. I used to advocate being an entrepreneur, but I started questioning this Brule when I noticed that many of the best people I've hired at Mindvalley were former entrepreneurs. Sometimes they made this change because they started businesses solely to earn a living but discovered something—the mission—was missing. Others had businesses with an educational mission but realized that being part of a larger, more estab-lished entity would add to their momentum, so they came onboard with us.

Many of the most important people in the world today are not entrepre-neurs. Many leading scientists, engineers, and innovators who are changing the world are doing it as employees at large, well-run, mission-driven organizations.

Entrepreneurism is a means goal, not an end goal. The end goal is usually living a life of purpose, combined with the experiences that freedom and money can bring. But in today's world, you can get those things by working for the right company. Extraordinary people focus on whatever actions they need to take to move their mission forward. So, instead of thinking, *I have to become an entrepreneur so I can fulfill my mission,* focus on your mis-sion as the end goal, and let it guide you. Start with your mission and then decide if it will mean becoming an entrepreneur, joining an established team, funding a company, or going to work for one. Don't get stuck in the entrepreneur-versus-employee model. Bottom line: Entrepreneurship is not a goal in itself. It is the side effect of having the right end goals.

Brule 2: The Career Myth

Let's talk about your career. Are you really in the right career for you? Too often, people pursue careers solely for money or titles. Both can be danger-ous to your long-term happiness. Getting sucked into these models can happen to anyone choosing a career path because they majored in a particu-lar field in college, or their parents nudged them into it, or the culturescape suggests a certain career as the proper path—and not because it's meaning-ful to them. You could be damning yourself to soul-stealing work for years or decades in that kind of job.

I know that at times you may have no choice—you might have to pay the bills, just as I did when I took my dialing-for-dollars job. If that happens to you, it's important to be doing things in other parts of your life that reflect movement toward a mission you believe in. In my case, for example, I started teaching meditation on the side because I felt it gave me the meaning my job did not.

But on the flip side, company jobs can get a bad rap. If you find a com-pany that matches your mission, you can have an incredibly rewarding career. But you must choose the right company. If working for a company is where you're at or where you're headed, here's the main thing to look for:

Is your company a humanity-plus or a humanity-minus company?

I believe that the key to long-term career happiness is the ability to differentiate between humanity-plus and humanity-minus settings. Here's how I define these terms.

Humanity-minus companies are often businesses that exist solely for a profit motive. There's nothing wrong with this, but it's harder to get excited about your company's mission when it's not adding any value to the world, or worse, if the company is selling harmful products like junk food or is engaged in unsustainable practices like fossil fuels.

Other humanity-minus companies are founded on artificial demand—that is, selling products we don't truly need and that might even be potentially harmful, but they are marketed as necessities for well-being or happiness. You know what I'm talking about. We see those ads on TV every day.

Humanity-plus companies, in contrast, push the human race forward. Some examples include companies focusing on clean, renewable energy sources, companies that promote healthy eating and living, or companies working on new ways to elevate and improve life on our planet. Ideally, these are the companies we should be working for, supporting, and starting.

You can work for a company in a traditional industry like airlines, insurance, electricity, and more, and that company might still have a powerful mission that inspires you and others. Think of Southwest Airlines, for example—it's a traditional industry, but they are contributing to the world by radically innovating on customer service and customers' experiences when they fly.

Whatever your mission turns out to be—whether it's starting your own business, joining a business, pursuing a cause outside of work, letting your creative light shine out to the world, or devoting yourself to raising amazing children, there's really only one thing you need to remember:

You don't have to save the world. Just don't mess it up for the next generation.

DISCOVERING YOUR QUEST

How do you get started with finding your mission?

This technique comes from my friend, author and speaker Martin Rutte, creator of projectheavenonearth.com. Martin suggests you ask yourself these three questions in order to help you identify your calling—fast. I've tested this out with people, and it's amazing how rapidly they come up with a purpose or mission they might want to explore.

The first question is: Recall a time when you experienced Heaven on Earth. What was happening?

The second question is: Imagine you have a magic wand and with it you can create Heaven on Earth. What is Heaven on Earth for you?

And now the final question: What simple, easy, concrete step(s) will you take in the next twenty-four hours to make Heaven on Earth real?

While asking yourself these questions, what words and phrases come to mind? What images do you see? Write them all down. Draw pictures. Record yourself speaking your thoughts if that helps the ideas flow.

As you do this, pay attention to your emotional reactions. (Remember: True end goals tend to be feelings.) Do you feel your heart open or beat faster? Does your gut literally respond? Does your breath catch or deepen? Do you gasp with excitement? These are your first big clues to your mission. Remember the words of Steve Jobs:

> Have the courage to follow your heart and intuition. They somehow already know what you truly want to become. Everything else is secondary.

Get guided: I've arranged with Martin Rutte to guide you through this process. You can access the video at www.mindvalley.com/extraordinary.

ADVICE FOR THE EXTRAORDINARY SOUL

At a certain point you might decide to take the plunge. Know that success might not come fast or easily. It sometimes seems that many of the people who make the news hit the jackpot fast. Not true.

I spoke to my friend Peter Diamandis, one of the most influential men in Silicon Valley, to ask his advice on what "makes someone extraordinary." Peter is the founder of Singularity University and the X Prize Foundation. He's been hailed as one of the foremost leaders in the world today. Peter associates with men like Larry Page of Google and Elon Musk (who sits on his board)—so I asked Peter what he thought made these individuals, as well as himself, so successful. This is what Peter said:

> I'll tell you that it's perseverance; it's having a heartfelt passion and emotionally driven passion—something you want to solve on the planet that wakes you up in the morning and keeps you up at night. For other people, it might be something they despise or some injustice in the world they want to solve. I know a lot of the time, doing anything big and bold in the world is hard, unless you have that emotional guiding star, that passion—most people fail by giving up—not by something that stops them.

Notice two things Peter mentioned. It won't be easy. But if you have a passion that keeps you going, you have an edge. This is yet another reason why identifying your particular calling—something that ignites that passion in your mind, heart, and soul—is so important.

Peter also once told me: "If I had one superpower, it would be persistence. X Prize took me ten years to get off the ground."

Elon Musk told me something similar: "I have a high tolerance for pain."

If you recall my story, you'll notice a similar pattern. My failures and misfortunes were often just as spectacular as my successes. I took a lot of jobs just to keep body and soul together. My career path looked oddly ordinary before a sudden burst of success in my later years.

Here's my list of jobs at various ages. Notice how plain and simple my career was, and the various dips in between. I hope this list inspires you to know that if you're on a dip at the moment, it may just be a *kensho* moment.

- TV commercial actor—(age) 18
- Stage actor—19

- Dishwasher—19

- Stagehand—19

- Web designer—20

- Theater troupe director—21

- Java programmer—21

- Photojournalist—21

- Bug tester at Microsoft—22

- Vice president of a nonprofit—23

- Unemployed—24

- B2B salesman—25

- Unemployed again—25

- Phone sales—25

- Director of sales—26

- Meditation instructor—27

- Small website owner—28

- Start-up founder—29

- CEO of Mindvalley—35

Despite the long slog, I kept going. So, stick with it—but to ensure that you're able to handle the bumps and dips, make sure that your mission is one that will sustain you.

As we part ways for now, I hope that you see the beautiful journey waiting for you. Perhaps like me, you grew up in a world where children were asked, "What do you want to be when you grow up?" That's a sure setup for a Brule-based life. I believe that in the future we'll instead be asking children, "What positive mark do you want to leave on the world in your lifetime?"

Remember that you can ask yourself that question now. It's never too late.

Is there any downside? you may ask.

People might tell you that you're crazy. They'll worry about you. They'll try to talk you out of it.

But some people will want to come play. There's nothing more captivating than a person vibrant with life and passion and pursuing their calling. They come from having end goals that bring meaning and from being happy in the now. People who radiate this energy are magnetic because they're living meaningful lives and helping others do the same. When you live at the level of extraordinary, you'll attract others who want to live there, too. And together, you'll create a better world for the generations who follow.

Your true greatness comes when you focus not on building a career but on finding your quest.

SO TAKE A STEP AND TRUST

I want to share some wise advice from the book *Think and Grow Rich* by Napoleon Hill. Basically, he says that if you aren't sure what to do, just take a step—a tiny baby step. When the universe calls on you, even if you don't know the exact path to success—take a baby step.

Baby steps show intention. They show that you're standing at attention and you received the marching orders. You may not know the optimal path to get where you're bound to go, but your boots are on and you're going. You may be stepping into the big wide unknown, but you'll take the marching orders anyway.

And something will come of that. You'll get some feedback and take the next step. If it's in the wrong direction, no worries. A little *kensho* or a nudge of intuition will be there to guide you. And then you'll take another step, which might lead you to a person who can help or to a resource you didn't even know existed.

Keep the steps as tiny as they need to be as you feel your way. One of my first baby steps was to register the company name Mindvalley. I had a piece of paper saying I owned that LLC. I didn't have anything more than that, but getting that piece of paper allowed me to begin to create a vision around a company that at least already had a name. Baby steps are more powerful than you think. They telegraph your intention to the universe: "I heard you loud and clear. Bring it on, baby! Tell me what you need done. I'll make it happen."

So, don't worry if you don't know exactly how to reach your goals. Just take one small step at a time.

1. Step out of the culturescape.

2. Toss away the Brules.

3. Grab your toolkit for consciousness engineering.

4. Pick up your empowering models of reality.

5. Don't forget to pack your systems for living.

6. Keep your mind firmly on bending reality.

7. Walk with Blissipline.

8. Hold your end goals firmly in your hand.

9. Be unfuckwithable.

10. Open that door and march firmly toward your quest.

The world can't wait to see what you're going to do next.

TOOLS FOR YOUR JOURNEY

Practice Transcendence: Where You Learn How to Integrate Key Systems from This Book into a Powerful Personal Practice

> It seems to me, therefore, that educated people no longer have a right to any form of spiritual provincialism. The truths of Eastern spirituality are now no more Eastern than the truths of Western science are Western. We are merely talking about human consciousness and its possible states. My purpose . . . is to encourage you to investigate certain contemplative insights for yourself, without accepting the metaphysical ideas that they inspired in ignorant and isolated peoples of the past.
>
> **—SAM HARRIS,** *WAKING UP*

WHAT IS TRANSCENDENCE?

Transcendence is the act of going beyond the physical world to embrace that which cannot be seen. In this book you learned about transcendent practices like gratitude and forgiveness. Here we'll go deeper and create a structured practice around these processes. You've learned a ton of new systems for living in this book. Here's where we bring it all together in one daily habit.

Often people ask me, "Vishen, what do you do daily to integrate these ideas—what is your daily practice?" In this section I'm going to share a transcendent practice that I custom-designed and use. I call it the Six-Phase.

The Six-Phase unifies several key ideas in this book into one integrated daily practice that spans fifteen to twenty minutes and leaves a powerful mark on your state of being. You can use it as a meditation, though it's actually a lot more than meditation alone.

The Six-Phase is rooted in science and personal study. The Six-Phase will not just make you happier and less stressed but will also make you healthier and more powerful at living your quest. Several professional sports teams are currently using it as part of their mental training as are several major entrepreneurs.

Over the last ten years, I've built many of the world's top meditation programs and apps, becoming one of the biggest promoters of meditation on the planet. I taught classes in New York and London, launched several meditation brands such as OmHarmonics, and my meditation app Omvana, which became the number-one highest-grossing health and fitness app on iTunes in more than thirty countries. I share this so you know I'm not just a dabbler in meditation. I've been researching and innovating on meditation practices for a decade. Yet the Six-Phase is NOT meditation by conventional definition. I cannot stress this enough. People who get bored with meditation or who simply cannot meditate thrive with the Six-Phase. And many people who practice traditional meditation switch to the Six-Phase because they find that they get the same health results as meditation, but as a bonus they also see their performance at work and life soar. This is why I prefer to call it a transcendent practice rather than a meditation practice.

What I'm about to share with you is the VERY BEST approach to combining transcendent practices that I've discovered. I'll explain it and give you clear directions on how to experience it.

This practice will help you:

- Make Blissipline part of your daily life and extend your happiness levels throughout the day.

- Focus on your end goals and the steps you need to take to get there.

- Become unfuckwithable by clearing out anxiety and practicing forgiveness.

- Connect to your intuition and inner voice, find an optimal path to your quest, and steer clear of Brules. Often during the Six-Phase, flashes of insight, ideas, and eureka moments will come.

■ Gain resilience to move past the inevitable bumps on the road to your calling.

And that's just the beginning. You also get the benefits of a meditation practice. The sheer number of benefits of meditation are at this point so vast that I won't cover them here. Just know that as of the time this book was published, there have been some 1,400 studies done on the benefits of meditation.

THE PROBLEM WITH MEDITATION

There are thousands of different styles of meditation, but they all fall into one of two categories: meditation methods derived from monastic practices and meditation practices designed for the modern human being.

All meditation is beneficial, but unless you're a monk, you don't want to meditate like one. It's inefficient and slow. Many of these practices are still rooted in dogma and haven't been updated for centuries.

According to Emily Fletcher, who founded the Ziva meditation school in New York City, the biggest misconception about meditation is that its purpose is to stop your mind from thinking. Just try to stop thinking. Difficult, huh? As Emily says, when people try that, it's usually "the beginning and end of their meditation career." She continues:

> But if we go into this thinking that the point of meditation is to get good at life—not to get good at meditation, and if we accept the reality that no one can give their mind a command to stop, then it's so much more innocent, so much more playful, and so much more enjoyable. Trying to give your mind a command to stop thinking is as effective as giving your heart a command to stop beating—it doesn't work.

The Six-Phase draws on many different methods to bring you an optimized meditation experience you can personalize to your schedule, needs, and life. It's rooted in science and allows you to incorporate every idea of this book into your life in just fifteen minutes a day. And you won't be asked to clear your mind.

INTRODUCING THE SIX-PHASE

The Six-Phase is a mental hack to get you to the level of extraordinary faster than ever before.

Each phase of the Six-Phase is designed to enhance one of six key skills. The first three contribute to happiness in the now. The next three contribute to your vision for the future.

1. Compassion
2. Gratitude
3. Forgiveness

} **Happiness in the Now**

4. Future Dreams
5. The Perfect Day
6. The Blessing

} **A Vision for the Future**

Here's why we're focusing on these six phases:

1. COMPASSION. I believe that all human beings need love and compassion in their lives. This phase is about helping you be kinder toward others and kinder toward yourself. It's a powerful self-love tool.

2. GRATITUDE. We may have many goals, but it's important to appreciate and be happy about what we've accomplished thus far. Gratitude has a high correlation with well-being and happiness.

3. FORGIVENESS. Being at peace with the world and the people around you is one of the most effective ways to maintain Blissipline. Plus, it makes you unfuckwithable.

4. **FUTURE DREAMS.** As you learned in chapters 7 and 8, it's hugely energizing to have a vision pulling you forward—a picture of how you want your life to unfold in the future.

5. **THE PERFECT DAY.** This phase gives you a sense of control over how life unfolds every day. It translates your future dreams into actionable steps.

6. **THE BLESSING.** We need to feel supported, resting in the knowledge that whatever big projects we're setting out to do, things are going to be okay. This phase is about making you feel safe and supported in your quest.

We'll first review each phase so you can familiarize yourself with how they unfold. Then I'll share exactly how to perform each phase.

At the end of this chapter, I'll also make available an app and a video you can watch that will easily guide you through this meditation anytime you want.

Phase I: Compassion

This phase is about feeling connected to others and feeling a sense of kinship with and kindness toward all of life, which we discussed in Chapter 10. In this phase, you express your intention of extending greater compassion and love to an ever-widening circle of humanity, starting with your family and friends and then widening all the way to encompass the planet. Compassion practices make you a better human being, and some studies have found that men and women found compassion or kindness to be one of the most attractive qualities in the opposite sex (so this might improve your love life, too).

Phase 2: Gratitude

Science shows that gratitude increases energy, reduces anxiety, improves sleep, and creates feelings of social connection—that's why several exercises in this book focus on it. In this phase, just think about three things you're grateful for in your personal life, three things you're grateful for in your career, and three things you're grateful for about yourself. This last one is important. Often we look for love from others but fail to truly love ourselves.

Phase 3: Forgiveness

As I shared in Chapter 7, forgiveness is critical to Blissipline and the peak states needed for extraordinary living. Here you'll incorporate the forgiveness exercise from that chapter into your daily practice.

Science is now showing that forgiveness can lead to profound health benefits, including reduced back pain, higher athletic performance, better heart health, and greater feelings of happiness. One study of a small group of people with chronic back pain showed that those who meditated with a focus on moving from anger to compassion reported less pain and anxiety compared to those who got regular care. Another study found that forgiving someone improved blood pressure and reduced the workload on the heart. Interesting that lightening the heart of negativity should literally help it.

Research on the impact of forgiveness by Xue Zheng of Erasmus University's Rotterdam School of Management showed that forgiveness makes the body seemingly stronger. "Our research shows that forgivers perceive a less daunting world and perform better on challenging physical tasks," said Zheng.

In one study, participants could actually jump higher after writing an account of forgiving someone who had harmed them. In another study by Zheng, participants who were asked to guess at the steepness of a hill described the hill as less steep after they had written down an account of an incident where they had forgiven someone. In a previous chapter, I described my own powerful experiences with forgiveness during meditation. That's why forgiveness is one of the components of the Six-Phase—it strengthens not only your body, but also your soul.

Phase 4: Future Dreams

Up to this point, you've focused on the present. In this phase, you express intentions for your future happiness. I credit this phase with the massive growth and joy I've experienced in my career. Years ago, I visualized the life I have today. Today, I visualize years ahead while still being happy in the now. Doing this on a daily basis seems to help my brain find the optimal paths to realizing my dreams.

When I'm visualizing my future life, I think three years ahead, and I suggest you do the same in this phase. And whatever you see three years ahead—double it. Because your brain will underestimate what you can do. We tend to underestimate what we can do in three years and overestimate what we can do in one year.

Some people think that being "spiritual" means having to be content with one's current life. Rubbish. You should be happy no matter where you are. But that shouldn't stop you from dreaming, growing, and contributing.

Choose an end goal from your answers to the Three Most Important Questions in chapter 8 and spend a few minutes just imagining and thinking with joy about what life would be like if you had already attained this end goal.

Phase 5: The Perfect Day

Knowing what you want your life to look like three years from now, what do you need to do today to make this happen? This phase brings you to your perfect day—today—and you can see how you'd like your day to unfold: starting your morning alert and excited, having a great meeting with amazing colleagues, feeling full of ideas, nailing that presentation, meeting up with friends after work, having a delicious dinner with your mate, playing with your kid before bed.

When you see your perfect day unfolding, you're priming your brain's reticular activating system (RAS) to notice the positives. The RAS is that component of your brain that helps you notice patterns. In a common example, when you buy a new car, say, a white Tesla Model S, all of a sudden you start to notice more Model S cars on the roads. The same effect happens here. So, let's say you imagine your lunch meeting today going well—great ideas, wonderful food, amazing ambiance. A few hours later, you're actually at that meeting—and the waiter screws up your order. Because you've imagined a beautiful reality, your RAS is more likely to pay attention to the ambiance, the company, and the food than to the screw-up, because you told it to. You see? You're training your brain to ignore the negative and embrace the positive. You don't have to change the world. You just have to change what you pay attention to in the world. And that, it turns out, is hugely powerful.

Phase 6: The Blessing

You can do this final phase no matter what your religious or spiritual beliefs are. If you believe in a higher power, you imagine that you can tap into it, call upon it, and feel the energy of this higher power flowing down into you, through your head and all the way to your toes—you feel loved and supported. That's it. It takes thirty seconds. If you don't believe in a higher power, you can imagine that you're rebooting yourself, fine-tuning yourself, or calling on your inner strength. Likewise, you feel this energy coursing through you. You're now ready to hit the ground running to pursue your quest.

GOING BEYOND "MEDITATION" WITH THE SIX-PHASE

If meditation has so many benefits, why do only about 20 million Americans meditate daily? I asked this question of 70,000-plus followers on my Facebook profile, and many of you completed a survey. I found that if you're not meditating daily, you're likely to have one of the three outdated models of reality about meditation below. Here's a snapshot of each and how the Six-Phase solves them.

I. "I'm Too Busy for This."

I call this the busyness paradox because it simply does not make logical sense. It's like saying, "I'm too hungry to eat." People who meditate regularly like Arianna Huffington, futurist Ray Kurzweil, and I all know that the massive beneficial impact of meditation on your productivity makes up for the fifteen minutes a day you might spend meditating. And that's not even counting other benefits such as the extension to life span, the boost in creativity and problem solving, or the fact that meditation makes you happier during the day. If I start my workday without it, I'm simply not going to be as efficient or productive. Yet many people buy into this paradox. The reason is not so much that they can't spend fifteen minutes, but that they are unaware of exactly how they should be meditating or what to do. The Six-Phase adds hours to your day by priming your mind to be more productive and efficient. It's not worth skipping.

2. "I Can't Do It Right."

The issue with meditation, unlike, say, jogging, is that with jogging it's easy to know if you're doing it right. You've gone from point A to point B in X amount of time. Yet with meditation, you might feel yourself fluttering from thought to thought, falling asleep, getting bored, or just waiting for it to end. So you may conclude that meditation is ineffective, but these things are only happening because you're not using the right system. The right system—the Six-Phase—keeps you engaged, isn't boring, and actually gives you specific milestones to reach during your fifteen-minute session. It makes a world of difference.

3. "That 'Clear Your Mind' Thing Never Works for Me."

There's an old Chinese saying: "The mind is like a drunken monkey always jumping from tree to tree." This is true. Do not think that you must clear your mind in order to meditate. This is one of the biggest myths about meditation. It may have been easier for hermits centuries ago to sit in a cave and clear their minds. They didn't have jobs, careers, families, kids, text messages, or Facebook alerts to deal with. Our world is different, and meditation needs to adapt. So I don't advocate starting with clear-the-mind methods. The Six-Phase engages your mind. It can even be used for solving problems. If there's a pressing problem at work or in your personal life, you can bring the thought of it into your meditation and turn the *problem* into a *project*. In this style of meditation, your mind is active—but you're STILL in meditation and are reaping all the rewards of stillness.

Many intensely busy entrepreneurs and people with ADD who could never meditate before now do it daily, thanks to the Six-Phase and the common meditation challenges it solves. I get letters about it daily.

John Davy, a British entrepreneur who founded and sold the world's largest comedy club, told me this the first time I met him:

> I started doing the Six-Phase for about one hundred days straight. And then I felt normal, so I stopped. All of a sudden within weeks of stopping, my friends would come to me and go, "John, what happened? You're all scratchy again. You're all stressed again." And then

I realized it. As I had been doing the Six-Phase, I was dramatically changing myself. When I stopped, some of the old stress and behavior came back. My friends thought I was off my meds. I'm now back to it. And I'm not stopping again. It's amazing.

Ready to begin?

HOW TO PRACTICE THE SIX-PHASE

There's a lot of freedom in how to do this method, but here are some guidelines:

WHEN TO DO IT. Typically it's easiest to do it in the morning or at night before bed. Some people can do it in their offices. The main thing is to find ten to twenty minutes of uninterrupted time. I like to do it in the morning because it charges me up for the day. But you can do it at night if that works better for you: Just visualize the next day unfolding, having an incredible sleep, and then exploding into your day.

HOW TO SIT. You can sit any way you want. There's no major method to it.

STAYING FOCUSED AND KEEPING AWAKE. A lot of people have random thoughts during meditation, or they drift off to sleep. The Six-Phase is geared to the way the mind naturally works—which is to always be active. You don't have to silence your mind. If a random thought arises, that's okay. Just push it aside. Or maybe you can use it in a later phase. Is there a goal you're excited about? Great! Save it for Phase 4: Future Dreams. Got a work meeting on your mind? Play it out in Phase 5: The Perfect Day. Are there things you're worried about? Pour the power of The Blessing over it all.

Many people doze off during conventional meditation because it gets boring. You're less likely to fall asleep during the Six-Phase because your mind is active. If you still have problems with this, fear not—you can download the audio (see opposite) and be guided through the phases.

Let's Get Started

In this section I explain exactly what to do in each phase. If you're doing this process for the first time, start slowly. Begin with Phase 1 on Day 1. On

Day 2, do Phase 1 and add Phase 2. And so on, until by Day 6, you're doing the full Six-Phase Meditation.

Read the instructions below before you begin. If you'd rather listen to the instructions, I've put together a simple six-day course you can download for free that will train you from Day 1 to Day 6 to master the full the Six-Phase. By Day 6, you're running the full meditation. At that point you can continue with your practice by listening to the Six-Phase track provided in the final chapter of the course. The course is available at this site for this book's online experience www.mindvalley.com/extraordinary.

Now, let's explore exactly what you should do in each phase.

Phase 1: Compassion

Think of someone you truly love—a face or smile that makes your heart glow. For me, it's my daughter, Eve. At the time of this writing, she's two years old. Eve's smile is a question I could spend my entire life answering. I start by picturing her and her smile.

As you picture your loved one—a partner, parent, child, close friend, mentor, or even a pet—make a mental note of the feelings of compassion and love that well up. This sensation becomes an anchor.

Now imagine this love as a bubble surrounding you. See yourself in a white bubble of love.

Now imagine this bubble expanding to fill the entire room. If there's anyone else in the room, imagine their being included in your bubble of compassion and love.

Now imagine the bubble filling your entire house. Mentally project a feeling of love to everyone in that house. You could "feel" love sent to them. Or you could simply mentally repeat a statement such as, "I send you love and compassion and wish you well."

Now imagine the bubble filling up your entire neighborhood or building . . .

Your entire city . . .

Your country . . .

Your continent . . .

And now the entire planet Earth.

For each, see yourself sending love and compassion to all living things within the bubble.

Don't get hung up on *how* you see or feel the bubble. Just the thought of sending love and compassion to all the citizens of Earth is enough.

You've just completed the compassion phase. Now on to Phase 2.

Phase 2: Gratitude

Start by thinking of three to five things you're grateful for in your personal life. It could be the fact that you have a warm bed or the fact that you have a terrific job. It could also be something simple, like the fact that you have a warm cup of coffee waiting for you in the kitchen.

Now think of three to five things you're grateful for in your work life. Perhaps the easy commute you have. Or that coworker whose smile always lights you up. Or a boss who appreciates you.

So far, so good.

Now for the most important part. Think of three to five things you're grateful for about yourself.

It could be the fact that you look so damn good in that favorite dress of yours. Or that you can really think on your feet in meetings. Or that you never forget a friend's birthday. Or your remarkable intellect and your knack for picking incredible books to read.

Self-appreciation is something we all need to do in abundance.

Phase 3: Forgiveness

Forgiveness is like a muscle: The more you flex it, the stronger it gets. Get it strong enough and you become unfuckwithable—negative people and events just won't affect you as much.

Start with the list of people or events to forgive that you made in Chapter 7. Each time you do the Six-Phase, focus on just *one* person or event. Keep in mind that the person could be you. You could be forgiving yourself for something you did in the past that still gnaws at you.

Next, bring up in your imagination the person or event.

You will now repeat the three steps we discussed in the forgiveness exercise in Chapter 7.

STEP I IS SET THE SCENE. Bring to mind the scene or image where you will do the forgiveness exercise. For example, when I was forgiving myself for a bad business decision that cost me millions, I imagined seeing a younger version of myself facing me in my office from 2005.

STEP 2 IS FEEL THE ANGER AND PAIN. For no more than two minutes (it's okay to estimate), allow yourself to feel the pain and anger. It's even okay to yell or pound a pillow. Let the emotions out, but don't spend too long on this.

STEP 3 IS FORGIVE INTO LOVE. Practice asking the questions I mentioned in Chapter 7: *What did I learn from this? How did this situation make my life better?* Also remember the idea of "hurt people, hurt people." Ask: *What could have happened in the past to this person to cause them to hurt me so?*

As you start asking these questions, you learn to see the situations from another's perspective. The forgiveness may not come from one session, but no matter how grave the wrongdoing, the forgiveness can come. It just takes practice.

When the forgiveness comes, it often is so thorough and complete it can be surprising. As Khaled Hosseini wrote in the *The Kite Runner:* "I wondered if that was how forgiveness budded; not with the fanfare of epiphany, but with pain gathering its things, packing up, and slipping away unannounced in the middle of the night."

And now you've wrapped up the first half of the Six-Phase. This segment should have taken six to fifteen minutes. I usually do it in seven. Now we move to Phases 4 through 6—all of which have to do with your vision for the future.

Phase 4: Future Dreams

Remember your answers to the Three Most Important Questions from Chapter 8? Here you start making use of them. Bring up one to three items from your list of answers.

Now just allow yourself to daydream. See yourself having the experiences, growth, and ability to contribute that you wrote on your list. Remember to take a longer-term view—I suggest three years.

Bring in emotions. Emotions are key. If you're seeing yourself visiting a new country, imagine the awe and excitement you would feel from making such a journey. Or imagine the pride and accomplishment you might feel as you easily pick up a new skill.

I like to spend three to five minutes on this phase. If you have problems visualizing, don't fret. Instead of seeing the goal, think about it using a technique called lofty questions by author Christie Marie Sheldon. Here you phrase the vision that you want for yourself as a question in the present tense. For example: *Why am I so easily able to visit incredible countries? Why am I so good at making, keeping, and multiplying money? Why am I so successful in love? Why am I at my ideal weight?* For many people, the phrases are easier to do than the visualization. Or you could combine them. Ultimately it's having the thought that matters. Just so you can hear the idea, see the idea, even smell the idea . . . and it will all work out fine.

Phase 5: The Perfect Day

Here you start with a simple question: *In order for me to start achieving the items on my Three Most Important Questions list, what should I be doing today?*

Now think of your day unfolding—the commute, the morning huddle with your team, your noon assignment, then that lunch meeting . . . all the way to wrapping up at work, coming home, and meditating or reading before going to bed.

For each of these tiny slices of your day, imagine the moment unfolding *perfectly.* Author Esther Hicks suggests that if you're prone to skepticism or negative thoughts, start with the phrase, "Wouldn't it be wonderful if _____". For example, ask yourself: *Wouldn't it be wonderful if I had a stress-free commute, listening to my favorite songs?*

Do this for every segment of your day until bedtime.

As you do this, just imagine, just pretend, that you have power over how your life and day will unfold. Just pretending that it's so tends to give you more control and power and will lead to your having more positive experiences throughout the day, even if you're simply noticing positive experiences over negative ones.

Now we come to Phase 6.

Phase 6: The Blessing

Here you imagine that there's a higher power ready to support you on your quest. It doesn't matter if you're an atheist or what religion you subscribe to. Your higher power could be your cultural or mythological god, your saints or prophets, or even a spiritual or angelic being. If you're an atheist, your higher power may simply be your own inner reserves of strength and fortitude.

Feel this higher power flow from the top of your scalp down over your forehead, eyes, face, neck, shoulders, arms, abdomen, hips, thighs, legs, and feet.

Imagine yourself protected and surrounded by a force that's ready to protect you and keep you on the right path to your dreams.

Now imagine yourself thanking this higher power or energy, and see yourself ready to face the day.

When you're ready, open your eyes. And you're done.

THE RESULTS YOU SEE AND THOSE YOU DON'T

When you practice the Six-Phase, you start to reap all the benefits of meditation that you might read about. But since this system goes beyond just relaxation, you also reap the rewards of compassion, forgiveness, and much more.

The Six-Phase reminds you that you can be happy and peaceful—but that you can still be a force for positive change in the world. And that we should never, ever stop aiming for our beautiful dreams.

I consider the Six-Phase the most important thing I do every day. It's the number-one secret to my success and the most important skill I teach. I cannot emphasize enough just how *powerful* it is. I look forward to hearing how it has benefited you. Write to me at hellovishen@mindvalley.com and share your stories and experiences.

I update and refine the Six-Phase on average every six months. (That's my refresh rate for the Six-Phase.) I'm continuously experimenting and improving. So you might find that some older recordings of the exercise on the Internet may be slightly different from what's in this book. Know that the most updated and current version of the exercise will always be on Mindvalley's learning platform. Just sign up at www.mindvalley.com/extraordinary to get your free six-day course and guided meditation on the Six-Phase.

TOOLS FOR YOUR JOURNEY

Following the Code of the Extraordinary Mind

Here's a list of all the laws and major exercises in the book to use as a reference guide.

CHAPTER 1: TRANSCEND THE CULTURESCAPE

We live in two worlds. There's the world of absolute truth—the things we can all agree on (fire is hot)—and the world of relative truth—the ideas, models, myths, and rules we've developed and passed from generation to generation. This is where concepts such as marriage, money, and religion reside. Relative truths aren't true for *all* human beings, yet we tend to live by them as if they're absolute truths. They can be incredibly empowering or incredibly limiting. I call this world of relative truth the culturescape.

Law 1: Transcend the culturescape.

Extraordinary minds are good at seeing the culturescape and are able to selectively choose the rules and conditions to follow versus those to question or ignore. Therefore, they tend to take the path less traveled and innovate on the idea of what it means to truly *live*.

CHAPTER 2: QUESTION THE BRULES

Many of us live according to outdated rules imposed on us through the culturescape. I call them Brules. A Brule is a bulls**t rule that society adopts to simplify its understanding of the world. To question the Brules is to take a step into the extraordinary.

COMMON BRULES WORTH CHALLENGING

1. **THE COLLEGE BRULE.** We should get a college degree to guarantee our success.

2. **THE LOYALTY TO OUR CULTURE BRULE.** We should marry within our religion or ethnicity.

3. **THE RELIGION BRULE.** We should adhere to a single religion.

4. **THE HARD WORK BRULE.** We should work hard to be successful.

Exercise: The Brule Test

How can you quickly recognize a Brule? Ask yourself these five questions:

Question 1: Is it based on trust and hope in humanity?

Question 2: Does it violate the Golden Rule?

Question 3: Did I take it on from culture or religion?

Question 4: Is it based on rational choice or contagion?

Question 5: Does it serve my happiness?

Law 2: Question the Brules.

Extraordinary minds question the Brules when they feel those Brules are out of alignment with their dreams and desires. They recognize that much of the way the world works is due to people blindly following Brules that have long passed their expiration date.

CHAPTER 3: PRACTICE CONSCIOUSNESS ENGINEERING

Think of consciousness engineering as an operating system for the human mind—one that you control. Your models of reality are like the hardware: They're your beliefs about yourself and the world. Your systems for living are like the software: what you do to "run" your life—from your daily habits to how you solve problems, raise your kids, make friends, make love, and have fun. We constantly upgrade our electronic models and systems, but many of us live with outdated beliefs and habits without even knowing it. When you swap out old, expired models and systems that limit you, you're elevating your consciousness and opening the path to extraordinary living.

Exercise: The Twelve Areas of Balance

For each category in the Twelve Areas of Balance below, rate your life on a scale of 1 to 10, with 1 being "very weak" and 10 being "extraordinary":

1. **YOUR LOVE RELATIONSHIP.** This is a measure of how happy you are in your current state of relationship. Your rating: _____

2. **YOUR FRIENDSHIPS.** This is the measure of how strong a support network you have. Your rating: _____

3. **YOUR ADVENTURES.** How much time do you get to experience the world and do exciting things? Your rating: _____

4. **YOUR ENVIRONMENT.** This is the quality of your home, car, workspace, living space, travel accommodations, etc. Your rating: _____

5. **YOUR HEALTH AND FITNESS.** How would you rate your health, given your age and any physical conditions? Your rating: _____

6. **YOUR INTELLECTUAL LIFE.** How much/how fast are you learning and growing? Your rating: _____

7. **YOUR SKILLS.** Are you growing the skills that make you unique or are you stagnating? Your rating: _____

8. **YOUR SPIRITUAL LIFE.** How much time to you devote to spiritual, meditative, or contemplative practices that keep you feeling balanced and peaceful? Your rating: _____

9. **YOUR CAREER.** Are you growing or stuck in a rut? Your rating: _____

10. **YOUR CREATIVE LIFE.** Do you engage in any activity that channels your creativity? Your rating: _____

11. **YOUR FAMILY LIFE.** How's your relationship with your mate, children, parents, and siblings? Your rating: _____

12. **YOUR COMMUNITY LIFE.** Are you playing a role in your community? Your rating: _____

> ## Law 3: Practice consciousness engineering.
> Extraordinary minds understand that their growth depends on two things: their models of reality and their systems for living. They carefully curate the most empowering models and systems and frequently update themselves.

CHAPTER 4: REWRITE YOUR MODELS OF REALITY

It's up to us to choose what we want to believe about ourselves and our lives—and give our children the power to do the same. The exercises below will help you rewire your models of reality. Try doing them with your children, too—and if they can't think of something they love about themselves, tell them something you love about them.

Exercise: The Gratitude Exercise

Think of three to five things you're grateful for today—they could be as small as a shared smile or as large as a promotion at work.

Exercise: The "What I Love about Myself" Exercise

Think of three to five things you love about yourself. Perhaps it's a quality or an action that made you proud today. Or perhaps it's your sense of humor, your calm in a crisis, your hair, or your jump shot. For a few minutes each day, acknowledge just how great that "you" is.

External Models of Reality

Our internal models of reality, or our beliefs about ourselves, are hugely powerful. But our external models—what we believe about the world—are just as powerful. Here are four of the most powerful new external models I've decided to believe have added immense value to my life:

- We all possess human intuition.
- There is power in mind-body healing.
- Happiness at work is the new productivity.
- It is possible to be spiritual but not religious.

Exercise: Examining Your Models of Reality in the Twelve Areas of Balance

1. YOUR LOVE RELATIONSHIP. What do you expect from a love relationship, both to receive and to give? Do you believe you deserve to be loved and treasured?

2. YOUR FRIENDSHIPS. How do you define friendship?

3. YOUR ADVENTURES. What's your idea of an adventure?

4. YOUR ENVIRONMENT. Where do you feel happiest? Are you content with where and how you live?

5. YOUR HEALTH AND FITNESS. How do you define physical health? How do you define healthy eating? Do you believe you're aging well or poorly?

6. YOUR INTELLECTUAL LIFE. How much are you learning and growing?

7. YOUR SKILLS. What holds you back from learning new things?

8. YOUR SPIRITUAL LIFE. What type of spiritual values do you believe in?

9. YOUR CAREER. What is your definition of work? Do you feel you have what it takes to succeed?

10. YOUR CREATIVE LIFE. Do you believe that you are creative?

11. YOUR FAMILY LIFE. What do you believe is your main role as a life partner, son, or daughter? Is your family life satisfying to you?

12. YOUR COMMUNITY LIFE. What do you believe is the highest purpose of a community? Do you believe you're able to contribute?

Two Tools to Rewrite Your Models of Reality

Here are two instant techniques you can apply to remove negative models of reality that you might develop on a day-to-day basis. Both are based on the idea of activating your rational mind before you unconsciously adopt a model. Ask yourself the following questions:

Question 1: Is my model of reality absolute or relative truth?

Question 2: Does this really mean what I think it means?

Law 4: Rewrite your models of reality.

Extraordinary minds have models of reality that empower them to feel good about themselves and powerful in shifting the world to match the visions in their minds.

CHAPTER 5: UPGRADE YOUR SYSTEMS FOR LIVING

Many of us are so busy *doing* that we never step back and think about *how* we're doing—or *why* we're doing it. Extraordinary minds are always looking to discover and refresh their systems for living. Then they evaluate to see how well those systems are working.

How well are your systems for living serving you? Is it time to upgrade?

Exercise: What's Your Refresh Rate?

Have you updated the systems in any of the Twelve Areas of Balance recently? I've listed the twelve areas below along with a favorite book or course for each that could offer a new perspective:

1. YOUR LOVE RELATIONSHIP. *Men Are from Mars, Women Are from Venus* by John Gray

2. YOUR FRIENDSHIPS. *How to Win Friends and Influence People* by Dale Carnegie

3. YOUR ADVENTURES. *Losing My Virginity* by Richard Branson

4. YOUR ENVIRONMENT. *The Magic of Thinking Big* by David J. Schwartz, PhD

5. YOUR HEALTH AND FITNESS. *The Bulletproof Diet* by Dave Asprey (for men) and *The Virgin Diet* by JJ Virgin (for women)

6. **YOUR INTELLECTUAL LIFE.** What better way to optimize your intellectual life than by learning to speed-learn and improve your memory? I recommend courses by Jim Kwik.

7. **YOUR SKILLS.** *The 4-Hour Workweek* by Timothy Ferriss

8. **YOUR SPIRITUAL LIFE.** *Conversations with God* by Neale Donald Walsch and *Autobiography of a Yogi* by Paramahansa Yogananda

9. **YOUR CAREER.** *Originals* by Adam Grant

10. **YOUR CREATIVE LIFE.** *The War of Art* by Steven Pressfield

11. **YOUR FAMILY LIFE.** *The Mastery of Love* by Don Miguel Ruiz

12. **YOUR COMMUNITY.** *Delivering Happiness* by Tony Hsieh

Exercise: Your Non-Negotiable Set Points

Once you refresh your systems for living, use non-negotiable set points to prevent backsliding and progress toward even higher levels of achievement.

Step 1. Identify the areas of your life where you want to create set points.

Pick a couple of areas from the Twelve Areas of Balance where you'd like to see progress.

Step 2. Determine your set points.

Set specific *achievable* goals in these areas.

Step 3. Test your set points and correct if you miss.

If you slip off your set point, initiate a set-point correction procedure (see Step 4).

Step 4. Turn up the heat—in a good way.

When you slip off your set point, set a goal to get back to your set point—*plus a little more*. Now you've not just prevented stagnation, you're actually growing.

The Systems of the Future

We pay far more attention to systems for taking care of our bodies than to systems that take care of our mind and spirit. We've created a society where it's considered normal to wake up with feelings of stress, anxiety, fear, and worry. But it isn't. We can install systems for living to be free of them. I call these systems transcendent practices. They include gratitude, meditation, compassion, bliss, and other practices. Just a few minutes each day will clear your mind and give you energy, optimism, and clarity for the day ahead.

Law 5: Upgrade your systems for living.

Extraordinary minds consistently spend time discovering, upgrading, and measuring new systems for living applied to life, work, heart, and soul. They are in a perpetual state of growth and self-innovation.

CHAPTER 6: BEND REALITY

As you start playing with consciousness engineering, questioning the Brules, and experimenting with new models of reality and systems for living, life starts to feel spacious and exciting. You're moving toward a powerful upgrade. I call it bending reality. There are two key things you feel in this state:

- You have a bold vision for the future pulling you forward.

- You're happy in the NOW.

Your vision is continuously pulling you forward—but it doesn't feel like work. It feels like a game, a game you love to play.

Exercise: The Eight Statements

The simple set of eight statements below will help you gauge where you are on the path to bending reality. There are no right or wrong answers. This is just for you to see where you are right now.

1. I love my current job to the point where it does not feel like work.

NOT AT ALL TRUE   SOMETIMES TRUE   VERY TRUE

2. My work is meaningful to me.

    NOT AT ALL TRUE   SOMETIMES TRUE   VERY TRUE

3. There are often moments at work that make me so happy the time just flies by.

    NOT AT ALL TRUE   SOMETIMES TRUE   VERY TRUE

4. When things go wrong, I don't worry at all. I just know something good is on the horizon.

    NOT AT ALL TRUE   SOMETIMES TRUE   VERY TRUE

5. I feel excited about my future, knowing even better things are always on their way.

    NOT AT ALL TRUE   SOMETIMES TRUE   VERY TRUE

6. Stress and anxiety don't seem to faze me much. I trust in my ability to attain my goals.

    NOT AT ALL TRUE   SOMETIMES TRUE   VERY TRUE

7. I look forward to the future because I have unique and bold goals on the horizon.

    NOT AT ALL TRUE   SOMETIMES TRUE   VERY TRUE

8. I spend a good amount of time thinking excitedly about my visions for the future.

    NOT AT ALL TRUE   SOMETIMES TRUE   VERY TRUE

If you answered "Very true" to statements 1 through 4, you are likely happy in the now.

If you answered "Very true" to statements 5 through 8, you likely have a good vision for your future.

If you can answer "Very true" for all eight statements, you're likely in the state of bending reality.

Most people, however, find that they tend to be able to answer "Very true" to either the happiness-related statements or to the vision-related questions, but not to both.

Law 6: Bend reality.

Extraordinary minds are able to bend reality. They have bold and exciting visions for the future, yet their happiness is not tied to these visions. They are happy in the now. This balance allows them to move toward their visions at a much faster rate while having a ton of fun along the way. To outsiders, they seem "lucky."

CHAPTER 7: LIVE IN BLISSIPLINE

Did you know that there's a simple system for mastering happiness in the now and feeling truly joyous? I call it Blissipline: the discipline of daily bliss. It consists of three key systems:

Blissipline System 1: The Power of Gratitude

Blissipline System 2: Forgiveness

Blissipline System 3: The Practice of Giving

Happiness is not some amorphous state outside of your control. It's a trainable skill. The exercises below are powerful pathways to Blissipline.

Exercise: Daily Gratitude

Most of us look toward the future when seeking happiness. But happiness is right in our own backyard. Focusing on the good things that have already happened in our lives provides instant happiness in the now. Each morning and evening, spend a few minutes thinking about:

Three to five things you're grateful for in your personal life

Three to five things you're grateful for in your work life

They can be big or small—as long as they're meaningful to you. Spend five to ten seconds letting the positive feelings well up about each thing. Try sharing the bliss: Try doing these exercises with your kids or with your partner.

Exercise: Liberate Yourself and Truly Forgive

Letting go of grudges and anger is the single most powerful conduit to a relaxed, powerful state of mind. Like happiness, forgiveness is a trainable skill. It is key to mastering Blissipline. Here is a simplified variation of the forgiveness exercise I learned at the program 40 Years of Zen.

Preparation

Make a list of people you feel have wronged you or situations where you've been hurt. This may not be easy to do, especially for a very hurtful or longstanding situation. Be gentle with yourself. When you're ready, pick one of the people on the list and start the exercise.

Step 1. Set the scene.

With your eyes closed, for two minutes or so, feel yourself in the moment it happened. Picture the environment.

Step 2. Feel the anger and pain.

As you picture the person who wronged you, get emotional, but don't do this for more than a few minutes.

Step 3. Forgive into love.

As you picture that person, feel compassion for him or her. What pain or anguish might they have suffered that made them do what they did? Ask yourself: *What did I learn from this? How did this situation make my life better?*

Afterward, you should feel a slightly lesser negative charge toward this person. Repeat the process until you feel comfortable forgiving into love. For a serious offense, this could take hours or days. "Forgiveness into love" does not mean to simply let go. You still need to protect yourself and take action if need be. Criminal acts, especially, need to be reported to authorities. But with forgiveness, the pain of what happened no longer eats at you.

Exercise: Ways of Giving

Step 1. List all the things you could give to others.

Ideas include: time, love, understanding, compassion, skills, ideas, wisdom, energy, physical help, and what else?

Step 2. Drill down and get specific.

What skills (accounting, tech support, tutoring, legal assistance, writing, office skills, art skills)? What kinds of wisdom (career counseling; working with kids; helping others deal with an experience you've had, such as going through an illness or being the victim of a crime)? What types of physical help (fixing things, assisting the elderly, cooking, reading to the blind)?

Step 3. Think about where you could give help.

Within your family or extended family? At work? In your neighborhood? Your city? Local businesses? Spiritual community? Local library? Youth organizations? Hospitals or nursing homes? Political or nonprofit organizations? What about starting a group or raising awareness about an underserved cause??

Step 4. Follow your intuition.

Review your lists and mark the items where you feel a surge of excitement.

Step 5. Take action.

Put out feelers, watch for coincidences that bring opportunity your way, and explore the possibilities.

Law 7: Live in Blissipline.

Extraordinary minds understand that happiness comes from within. They begin with happiness in the now and use it as a fuel to drive all their other visions and intentions for themselves and the world.

CHAPTER 8: CREATE A VISION FOR YOUR FUTURE

Most of us are asked to choose a career before we can legally buy a beer. How can we possibly know what we want from life at that age? But even when we try to be "mature" and systematic about goal setting, we may end up dissatisfied because most modern goal-setting methods are fundamentally flawed.

We're trained to set "means goals"—goals that are a means to an end—and usually about meeting or conforming to society's Brules. In contrast, "end goals" follow our heart, excite and inspire us, and put our ultimate target in our sights. Pursuing end goals accelerates our momentum toward the extraordinary. The Three Most Important Questions exercise can help you get straight to the end goals that really matter in your life:

Exercise: Ask Yourself the Three Most Important Questions

Question 1: What Experiences Do You Want to Have?

If time and money were no object and I did not have to seek anyone's permission, what kinds of experiences would my soul crave?

- **YOUR LOVE RELATIONSHIP.** Vividly imagine your ideal love relationship. Whom do you want to wake up next to in the morning?

- **YOUR FRIENDSHIPS.** Picture your social life in a perfect world—the people, the places, the conversation, the activities.

- **YOUR ADVENTURES.** What kinds of adventures would make your soul sing?

- **YOUR ENVIRONMENT.** Conjure up the feelings of being in environments you love. What would your ideal home, car, travel destinations look like?

Question 2: How Do You Want to Grow?

In order to have the experiences above, how do I have to grow? What sort of man or woman do I need to evolve into?

- **YOUR HEALTH AND FITNESS.** Describe how you want to feel and look every day. What about five, ten, or twenty years from now?

- **YOUR INTELLECTUAL LIFE.** What do you need to learn in order to have the experiences you listed above? What would you love to learn?

- **YOUR SKILLS.** What skills would help you thrive at your job? If you'd love to switch gears professionally, what would it take to do that? What are some skills you want to learn just for fun?

- **YOUR SPIRITUAL LIFE.** What is your highest aspiration for your spiritual practice?

Question 3: How Do You Want to Contribute?

If I have the experiences above and have grown in these remarkable ways, then how can I give back to the world?

- YOUR CAREER. What are your visions for your career? What contribution to your field would you like to make?

- YOUR CREATIVE LIFE. What creative activities do you love to do or what would you like to learn? What are some ways you can share your creative self with the world?

- YOUR FAMILY LIFE. Picture yourself being with your family, not as you think you "should" be but in ways that fill you with happiness. What wonderful experiences are you having together? What can you contribute to your family that is unique to you? Remember, your family doesn't have to be a traditional family—define "family" as those whom you truly love and want to spend time with.

- YOUR COMMUNITY LIFE. Your community could be your friends, neighborhood, city, state, nation, religious community, ethnicity, or the world community. Looking at everything that makes you who you are, what is the mark that you want to leave on the world that excites and deeply satisfies you?

Law 8: Create a vision for your future.

Extraordinary minds create a vision for their future that is decidedly their own and free from expectations of the culturescape. Their vision is focused on end goals that strike a direct chord with their happiness.

CHAPTER 9: BE UNFUCKWITHABLE

Extraordinary minds are full of energy and are prepared to take on the world to manifest their bold goals and visions. If you want to do the same, you must step past your fears. Fortunately, like much of what you've learned in this book, becoming unfuckwithable is a trainable skill. It involves understanding two particular models of reality:

SELF-FUELED GOALS. These are end goals that you have absolute control over. No one can take them away from you. Example: to be consistently surrounded by love.

YOU ARE ENOUGH. Feeling that you must prove yourself will infect your life with the need to seek validation from the outside world. It gives away control over your life. Knowing that you are enough takes you from having a hole in your heart to being whole-hearted—and with your heart whole, you will have so much more to give to life, love, yourself, and the planet.

Exercise 1: The Person in the Mirror (for Creating Self-Love)

Stand before a mirror, look directly into your eyes, and repeat to yourself, "I love you." Do this as many times as feels right to you.

Exercise 2: Self-Gratitude (for Appreciating Yourself)

Make sure you do the "What I Love about Myself" exercise every day (see Chapter 4).

Exercise 3: Becoming Present (to Remove Sudden Fear and Anxiety)

Use present-centeredness to pull yourself out of stress and anxiety and return to happiness in the now. Simply spend a minute or so focusing on a specific detail in the present moment: the way the light is falling on an object, the beautiful design of your own hand, or the rise and fall of your breath.

Law 9: Be unfuckwithable.

Extraordinary minds do not need to seek validation from outside opinion or through the attainment of goals. Instead, they are truly at peace with themselves and the world around them. They live fearlessly—immune to criticism or praise and fueled by their own inner happiness and self-love.

CHAPTER 10: EMBRACE YOUR QUEST

When I think about the extraordinary people I know, their uniqueness is that they're driven by a vision so big that they're operating beyond the conventional limitations of work and life. Their energy is inherently positive, and they pour it into a mission that they're passionate about.

The most extraordinary people in the world do not have careers. What they have is a calling.

A calling is your contribution to the human race. It's something that helps us leave the planet better for our children. It can be a book you're working on. It could be dedicating your life to raising remarkable children. It could be working for a company with a mission to change the world in a way that resonates with you. When you pursue a calling, your life is filled with passion and meaning. With the right practices, anyone can reach this stage of supreme fulfillment.

Discovering Your Quest

How do you get started with finding your mission? There are two approaches I know of: the approach for the brain and the approach for the heart. You can also combine both.

Author and speaker Martin Rutte, creator of projectheavenonearth. com, suggests you ask yourself these three questions in order to help you identify your calling—fast.

The first question is: Recall a time when you experienced Heaven on Earth. What was happening?

The second question is: Imagine you have a magic wand and with it you can create Heaven on Earth. What is Heaven on Earth for you?

And now the final question: What simple, easy, concrete step(s) will you take in the next twenty-four hours to make Heaven on Earth real?

Law 10: Embrace your quest.

Extraordinary minds are motivated by a quest or calling—a drive to create some positive change in the world. This drive propels them forward in life and helps them to gain meaning and make a meaningful contribution.

TRANSCEND THE CULTURESCAPE

QUESTION THE BRULES

PRACTICE CONSCIOUSNESS ENGINEERING

REWRITE YOUR MODELS OF REALITY

UPGRADE YOUR SYSTEMS FOR LIVING

BEND REALITY

LIVE IN BLISSIPLINE

CREATE A VISION FOR YOUR FUTURE

BE UNF*CKWITHABLE

EMBRACE YOUR QUEST

THE CODE OF
THE EXTRAORDINARY MIND

THE CODE OF THE EXTRAORDINARY MIND:

The Online Experience

Create Your Account to Experience a Book Like Never Before. Free with this Book.

THE APP: GO DEEPER INTO TOPICS YOU CARE ABOUT

This book comes with its own custom-designed app with hours of additional content, practices, training, and more. Do you especially like a particular idea from one of the thinkers I mention in the book? You can use the app to dive in deeper and listen to my full interview with them. Inspired by a particular technique I share? The app will let you play a video of me guiding you through the technique. You'll find gorgeous images, photos, ideas, and more, all on the Online Experience available for Web, Android, and iOS. You can therefore read this book in a few hours, or you can choose to spend days exploring and deep-diving into the full content. Access it from www.mindvalley.com/extraordinary.

THE SOCIAL LEARNING PLATFORM: TALK TO VISHEN AND OTHER READERS

Since this book is about questioning life, as I wrote it I began questioning the way traditional ways books are made. One of my big annoyances with the idea of the "'book"' in today's world is that you cannot easily interact with fellow readers or with the author. For this book, I decided to fix this flaw. I had my team develop a social learning platform to allow authors and readers to interact and learn from each other. As far as I know, this is the first of its kind in the world. You can interact with other readers, share ideas, and even communicate with me directly from your phone or computer when you sign up for the online experience. This makes this book perhaps one of the most technologically hooked up volumes in history. You can access the Social Learning Platform via the Online Experience on www.mindvalley.com/extraordinary.

To Get Started, Just Visit:
www.mindvalley.com/extraordinary
And Create an Account.

TEN THINGS YOU CAN DISCOVER IN THE ONLINE EXPERIENCE

1. **An online course** that guides you through the key exercises in every chapter. Get videos, audio and deeper instructions.

2. **The Six-Phase Online Program** that trains you to apply many of the transcendent practices discussed in this book. Download for Android or iPhone or play on your computer.

3. **Complete video and audio interviews** for key figures in this book, including Peter Diamandis, Arianna Huffington, Ken Wilber, Michael Beckwith, Emily Fletcher, and more.

4. **Videos from A-Fest** of key figures in this book discussing the ideas shared here in more detail, including Morty Lefkoe and Marisa Peer.

5. **A beautiful course called Extraordinary by Design,** which will guide you into consciously creating extraordinary results in all twelve areas of your life.

6. **Guided Exercise on the Three Most Important Questions** to help you create your blueprint in less than ten minutes.

7. **Guided Exercise on the Heaven on Earth Tool** to help you identify your quest.

8. **Join our online community** of readers discussing and practicing The Code on our custom-built Social Learning Platform. You can share your learnings and ideas and learn from other readers.

9. **Behind-the-scenes pics** from the encounters and stories described in this book, from meeting Branson to visiting the Amazon Rainforest.

10. **Free updates and communication** from me, including future chapters, videos, and insights all delivered on the online Learning Platform.

EXPERIENCE A *BOOK* LIKE NEVER BEFORE

Get all videos and further trainings free plus interact with Vishen and other readers in our one-of-a-kind learning platform. Just visit: www.mindvalley .com/extraordinary

CONNECT WITH VISHEN LAKHIANI

I love being in touch with my readers. Here's how to connect with me:

1. Follow me on Facebook. This is the real me. Not a fanpage. Go to www.facebook.com/vishen and click +FOLLOW. This is by far the best way to connect with me. I share insights and thought-provoking posts weekly.

2. Join the online community for Code of the Extraordinary Mind. I frequently answer questions and share insights. Visit www.mindvalley.com/extraordinary to connect.

3. Sign up for my newsletter on VishenLakhiani.com

4. For feedback or ideas, you can write to me at hellovishen@mindvalley.com.

GLOSSARY

BEAUTIFUL DESTRUCTION: A situation where a part of your life is destroyed, only to make way for better and bigger things to come to you.

BENDING REALITY: The idea that our consciousness can shape the world around us and that luck is within our control.

BLISSIPLINE: The discipline of daily bliss. The process of consciously raising one's happiness level by adopting specific systems for living, including transcendent practices. See also Transcendent practices.

BLUEPRINT FOR THE SOUL: A person's written answers to the Three Most Important Questions.

BRULE: A bulls**t rule. An element of the culturescape that an individual has decided to ignore or dismiss as untrue or irrelevant to that individual's worldview.

BUSYNESS PARADOX: The fallacy of thinking one is too busy to meditate—similar to saying, "I'm too hungry to eat."

COMPUTATIONAL THINKING: A process that generalizes a solution to open-ended problems. Open-ended problems encourage full, meaningful answers based on multiple variables, which require using decomposition, data representation, generalization, modeling, and algorithms.

CONSCIOUSNESS ENGINEERING: A method to optimize learning and hacking of the culturescape by gaining awareness of the models of reality and systems for living that may have intentionally or unintentionally been adopted from the culturescape.

CULTURE HACKING: The technique of changing the culture (beliefs and practices) of a group (as in workspace, company, family, school) by using tools to create positive advancements in the group culture. It's applying consciousness engineering within a group to allow the members to grow and work together better. See also Consciousness Engineering.

CULTURESCAPE: The world of relative truth, which is made up of human ideas, cultures, mythologies, beliefs, and practices.

CURRENT REALITY TRAP: The state of feeling happy in the now but without a vision for the future. While this state may bring temporary happiness, it won't bring fulfillment.

DO-DO TRAP: The condition of being so busy *doing* that there is no time to step back and think about *how* and *why* one is doing things.

END GOAL: An ultimate aim or destination—often discerned by following one's heart and feelings; the opposite of a means goal. See also Means goal.

FOUR STATES OF HUMAN LIVING: Four conditions of life, each having a different level or balance (being pulled forward by a bold vision for the future and being happy in the now): 1) the negative spiral, 2) the current reality trap, 3) stress and anxiety, and 4) bending reality.

GODICLE THEORY: The idea that human beings are particles of God and are thus endowed with certain God-like abilities such as the ability to bend reality.

HUMANITY-MINUS COMPANY: A business whose product may fill an unsustainable or artificially-created demand and that leaves the world and the human race worse off.

HUMANITY-PLUS COMPANY: A company that pushes the human race forward; for example, companies focusing on clean, renewable energy sources, companies that promote healthy living, or companies working on new ways to live on the planet.

KENSHO: A gradual process of positive personal growth that often happens through the tribulations of life. This positive growth may not be noticeable while it is happening. See also Satori.

LOFTY QUESTIONS: A method of asking positive questions during a transcendent practice as described by author Christie Marie Sheldon; an alternative to affirmations and problem-focused personal growth practices; for example, How am I finding so many ways to give and receive love? instead of Why can't I find a love relationship?

MEANING-MAKING MACHINE: A syntax in the human brain that attempts to attach meaning to situations that often are random, have no implied meaning, or do not have the meaning that has been attached.

MEANS GOAL: A goal (sometimes a Brule) mistakenly identified and pursued as an end in itself, when in fact it is simply a means to a larger, more fulfilling end. See also Brule and End goal.

MODELS OF REALITY: Beliefs about the world that play out in one's experiences of the world, unconsciously or consciously; analagous to hardware in a computer. See also Systems for living.

NEGATIVE SPIRAL: The painful state of not being happy in the now and not having a vision for the future.

PRESENT-CENTEREDNESS: Becoming focused on the present as a technique for finding happiness in the now and raising one's happiness set point.

REFRESH RATE: How frequently a person updates his or her systems for living.

RETICULAR ACTIVATING SYSTEM (RAS): The component of the brain that registers patterns; certain transcendent practices prime the RAS to notice the positives over the negatives in life situations.

REVERSE GAP: As explained by Dan Sullivan, the space, or gap, between the past and the present and the events that fill it—the best place to focus on when practicing gratitude and a far more reliable source of happiness than focusing on the forward gap (anticipating happiness in the future), as most people do.

SATORI: A sudden spurt of positive personal growth that happens by awakening; a life-changing insight that occurs without warning and lifts a person immediately to a new plane. See also *Kensho.*

SET POINT: A non-negotiable benchmark that is easily measurable and helps you measure your level of growth or maintenance.

SIX-PHASE MEDITATION: A meditation program rooted in science that takes just fifteen minutes a day and draws on many different methods to bring practitioners a rewarding and optimized meditation experience they can personalize to their own schedule, needs, and life.

SYSTEMS FOR LIVING: Structured habits and processes for living aspects of life, from play to work to growth. A repeated (and, ideally, an optimized) pattern for getting things done; analogous to software in a computer or apps. See also Models of reality.

THREE MOST IMPORTANT QUESTIONS: Three pivotal questions for setting expansive, fulfilling goals on the path to bending reality.

TRANSCENDENT PRACTICES: Optimized systems for living that nurture the mind and spirit and take practitioners beyond or above the range of normal or merely physical human experiences. Examples include exercises in gratitude, meditation, compassion, and bliss. See also Blissipline.

TWELVE AREAS OF BALANCE: Twelve key domains of a balanced life: your love relationship, your friendships, your adventures, your environment, your health and fitness, your intellectual life, your skills, your spiritual life, your career, your creative life, your family life, your community.

UNFUCKWITHABLE: According to Internet memes: "When you're truly at peace and in touch with yourself. Nothing anyone says or does bothers you and no negativity can touch you."

SOURCES

CHAPTER 1

"Adult Obesity Facts." Centers for Disease Control and Prevention. Page last reviewed: September 21, 2015. http://www.cdc.gov/obesity/data/adult.html (accessed December 22, 2015).

"Bill Gates, Founder and Technology Advisor." www.microsoft.com http://news.microsoft.com/exec/bill-gates/ (accessed August 13, 2015).

Gates, Bill. "About Bill." Gatesnotes (the blog of Bill Gates). www.gatesnotes.com. http://www.gatesnotes.com/GlobalPages/bio (accessed August 13, 2015).

Gregoire, Carolyn. "Happiness Index: Only 1 in 3 Americans Are Very Happy, According to Harris Poll." *The Huffington Post,* Posted: June 1, 2013, Updated: June 5, 2013. http://www.huffingtonpost.com/2013/06/01/happiness-index-only-1-in_n_3354524.html (accessed November 29, 2015).

Harari, Yuval Noah. *Sapiens.* New York: HarperCollins, 2015.

Holland, Kelley. "Eight in 10 Americans Are in Debt: Study." CNBC Personal Finance, July 29, 2015. http://www.cnbc.com/2015/07/29/eight-in-10-americans-are-in-debt.html (accessed December 22, 2015).

Loria, Kevin. "No One Could See the Color Blue until Modern Times." Business Insider, February 27, 2015. http://www.businessinsider.com/what-is-blue-and-how-do-we-see-color-2015-2 (accessed August 10, 2015).

"Marriage & Divorce." American Psychological Association, Adapted from the *Encyclopedia of Psychology,* n.d. http://www.apa.org/topics/divorce/ (accessed November 29, 2015).

Smith, Chandler. "Gallup Poll: 70% of Americans Hate Their Stupid Jobs." RYOT, 2 years ago. http://www.ryot.org/gallup-poll-70-americans-disengaged-jobs/376177 (accessed November 29, 2015).

CHAPTER 2

Bryant, Adam. "In Head-Hunting, Big Data May Not Be Such a Big Deal." *New York Times,* June 19, 2013. http://www.nytimes.com/2013/06/20/business/in-head-hunting-big-data-may-not-be-such-a-big-deal.html?_r=1 (accessed December 18, 2015).

Friedman, Thomas L. "How to Get a Job at Google." *New York Times,* Sunday Review, February 22, 2014. nytimes.com/2014/02/23/opinion/sunday/friedman-how-to-get-a-job-at-google.html?hp&rref=opinion&_r=1 (accessed August 30, 2015).

Harari, Yuval Noah. *Sapiens.* New York: HarperCollins, 2015.

Marsden, P. "Memetics and Social Contagion: Two Sides of the Same Coin?" *Journal of Memetics—Evolutionary Models of Information Transmission,* vol. 2., 1998. cfpm.org/jom-emit/1998/vol2/marsden_p.html.

"Original sin." merriam-webster.com, n.d. (accessed November 14, 2015).

"Our Founder." dekaresearch.com, n.d. (accessed November 14, 2015).

Ravo, Nick. "Our Towns; From L. I. Sound, A New Nation Asserts Itself." *New York Times,* April 22, 1988. nytimes.com/1988/04/22/nyregion/our-towns-from-li-sound-a-new-nation-asserts-itself.html (accessed August 26, 2015).

Sanchez, Hanna. "Ernst and Young Removes College Grades from Recruitment Criteria, Saying It Does Not Guarantee Success Later in Life." iSchoolGuide, September 29, 2015. ischoolguide.com/articles/27528/20150929/ernst-young-college-grades-recruitment-criteria-success.htm (accessed December 23, 2015).

Urban, Tim. "The Cook and the Chef: Musk's Secret Sauce." waitbuywhy.com, November 6, 2015. waitbutwhy.com/2015/11/the-cook-and-the-chef-musks-secret-sauce.html (accessed November 22, 2015).

"Vision & Mission." usfirst.org, n.d.usfirst.org/aboutus/vision (accessed November 14, 2015).

CHAPTER 3

Crum, Alia J., and Ellen J. Langer. "Mind-Set Matters: Exercise and the Placebo Effect." *Psychological Science* 18, no. 2:165-17. 2007. dash.harvard.edu/bitstream/handle/1/3196007/Langer_ExercisePlaceboEffect.pdf?sequence=1 (accessed August 26, 2015).

Shea, Christopher. "Mindful Exercise." *New York Times* Magazine, December 9, 2007. nytimes.com/2007/12/09/magazine/09mindfulexercise.html?_r=0 (accessed August 26, 2015).

Steineckert, Rachael. "Achuar Rituals: Nurturing a Connection with Pachamama." Pachamama Alliance, September 9, 2014. pachamama.org/blog/achuar-rituals-connection-pachamama (accessed August 26, 2015).

CHAPTER 4

Crum, Alia J., and Ellen J. Langer. "Mind-Set Matters: Exercise and the Placebo Effect." *Psychological Science* 18, no. 2:165-17. 2007. dash.harvard.edu/bitstream/handle/1/3196007/Langer_ExcersisePlaceboEffect.pdf?sequence=1 (accessed August 26, 2015).

Dewey, PhD, Russell A. "Psychology: An Introduction." Psych Web, 2007–2014. intropsych.com/ch15_social/expectancy.html (accessed September 16, 2015).

Epstein, Greg M. *Good without God.* New York: William Morrow, 2010.

Feloni, Richard. "Branson: Wild Parties Are Essential to a Company's Success." *Business Insider,* January 1, 2015. businessinsider.sg/richard-branson-on-the-importance-of-parties-2014-12/#.VlyzPXtu7Io (accessed November 30, 2015).

Moore, Thomas. *A Religion of One's Own.* New York: Avery, 2014 (reprint edition).

Silberman, Steve. "Placebos Are Getting More Effective. Drugmakers Are Desperate to Know Why." *Wired,* August 24, 2009. archive.wired.com/medtech/drugs/magazine/17-09/ff_placebo_effect?currentPage=all (accessed November 14, 2015).

Talbot, Margaret. "The Placebo Prescription." *New York Times* Magazine, January 9, 2000. nytimes.com/2000/01/09/magazine/the-placebo-prescription.html (accessed August 26, 2015).

Turner, PhD, Kelly. "The Science behind Intuition." *Psychology Today,* May 20, 2014. psychologytoday.com/blog/radical-remission/201405/the-science-behind-intuition (accessed August 26, 2015).

CHAPTER 5

Jensen, Bill. *Future Strong.* Carlsbad, California: Motivational Press, 2015.

CHAPTER 7

Achor, Shawn. *The Happiness Advantage.* New York: Crown Business, 2010.

Baumeister, Roy F., Kathleen D. Vohs, Jennifer L. Aaker, and Emily N. Garbinsky. "Some Key Differences Between a Happy Life and a Meaningful Life."

Forthcoming. *Journal of Positive Psychology.* faculty-gsb.stanford.edu/aaker/pages /documents/somekeydifferenceshappylifemeaningfullife_2012.pdf (downloaded October 8, 2015).

"Item 5: My Supervisor Cares about Me." *Business Journal,* gallup.com, April 19, 1999. gallup.com/businessjournal/493/item-supervisor-cares-about.aspx (accessed November 8, 2015).

Owen, Jo. *The Mindset of Success.* London: Kogan Page, 2015.

Robbins, Ocean. "The Neuroscience of Why Gratitude Makes Us Healthier." *Huffington Post,* November 4, 2011, Updated January 4, 2012. huffingtonpost.com/ocean-robbins/ having-gratitude-_b_1073105.html (accessed October 6, 2015).

Sullivan, Dan. "Escape 'The Gap'!" Coach Insider, Strategic Coach, n.d. private. strategiccoach.com/enews/ci_gap20130117.html (accessed December 26, 2015).

"12: The Elements of Great Managing." gallup.com, n.d. gallup.com/press/176450/ elements-great-managing.aspx (accessed November 8, 2015).

Wagner, Rodd, and Jim Harter. "The Fifth Element of Great Managing." *Business Journal,* adapted from *12: The Elements of Great Managing,* gallup.com, September 13, 2007. gallup.com/businessjournal/28561/fifth-element-great-managing.aspx (accessed November 8, 2015).

CHAPTER 9

"How to Love Yourself" training by Kamal Ravikant with Vishen Lakhiani. Consciousness Engineering Program. 2014.

"Unleash Your Intuition" training by Sonia Choquette with Vishen Lakhiani. Consciousness Engineering Program. 2014.

Wilber, Ken. *The Essential Ken Wilber.* Boulder, Colorado: Shambhala, 1998.

CHAPTER 10

Gilbert, Elizabeth. *Big Magic.* New York: Riverhead Books, 2015.

"The Friendly Universe with Michael Beckwith" training by Michael Beckwith with Vishen Lakhiani. Consciousness Engineering Program. 2015.

"Meditation for Performance" training by Emily Fletcher with Vishen Lakhiani. Consciousness Engineering Program. 2015.

TOOLS FOR YOUR JOURNEY

Carson, J. W., F. J. Keefe, V. Goli, A. M. Fras, T. R. Lynch, S. R. Thorp, and J. L. Buechler. "Forgiveness and Chronic Low Back Pain: A Preliminary Study Examining the Relationship of Forgiveness to Pain, Anger, and Psychological Distress." *The Journal of Pain,* vol. 6, no. 2 (2005): pp. 84–91.

Gregoire, Carolyn. "Kindness Really Does Make You More Attractive." *The Huffington Post,* updated October 30, 2014. huffingtonpost.com/2014/10/29/kindness-attractive_n_6063074.html (accessed December 28, 2015).

Jacobs, Tom. "The Tangible Benefits of Forgiveness." Pacific Standard, January 6, 2015. psmag.com/books-and-culture/tangible-benefits-forgiveness-97627 (accessed December 28, 2015).

Westervelt, Amy. "Forgive to Live: New Research Shows Forgiveness Is Good for the Heart." Good, August 25, 2012. magazine.good.is/articles/forgive-to-live-new-research-shows-forgiveness-is-good-for-the-heart (accessed December 2, 2015).

ACKNOWLEDGMENTS

My thanks to:

Ajit Nawalkha and Kshitij Minglani—for being some of the best business advisors I could hope for.

My leadership team at Mindvalley: Veena Sidhu, Hannah Zambrano, Ezekiel Vicente, Eric Straus, Klemen Struc, Jason Campbell, Troy Allen, and Gareth Davies for ensuring that our company ran so smoothly as I stepped away briefly from being a CEO to write this book.

Allies, supporters, and teachers through the ages who were there for me and taught me so much, including: Juan Martitegui, Luminita Saviuc, Mia Koning, Kadi Oja, Tanya Lopez, Khailee Ng, Amir Ahmad, Ngeow Wu Han, Mike Reining, Cecilia Sardeo, Ewa Wysocka, Justyna Jastrzebska, Renee Airya, and Carl Harvey.

Teachers and healers in my life: Christie Marie Sheldon, Yanik Silver, Greg Habstritt, Burt Goldman, Jose Silva, Harv Eker, Jack Canfield, and Neale Donald Walsch.

My collaborator Toni Sciarra Poynter for keeping me on track, kicking my butt, and going above and beyond anything I expected to help make this book a success.

My editor Leah Miller and the team at Rodale for believing in me. And Maria Rodale for her support.

Celeste Fine and John Maas, my agents at Sterling Lord Literistic, who started this journey for me.

My book production and tech team: Colton Swabb, Gavin Abeyratne, Chee Ling Wong, Paulius Staniunas, Ronan Diego, Krysta Francoeur, Siddharth Anantharam, Tania Safuan, Mariana Kizlyk, Shafiu Hussain, John Wong, and TS Lim for the copy, websites, and technology that made this book special.

Ashley and Carrie and the team at Triple 7 PR.

Mindvalley's film production, for their work filming the online experience: Crystal Kay, Anton Veselov, Kuhan Kunasegaran, Mildred Michael, Matej Valtrj, Al Ibrahim, Mimi Thian, Shan Vellu, Khairul Johari, Triffany Leo, Alexandria Miu, Angela Balestreri, and Jacqueline Marroquin.

The entire team at Mindvalley, our customers, subscribers, and fans.

My tribe at A-Fest, students of Consciousness Engineering, and Facebook fans for being amazing students and making me love my job every day.

Peter Diamandis, Anousheh Ansari, and members of the X Prize Innovation Board for always inspiring me to reach for the stars and dream bigger.

Members of the Transformational Leadership Council for helping me learn and grow from some of the wisest souls on Earth.

The AIESEC Michigan crew: Jon Opdyke, Vardaan Vasisht, Cindy Vandenbosch, Jennifer Starkey, Hana Malhas, and Omar Kudat.

The teachers who provided wisdom for this book: Richard Branson, for suggesting I write this book; His Holiness the 14th Dalai Lama, for living the truth; Elon Musk, for being a powerful Godicle; Arianna Huffington, for being a role model for my daughter; Dean Kamen, American inventor, for his inspiration; Jon Butcher, for sharing your Lifebook; Ken Wilber, for teaching me models to understand the world; Michael Bernard Beckwith, for introducing me to amazing wisdom; Marisa Peer, for the transformational hypnotherapy sessions; Dave Asprey, for 40 Years of Zen; Patrick Grove, for inspiring me to think impossibly big; Emily Fletcher, for giving me great insights on the truth of meditation; Christie Marie Sheldon, for the healings; Tony Robbins, for inviting me to learn at his private resort; T Harv Eker, for friendship and mentoring; Shelly Lefkoe, for making me a better parent; Mike Dooley, for inspiring me with his daily notes; Sonia Choquette, for teaching me to use my intuition; Joe Vitale, for teaching me inspiration vs. intention; JJ Virgin, for setting the wheels in motion for this book; Joe Polish, for the connections and big-ass heart; Lisa Nichols, for believing in me; and Bob Proctor, for pushing me to dream bigger.

To Morty Lefkoe. Hope you're having a blast in heaven. I'm honored to be able to share your final speeches and interviews with the audience for this book.

INDEX

Boldface references indicate illustrations.

P

Parenthood paradox, 132–33
Parents, role in spreading Brules, 28–29, 30
Pattern recognition, in computational thinking, 45
PayPal, 14
Peer, Marisa, 70–72, 178, 184, 186
Perfect day phase, Six-Phase, 213, 215, 222
Performance, happiness and, 130–31
Personal growth. *See* Growth
Personal life, gratitude for, 137
Person in Mirror exercise, 181–82, 238
Pessimism, relation to results, 131
Placebo effect, 52, 74–75
Polish, Joe, 143
Politics, fear-based, 30
Praise, immunity to, 181
Precious Moments, 62
Present-centeredness, 183–84, 238, 246
Present moment, in bending reality, 120
Pressfield, Steven, 99
Problems, positive side of, 15–17
Psychological Science, 51–52, 74
Purpose, living with, 200
Pygmalion Effect, 75–76

Q

Quantified Self movement, 139
Quest, finding
advice regarding, 204–7
baby steps toward, 207–8
beautiful destruction, 191–92
callings, 189–91
career myth, 202–3
embracing quest, 201
entrepreneurship Brule, 201–2
Godicle Theory, 196–201, **197**
kensho and *satori* concepts, 192–94, **194**
overview, xxi, 187–89, 238–39
technique for, 204
when universe comes calling, 194–96
Questions. *See also* Three Most
Important Questions
lofty, 222, 246
what, 78
why, 28–29, 78

R

RAS (reticular activating system), 215, 246
Rational choice
Brule Test, 39
vs. social contagion, 20
Ravikant, Kamal, 181–82
Reading, boosting refresh rate through, 98–99
Reality. *See* Bending reality; Models of reality
Rebels, as making dent in universe, 33
Recoding yourself (Level 3), **xviii**, xx, 111–12, **187**, 188. *See also* Bending reality; Blissipline; Vision for future
Refresh rate
defined, 246
exercise, 98–100, 229–30
overview, 95–96, 98
Relationships. *See* Friendships; Love relationships
Relative truth
models of reality as, identifying, 87–88
world of. *See* Culturescape
Religion
Brules about, 22–23, 25–27
Brule Test, 38, 39
spirituality without, 26, 83–84
Religion of One's Own, A, 84
Reticular activating system (RAS), 215, 246
Retirement, as real mental construct, 11
Reverse gap, 136–37, **136**, 138, 246–47
Robbins, Tony, 65
Rockefeller, John D., 123
Rosenthal, Robert, PhD, 75–76
Ruiz, Don Miguel, 99
Rules. *See also* Brules (bulls**t rules); Culturescape
dawn of, 6–7
relation of language to, 9
tyranny of, 6
Rutte, Martin, 204, 239

S

Safety
as overrated, 15–17
problem with, 12–13